The Six Sigma
Yellow Belt Handbook

H. James Harrington, Ph.D.
Frank Voehl, Ph.D.

Paton
PROFESSIONAL

Chico, California

Most Paton Professional books are available at quantity discounts when purchased in bulk. For more information, contact:

Paton Professional
A division of Paton Press LLC
P.O. Box 44
Chico, CA 95927-0044
Telephone: (530) 342-5480
Fax: (530) 342-5471
E-mail: *books@patonprofessional.com*
Web: *www.patonprofessional.com*

Printed in the United States of America

V.2/2011
ISBN: 978-1-932828-24-5

Library of Congress Cataloging-in-Publication Data
Harrington, H. J. (H. James)
 The Six Sigma yellow belt handbook / by H. James Harrington, Frank Voehl.
  p. cm.
 ISBN 978-1-932828-24-5
 1. Total quality management. 2. Six sigma (Quality control standard) 3. Quality control--Management. 4. Production management. I. Voehl, Frank, 1946- II. Title.
 HD62.15.H3698 2009
 658.4′013--dc22
                                        2009017036

Notice of Liability
The information in this book is distributed on an "as is" basis, without warranty. Although every precaution has been taken in the preparation of the book, neither the author nor Paton Press LLC shall have any liability to any person or entity with respect to any loss or damage caused or alleged to be caused directly or indirectly by the information contained in this book.

Staff
Publisher: Scott M. Paton
Editor: Laura Smith
Book design: David Hurst
Cover design: Caylen Balmain

CONTENTS

Chapter 2
Being a Team Player

Chapter 3
Basic Six Sigma Yellow Belt Tools

Chapter 4
Statistical Tools for Yellow Belts

Chapter 5
DMAIC Overview

Chapter 6
The Six Sigma Define Phase

Chapter 7
The Six Sigma Measure Phase

Chapter 8
The Six Sigma Analyze Phase

About the Authors

H. James Harrington

In *Tech Trending* (Capstone, 2001), author Amy Zuckerman referred to H. James Harrington as "the quintessential tech trender." *The New York Times* commented on his "...knack for synthesis and open mind about packaging his knowledge and experience in new ways—characteristics that may matter more as prerequisites for new-economy success than technical wizardry . . . ." President Clinton appointed him to serve as an ambassador of goodwill. Harrington is recognized as a world leader in applying performance improvement methodologies to business processes. He wrote the books that other consultants use.

Present responsibilities

Harrington now serves as chief executive officer for the Harrington Institute and Harrington Middle East. He's the founder and president of the Walter L. Hurd Foundation, which manages the International Asia Pacific Quality Award. He also serves as chairman of the board for a number of businesses and as the U.S. chairman of technologies for project management at the University of Quebec.

Previous experience

In February 2002 Harrington retired as the COO of Systemcorp ALG, which was, before its purchase by IBM in 2004, the leading supplier of knowledge management and project management software solutions. Prior to that, he served as a principal and leader in the Process Innovation Group at Ernst & Young; he retired when it was purchased by Capgemini. Harrington joined Ernst & Young in 1989, when it purchased Harrington, Hurd & Rieker, a consulting firm that he started. Before that Harrington worked for IBM for more than forty years as a senior engineer and project manager.

Harrington served as past chairman and president of the prestigious International Academy for Quality and the American Society for Quality Control. He's an active member of the Global Knowledge Economics Council.

Credentials

The Harrington/Ishikawa Medal, presented yearly by the Asia Pacific Quality Organization, was named after Harrington to recognize his many contributions to the region. In 1997, the Quebec Society for Quality named its quality award "The Harrington/Neron Medal," honoring Harrington for his many contributions to Canada's quality movement. In 2000 Sri Lanka named its national quality award after him. The European Universities Network established the Harrington Best TQM Thesis Award in 2004, and Sudan University established the Harrington Chair in Performance Excellence in his honor.

Harrington's contributions to performance improvement around the world have brought him many honors and awards, including the Edwards Medal, the Lancaster Medal, ASQ's Distinguished Service Medal,

China's Magnolia Award, and many others. He is an honorary advisor to the China Quality Control Association, and he was elected to the Singapore Productivity Hall of Fame in 1990. He's been named lifetime honorary president of the Asia Pacific Quality Organization and honorary director of the Associácion Chilean de Control de Calidad.

Harrington has been elected a Fellow of the British Quality Control Organization and the American Society for Quality Control. He was also elected an honorary member of the quality societies in Taiwan, Argentina, Brazil, Colombia, and Singapore. He's also listed in *Who's Who Worldwide* and *Men of Distinction Worldwide*. He's presented hundreds of papers on performance improvement and organizational management structure at the local, state, national, and international levels.

Harrington is a prolific writer. He's written thirty-three books and ten software packages, and has published hundreds of technical reports and magazine articles. For the past eight years, he's published a monthly column in *Quality Digest* magazine and is syndicated in five other publications.

Harrington lives in Los Gatos, California, with his wife, Marguerite. He can be contacted via e-mail at *hjh@harrington-institute.com*.

Frank Voehl

Frank Voehl is president and chairman of Strategy Associates Inc. and a senior consultant and chancellor for the Harrington Institute. He also serves as the chairman of the board for a number of businesses and as a Master Black Belt instructor and technology advisor at the University of Central Florida in Orlando. He's recognized as one of the world leaders in applying quality measurement and Lean Six Sigma methodologies to business processes.

Voehl has extensive knowledge of Nuclear Regulatory Commission, Food and Drug Administration, Good Manufacturing Processes, and National Aeronautics and Space Administration quality system requirements. He's an expert in ISO 9001, ISO 14000, and Six Sigma quality system standards and processes. He has degrees from St. John's University and advanced studies at New York University, as well as a doctor of divinity degree.

Other Books By H. James Harrington

- *The Improvement Process* (McGraw-Hill, 1987, a best-selling business book that year)
- *Poor-Quality Cost* (Marcel Dekker, 1987)
- *Excellence—The IBM Way* (ASQ Quality Press, 1988)
- *The Quality-Profit Connection* (ASQ Quality Press, 1988)
- *Business Process Improvement* (McGraw-Hill, 1991, the first book about process redesign)
- *The Mouse Story* (Ernst & Young, 1991)
- *Of Tails and Teams* (ASQ Quality Press, 1994)
- *Total Improvement Management* (McGraw-Hill, 1995)
- *High-Performance Benchmarking* (McGraw-Hill, 1996)
- *The Complete Benchmarking Implementation Guide* (McGraw-Hill, 1996)
- *ISO 9000 and Beyond* (McGraw-Hill, 1996)
- *The Business Process Improvement Workbook* (McGraw-Hill, 1997)
- *The Creativity Toolkit—Provoking Creativity in Individuals and Organizations* (McGraw-Hill, 1998)
- *Statistical Analysis Simplified—The Easy-to-Understand Guide to SPC and Data Analysis* (McGraw-Hill, 1998)
- *Area Activity Analysis—Aligning Work Activities and Measurements to Enhance Business Performance* (McGraw-Hill, 1998)
- *Reliability Simplified—Going Beyond Quality to Keep Customers for Life* (McGraw-Hill, 1999)
- *ISO 14000 Implementation—Upgrading Your EMS Effectively* (McGraw-Hill, 1999)
- *Performance Improvement Methods—Fighting the War on Waste* (with Kenneth C. Lomax, McGraw-Hill, 1999)
- *Simulation Modeling Methods—An Interactive Guide to Results-Based Decision Making* (McGraw-Hill, 2000)
- *Project Change Management—Applying Change Management to Improvement Projects* (with Daryl R. Conner and Nicholas L. Horney, McGraw-Hill, 2000)
- *E-Business Project Manager* (ASQ Quality Press, 2002)
- *Process Management Excellence—The Art of Excelling in Process Management* (Paton Press, 2006)
- *Project Management Excellence—The Art of Excelling in Project Management* (Paton Press, 2006)
- *Change Management Excellence—The Art of Excelling in Change Management* (Paton Press, 2006)
- *Knowledge Management Excellence—The Art of Excelling in Knowledge Management* (Paton Press, 2006)
- *Resource Management Excellence—The Art of Excelling in Resource Management* (Paton Press, 2007)
- *The Six Sigma Green Belt Handbook* (Paton Professional, 2009)

x

Acknowledgments

First and foremost, I want to acknowledge my friend and associate, Candy Rogers, who converted and edited endless hours of dictation and inputs from two authors into a finished product. We couldn't have done it without her.

We would like to recognize the contributions made by Praveen Gupta and Ken Lomax for their inputs to this book.

Dedication

I would like to dedicate this book to my mother, Carrie Harrington,
who gave me so much love and encouragement throughout my life.
I miss her very much.

Foreword

"Six Sigma GE Quality 2000 will be the biggest, the most personally rewarding, and, in the end, the most profitable undertaking in our history. We plunged into Six Sigma with a company-consuming vengeance just over three years ago. We have invested more than a billion dollars in the effort and the financial returns have now entered the exponential phase."

—General Electric's letter to shareowners
February 12, 1999

Y ou are about to embark on a wonderful journey—one that will make you more valuable professionally and to your organization. It's a journey that will provide you with new insights and abilities that can be applied at work and at home. This book will identify a number of special tools that will help you address problems in your personal and business lives. It will prepare you to serve as a member of a Six Sigma team in a capacity that will allow you to help solve some of your organization's most important problems.

Don't fear the statistical terms addressed in this book; we use them to impress management. In truth, we have taken many of these complex tools and simplified them so that almost anyone can understand and be able to use them. To make these difficult statistical approaches easier to use, computer programs are available that take the raw data and perform all of the mathematical calculations for you.

The Six Sigma methodology is based upon two concepts:

■ *Concept No. one:* The more that variation is reduced around the midpoint of a specification, the less chance there is to create defects or errors. (See figure 0.1.)

This is a concept that was developed in the 1940s and popularized in the 1970s by Genichi Taguchi. In the 1920s, Walter A. Shewhart set the standard of performance in his control charts at plus-or-minus three sigma. In the 1960s, Phil Crosby advocated a philosophy of "Zero Defects" at ITT Corp. In the 1990s, executives at Motorola felt that Crosby's Zero Defects performance criteria was unattainable (and they were right) so they set a performance target of six sigma. This is

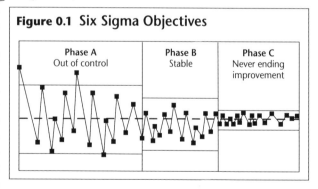

Figure 0.1 Six Sigma Objectives

| Phase A | Phase B | Phase C |
| Out of control | Stable | Never ending improvement |

known as a process capability (Cp) of 2.0. Motorola's executives felt that over time the process would drift plus-or-minus 1.5 sigma, so the long-term process capability (Cpk) target was set for 1.5, or 4.5 sigma. (See figure 0.2.)

The change in target variation from three sigma to six sigma is where the Six Sigma concept got its name. At the six sigma level, the long-term process capability results in 3.4 errors per million opportunities. This is near to perfection without requiring perfection. It's a goal to be sought after, not a performance standard that has to be met.

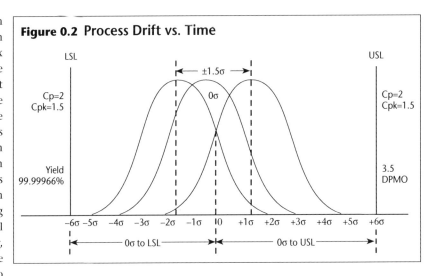

Figure 0.2 Process Drift vs. Time

Six sigma is calculated using ~~total~~ opportunities for error, not total output. For example, a car could have a million opportunities for failure due to the complexity of the processes that created it. In this case, at the six sigma level there would be an average of 3.4 defects per car produced. This is the reason that every car that rolls off the Toyota assembly line still has its brakes checked to be sure they work.

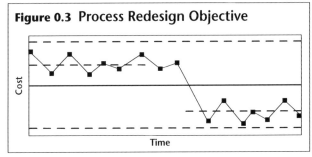

Figure 0.3 Process Redesign Objective

- *Concept No. two:* The lower the costs, cycle time, and error level, the higher the profits, market share, and customer satisfaction. This approach focuses on streamlining the process, driving out waste, and eliminating nonvalue-added activities. It was based upon the business process improvement concepts that were popularized in the early 1980s. (See figure 0.3.)

  In this concept, reducing the mean—not variation—is the objective. For example, it's better to manufacture a part for $100 plus-or-minus $10 than to manufacture the same part for $500 plus-or-minus $1. In fact, in some cases variation is welcomed as long as it is on the lower side of the midpoint. Often, investigating these lower levels of variation can lead to additional reductions in cost, cycle time, and error rate.

Lean is another aspect of the Six Sigma concept. This methodology nearly eliminates in-process stock, designs continuous flow lines, and error-proofs manufacturing equipment. Toyota has further refined this methodology into one of the most effective auto assembly processes in the world.

Using these two primary concepts as an objective, Motorola used Shewhart's PDCA cycle to implement them. Mikel Harry helped Motorola modify the PDCA approach to RDMAICSI (recognize-define-measure-analyze-improve-control-standardize-integrate). This was further refined to define, measure, analyze, improve, and control (DMAIC). Bill Smith, a Motorola engineer who became the leader of the company's Six Sigma efforts, felt that the complexity of Motorola's problems required more sophisticated techniques. Unfortunately, many of Motorola's quality engineers had left the company, taking with them the statistical analysis tools that were part of the quality engineering profession. As a result, Motorola's Six Sigma

program was heavily focused on statistical training and analysis. This resulted in a cadre of special problem solvers who became proficient in statistical tools such as design of experiments. They were called Six Sigma Black Belts.

Don't worry, we won't try to turn you into a statistician. As a Yellow Belt, you won't have to perform designs of experiments. Most of your training will be related to the basic problem-solving tools; most of these tools were used to train quality circle (or employee involvement team) members in the 1980s. You will also be introduced to some of the statistical tools, but they will not require advanced math to understand or use.

Why Six Sigma?

You may ask: "Why did Motorola take on the big jump from three sigma to six sigma?" We will give you a little of Motorola's history which will help you understand why it made this drastic decision.

In the early 1970s Motorola divested itself of its Quasar television and radio manufacturing division, which was acquired by Matsushita of Japan. Under Japanese management and using the same employees, the quality level of the products improved by 100 times and productivity doubled. In 1978 at one of its management meetings, Art Sundry, Motorola's vice president, stated the obvious: "Motorola's quality stinks," he said.

In the 1980s, business schools around the United States were using Quasar as an example of how poorly an organization could be managed, emphasizing the better management styles used in Japan to improve quality, productivity, and profits.

In 1981, Bob Galvin, CEO of Motorola, observed that John Young, CEO of Hewlett-Packard (HP), had set a tenfold improvement objective for all of HP's products to be met within the decade. As a result of this and his personal observations of Motorola's performance, he set a tenfold improvement goal in all of Motorola's measurements over the next five years. To accomplish this, Motorola embraced the "total quality management" concept.

In 1987 Motorola was still losing market share and although its quality and cycle time had improved over the previous five years, the improvements still didn't meet market demands. As a result, Motorola's management set a new goal of a tenfold improvement every two years. This led to the birth of Six Sigma.

Why is reaching the six sigma level so important to your organization? The following is an analysis of the effect that errors have on your organization related to various sigma levels:

■ At three sigma, errors cost you 25–40 percent of your gross
■ At four sigma, errors cost you 15–20 percent of your gross
■ At five sigma, errors cost you 5–15 percent of your gross
■ At six sigma, errors cost you less than 1 percent of your gross

Does Six Sigma generate results? You can bet your last dollar on it. Let's look at the savings from five organizations that reported their Six Sigma results.

Six Sigma Savings

Organization	Years	Savings (in billions of dollars)	Revenue (in billions of dollars)	Percent of revenue savings
Motorola	1986–2001	$16	$356.9	4.5 percent
AlliedSignal	1998	$0.5	$15.1	3.3 percent
General Electric	1996–1999	$4.4	$382.1	1.2 percent
Honeywell	1998–2000	$1.8	$72.3	2.4 percent
Ford Motor Co.	2000–2002	$1.0	$43.9	2.3 percent

As GE's 1996 annual report states, "It has been estimated that less-than-six sigma quality, i.e., the three-to-four sigma levels that are average for most U.S. companies, can cost a company as much as 10–15 percent of its revenues. For GE, that would mean $8–12 billion." With GE's 2001 revenue of $111.6 billion, this would translate into $11.2–16.7 billion of savings." (Source: GE Investor Relations Annual Report)

To summarize, Six Sigma added to proven best practices and combined them to effectively solve problems and turn improvement opportunities into results. As a Yellow Belt, you are starting down a road that will help you to discover your creative abilities and develop you for more responsible assignments.

"A Six Sigma system is an organization's best-value proposition."

CHAPTER 1

YOU, AS A YELLOW BELT

"One of the most gratifying assignments a person can have
is solving a difficult problem."

—HJH

There is special term for people who use Six Sigma to solve difficult business problems or take advantage of new improvement opportunities: Yellow Belts. To become a Yellow Belt is to reach the first level in the Six Sigma methodology. These levels are:

1. Yellow Belt
2. Green Belt
3. Black Belt
4. Master Black Belt

As a Yellow Belt, you will learn not only how to correct problems, but also how to transform and take products and processes to new levels of quality and performance. Becoming a Yellow Belt is not an end unto itself; it's part of your personal journey toward performance excellence. Once you have mastered the Yellow Belt tools, you can move on to more complex Green Belt performance improvement tools. Even then, there are more challenges ahead as you start to learn Black Belt tools. The ultimate goal is to progress to the Master Black Belt level, which indicates mastery of a complete set of performance improvement tools and the ability to apply them to save your organization money and improve customer satisfaction. Just one in 1,000 employees in the average organization reaches the Master Black Belt level.

As you can see, becoming a Yellow Belt is just the start of a long intellectual journey that has a number of milestones along the way. Some people go all the way to become Master Black Belts, others are happy with acquiring just the Yellow Belt skills. The decision of how far to progress on the Six Sigma continuum must be made jointly by the management team and the individual.

WHAT IS SIX SIGMA?

The term "Six Sigma" was coined by Bill Smith, a Motorola engineer, when he convinced William J. Weisz, then chief operating officer of Motorola, that the standard of performance for all business activities should be 3.4 defects per million opportunities. This was statistically equivalent to ±6 sigma when long-term drift was considered. Previously, most process control standards were 66.8 defects per million opportunities, or

±3 sigma. To meet this more rigid requirement, Motorola implemented an extensive training program that focused on teaching people how to solve problems. This program was called Six Sigma, and it was the start of a worldwide movement to produce products and services that were nearly perfect.

INTRODUCTION

Although process capability techniques have been used extensively in manufacturing for more than sixty years, a major breakthrough occurred when Motorola applied them to its business support functions and manufacturing processes. The new approach improved Motorola's business processes by ten to 100 times in just two years. When Motorola won the Malcolm Baldrige National Quality Award in 1988, it credited Six Sigma as the primary driver of its improvement. By the early 1990s, Six Sigma started to catch on at other organizations. General Electric (GE) implemented Six Sigma techniques in the mid-1990s and committed millions of dollars to implementing the program organizationwide. GE's program expanded from 200 projects in 1995 to 6,000 projects in 1997, resulting in more than $320 million in savings. By 1998, GE estimated that its savings were about $750 million.

OVERVIEW

Quality control has evolved significantly over the years. In the early 20th century, 100 percent inspection was the most-used approach; sampling plans were developed in the 1940s to define acceptable defect levels. In the 1970s quality guru Philip Crosby established the Zero Defects methodology, an inspirational way of explaining to employees the notion that everything should be done right the first time and no amount of failure or defect in the work output was an acceptable performance. Zero Defects focused on committing employees to performing error-free work. Employees even signed a pledge card, promising to do their work "right the first time."

The Zero Defects concept was somewhat controversial because some quality experts felt it focused on meeting internal design specifications instead of customer requirements or continuous improvement. Many quality professionals disagreed with the concept because they believed that it was impossible to produce zero defects all the time. These process-oriented professionals felt that process capability requirements were a better way of defining acceptable performance. However, the U.S. government embraced the Zero Defects concept and it became *the* quality trend of the 1970s.

DEFINITIONS

The following are some key definitions related to Six Sigma:
- *Process capability.* The determination of whether a process or activity is capable of meeting requirements, determined by comparing the ±3 sigma distribution of the process to the requirement's limits.
- *Short-term process capability (Cp).* An indicator of the potential performance capability of a centered or ideal process as indicated by a comparison of the voice of the customer (i.e., what the customer wants) to the voice of the process (i.e., what the process is able to provide). It's measured as the ratio of specification tolerance width to six standard deviations in process variation as indicated using short-term data.
- *Long-term process capability (Cpk).* An indicator of a process' performance capability, taking into account its real-world results. It's measured as the minimum of the difference between the process average and the distance to the upper and lower specification limits divided by six standard deviations in process variation

[handwritten margin notes: Cp, Cpk]

2

using short-term data that are collected over a long period of time. It allows the drift and variation in the process mean to be taken into account.

■ *Sigma (σ).* The Greek letter used to describe the standard deviation of a population.

■ *Standard deviation.* A measure of the spread or dispersion of a set of data. It's calculated by taking the square root of the variance and is symbolized by *s.d.* or *s.*

■ *Stationary process.* A process with an ultimate constant variance.

■ *Statistical process control (SPC).* The application of statistical techniques in the control of processes. SPC is often considered a subset of statistical quality control (SQC), in which the emphasis is on the tools associated with the process, but not product acceptance techniques.

■ *Statistical quality control (SQC).* The application of statistical techniques in the control of quality. SQC includes the use of regression analysis, test of significance, acceptance sampling, control charts, and distributions. (Note: appendix A contains a glossary of Six Sigma definitions.)

In the 1970s and early 1980s organizations such as IBM released requirements that their process capabilities (Cpk) reach the 1.40 level or an acceptable corrective action plan had to be in place before products could be shipped to customers. IBM's technical report entitled "Process Qualification—Manufacturing's Insurance Policy," by H. James Harrington, published September 15, 1980, required that a process' ±4 sigma limit fall within the specification limit when the following are considered:

■ Accuracy
■ Precision
■ Repeatability/reproducibility
■ Variation/stability
■ Linearity and resolution
■ Sensitivity
■ Variation between similar pieces of equipment used for the same purpose

HISTORY OF SIX SIGMA

In 1981 Motorola's chief operating officer, William J. Weisz, directed that all manufacturing processes should have a tenfold improvement within a five-year period. Five years later, he required another tenfold improvement—to be obtained within three years. These goals required radical changes, and Motorola applied Six Sigma to reach them.

To calculate the process performance, samples of the output were plotted on a histogram and the standard deviation was calculated. Once the standard deviation and mean were calculated, it was easy to compare the Six Sigma-calculated performance limit to the specifications and/or requirements. This required all organizations to define their requirements for each process and each activity within the process. Of course, this was not the case for most nonproduction activities. As a result, organizations that implement Six Sigma are forced into major upgrades of their internal requirements and measurement systems. To accomplish this, we recommend a technique called area activity analysis. (See H. James Harrington's book *Area Activity Analysis*, published by McGraw-Hill, 1998.)

Once the process variation and mean performance are compared to the requirements, most processes fail to meet Six Sigma requirements. Many nonproduction processes fail to even meet a ±3 sigma performance level (three errors per 1,000 opportunities). In many cases, nonmanufacturing process didn't even meet a ±1 sigma requirement (318 errors per 1,000).

Six Sigma gained popularity after Motorola won the Baldrige Award in 1988. The information packet that Motorola distributed to explain its quality improvement approach stated:

"To accomplish its quality and total customer satisfaction goals, Motorola concentrates on several key operational initiatives. At the top of the list is Six Sigma quality, a statistical measure of variation from a desired result. In concrete terms, Six Sigma translates into a target of no more than 3.4 defects per million products, customer services included. At the manufacturing end, this requires designs that accommodate reasonable variation in component parts but production processes that yield consistently uniform final products. Motorola employees record the defects found in every function of the business, and statistical technologies are increasingly made part of each and every employee's job."

Although Motorola called its program Six Sigma, it required that the measurement be applied only to one point (Cp = 2) and allowed the process to perform at lower levels when the process drift is considered (Cpk). Figure 1.1 relates the various levels of sigma to errors per thousand and per million (short-term variation).

Figure 1.1 Sigma Levels and Corresponding Number of Errors

Sigma Level	Errors Per Thousand Opportunities	Errors Per Million Opportunities
1 sigma	317	317,310
2 sigma	45	45,500
3 sigma	2.7	2,700
3.5 sigma	0.465	465
4 sigma	0.063	63
4.5 sigma	0.0068	6.8
5 sigma	0.00057	0.57
6 sigma	0.000002	0.002

USING SIGMA

Figure 1.2 depicts a histogram using the same data as shown in figure 1.1. By studying figure 1.1, it's easy to see that Six Sigma is ~~two errors per billion units processed,~~ not the 3.4 errors per million that Motorola accepts for its Six Sigma quality level. There's a difference between the two because Motorola considers a ±1.5 sigma shift of the process average over time as part of its total specification. For example, consider a manufacturing process whose specification limit is equal to Six Sigma (Cp = 2). If the process average is off-center by 1.5 sigma, the maximum number of errors is 3.4 per million based upon the standard normal distribution table.

Figure 1.3 shows the effect on the process' capability to meet specification when the center point drifts over time.

Note that the center point of a distribution will drift although the single sample calculations for the distribution shape and width has not changed. Motorola took this into consideration by subtracting ±1.5 sigma drift/shift in the process over time. For example, if a single sample had its specification limits as equal

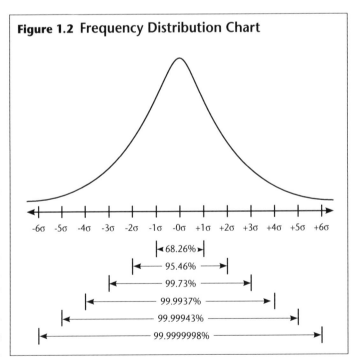

Figure 1.2 Frequency Distribution Chart

-6σ -5σ -4σ -3σ -2σ -1σ -0σ +1σ +2σ +3σ +4σ +5σ +6σ

68.26%
95.46%
99.73%
99.9937%
99.99943%
99.9999998%

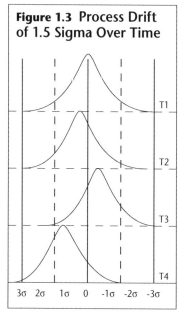

Figure 1.3 Process Drift of 1.5 Sigma Over Time

to ±6 sigma when its mean was centered on the center of the specification limit, Cp would be ±6 sigma/±3 sigma = 2. If the long-term sample mean drifted ±1.5 sigma from the specification midpoint, the long-term process capability (Cpk) would be 1.5.

Cpk = (short-term sigma value minus long-term drift) divided by 3 sigma)

Calculation is Cpk = (±6 sigma–±1.5 sigma)/3 sigma = 1.5)

It's important to note that this effect can occur due to many factors. For example, it can occur due to changing operators and between different sets of equipment used in the same process to do the same activity. Equipment presents an additional problem because it can produce slightly different products, even if it's built to the same specification. Figure 1.4 shows how quality levels vary based on off-center drifts expressed in sigmas.

There are a number of ways to have a quality level of 3.4 errors per million parts or less. The following are three typical examples:

■ With 0.5 sigma off-centering with 5 sigma quality
■ With 1 sigma off-centering with 5.5 sigma quality
■ With 1.5 sigma off-centering with 6 sigma quality

It's often easier to center the mean than it is to reduce variation significantly. Pandu R. Tadikamalla, a professor at the University of Pittsburgh, pointed this out in his November 1994 *Quality Progress* article:

"When companies embark on Six Sigma quality programs, what is their objective? Is it to reduce the process variance so that the half-tolerance of the product characteristic is equal to six times the standard deviation? Or is it to have very few defects, say in the neighborhood of 50 to 100 per million? From the technical viewpoint, it might make sense to talk in terms of the process variance. From the managerial or customer viewpoint, the quality standards can be described in terms of defects per million. In addition, in many situations,

Figure 1.4 Effect of Off-Center Drifts On Quality Level, Expressed In Per Million

Off-centering quality level	3 sigma	3.5 sigma	4 sigma	4.5 sigma	5 sigma	5.5 sigma	6 sigma
0	2,700	465	63	6.8	0.57	0.034	0.002
0.25 sigma	3,577	666	99	12.8	02	0.1056	0.0063
0.5 sigma	6,440	1,382	236	32	3.4	0.71	0.019
0.75 sigma	12,288	3,011	665	88.5	11	1.02	0.1
1 sigma	22,832	6,433	1,350	233	32	3.4	0.39
1.25 sigma	40,111	12,201	3,000	577	8.5	10.7	1
1.50 sigma	66.803	22,800	6,200	1,350	233	32	3.4
1.75 sigma	105,601	40,100	12,200	3,000	577	88.4	11
2 sigma	158,700	66,800	22,800	6,200	1,300	233	32

adjusting the process to move the process average closer to the target value is relatively easier than improving the process to reduce the variance. Thus, if the goal is to reduce the number of defects, it does not make much sense to improve the process to Six Sigma levels and not center the process. Planning or allowing for the process average to drift 1.5 standard deviations from the target value just in case is similar to building up inventories when implementing just-in-time inventory management."

A debate on Six Sigma or allowable off-center drift isn't going to be very productive. The important thing is that the output quality level should reach one digit in parts per million or—even better—in parts per billion. Figure 1.5 shows a chart prepared by Fred McFadden, a professor at the University of Colorado. It was published in an article entitled "Six Sigma Quality Programs" in the June 1993 issue of *Quality Progress*, and provides an excellent example of defect rate decrease as the sigma specification level ratio increases.

Figure 1.5 Error Rate vs. Sigma Level (Centered Process)

Sigma level	Error rate (ppm)	Duration of power outages per month	Number of misspelled words
1	317,400	228.5 hours	159 per page
2	45,600	32.8 hours	23 per page
3	2,700	1.94 hours	1.35 per page
4	63	2.72 minutes	1 per 31 pages
5	0.57	1.48 seconds	1 per several books
6	0.002	0.005 seconds	1 per small library
7	0.000003	0.00001 seconds	1 per large library

Although 3.4 errors per million fuses, bolts, screws, nuts, garden hoses, or brooms may not be an aggressive target, when you start to apply the same requirements to management decisions, drawings, books, letters, sales contracts, meals served, auto repairs, medical operations, sales calls, or lines of codes, it is a very aggressive target. This is particularly true in any type of service activity where quality can't be inspected or tested in. Few support or service processes have reached a 4 sigma error rate level. We have yet to find an executive team that is working at the 4 sigma level.

ERROR OPPORTUNITIES

The Six Sigma concept is based upon errors per opportunity. This is a major shift from measurements such as errors per unit, errors per output, or errors per operation, etc. An opportunity is defined as anything within an item, product, process, service, or system where an error would cause a failure to meet internal or external customer expectations.

Figure 1.6 Entry Errors Based Upon Different Sigma Levels

Single sample sigma	Sigma with a ± 1.5 drift	Percent errors	Percent errors per entry	Percent errors per day
1 sigma	-0.5	69.9	69.9	20,970
2 sigma	+0.5	30.9	30.9	9,270
3 sigma	1.5	6.7	6.7	2,010
4 sigma	2.5	0.6	0.6	180
5 sigma	3.5	0.02	0.02	6.0
6 sigma	4.5	0.00034	0.00034	0.1

For example, consider a situation where an individual is responsible for inputting financial data. He or she would record the customer's name, address, what the customer purchased, and the cost. This would require him or her to record about 100 characters for each entry. Assuming 300 entries per day would mean he or she recorded 30,000 characters each day, creating 30,000 error opportunities. Figure 1.6 shows the error rate based on different sigma performance levels.

Figure 1.7 Error Opportunities on a One-Page Memo

Single sample sigma	Long-term sigma drift + 1.5 sigma	Percent errors	Errors per memo	Errors per 1,000 memos
1	-0.5	69.9	1,398	1,398,000
2	+0.5	30.9	618	618,000
3	1.5	6.7	134	134,000
4	2.5	0.6	12	12,000
5	3.5	0.02	0.4	400
6	4.5	0.00034	0.0068	7

In this example at the 6 sigma performance level, there would be one entry error every ten working days.

In reviewing just a single print with 100 dimensions, a manufacturing engineer would have an error opportunity rate of 300. This is based on each of the dimensions having a ± 200 tolerance (200 error opportunities) for a total of 300 error opportunities (100 dimensions + 200 error opportunities).

This doesn't include error opportunities such as distributing the memo on time, sending it to the right people, that the addresses are correct, that it's put into the right envelope, etc. Figure 1.7 shows the calculated error rate per memo.

THE SIX SIGMA QUALITY SYSTEM

Because Six Sigma represents such a radically different way of measuring quality, it requires an organizationwide paradigm shift. It's for this reason that Motorola calls its quality effort a Six Sigma quality program. (The term "system" is better than "program" because a program has a start and an end to it. A Six Sigma system represents an ongoing focus directed at always improving.)

Motorola's Six Sigma quality program is divided into four major quadrants:
- Improvement processes
- Quality initiatives
- Quality measurements
- Improvement tools

To help with the implementation of the Six Sigma quality program, Motorola formed the Six Sigma Research Center to develop a set of reference books known as the *Encyclopedia of Six Sigma*. This encyclopedia consists of three main parts:
- A collection of statistical tools
- Application case studies
- Descriptive, specific optimization methods

> "I don't give a damn if we get a little bureaucracy as long as we get the results. If it bothers you, yell at it. Kick it. Scream at it. Break it!"
>
> —Jack Welch,
> former GE chairman
> *Business Week* magazine,
> June 1998

SIX SIGMA ORGANIZATIONAL STRUCTURE

Motorola established an innovative recognition system called the Black Belt program to support its Six Sigma quality program. Individuals progress through various levels that were designated as:
- *Green Belts.* Those who possess basic Six Sigma skills and are equipped to manage simple Six Sigma projects.
- *Black Belts.* Highly competent professionals who operate as on-site consultants for the application of Six Sigma methodologies.
- *Master Black Belts.* Those who have mastered the Six Sigma process and are capable of teaching it to others.

After the decision to implement a Six Sigma initiative, it's time to establish the Six Sigma organizational structure, which should be an integrated part of the total organization.

A Six Sigma system is designed to increase profits and customer satisfaction. It's an organized and documented approach to eliminating root causes of errors throughout the organization by reducing variation and developing streamlined, effective, and efficient processes. Figure 1.8 illustrates a typical Six Sigma structure.

Each level of management and every employee plays an important role in the Six Sigma system. Each is dependent on the other, and each role adds value to the system.

Figure 1.8 Motorola's Six Sigma Quality Program

Basic components	Enabling initiatives and tools
Improvement process	**Quality initiatives**
1. Define products and services.	1. Participative management
2. Identify customer requirements.	2. Short-cycle manufacture
3. Compare product with requirements.	3. Design for manufacturing
4. Describe the process.	4. Benchmarking
5. Improve the process.	5. Statistical process control
6. Measure quality and productivity.	6. Supplier qualification

Six Sigma quality program

Quality measurements	Improvement tools
1. Process mean and standard deviation	1. Quality function deployment
2. Capability index Cp and Cpk	2. Flowcharts
3. Defects per unit	3. Pareto charts
	4. Histograms
	5. Cause-and-effect diagrams
	6. Experimental design

THE EXECUTIVE TEAM/SIX SIGMA STEERING COMMITTEE

The executive committee (EC) sets the direction and priorities for the organization. As a result, it must be the owner of the Six Sigma system. It's responsible for managing the system to ensure that it's operating effectively. It needs to be a good role model by including Six Sigma thinking into the way it functions. It's responsible for developing the organization's strategic plan, which forms the basis for selecting the Six Sigma projects. It needs to understand the Six Sigma system well enough to be able to justify redirecting resources from routine work to attack waste that's causing less-than-perfect performance.

One of the key responsibilities of the executive team (ET) is to define what opportunities will be approved as a Six Sigma project. The following are typical rules used by the ET to select Six Sigma projects:

■ Is the project in line with the business objectives?
■ Will it have a net savings of at least $150,000 during the next three years considering the cost of the SST but not the cost of the implementation?

"The company cannot buy its way into quality. It must be led into quality by top management."
—W. Edwards Deming, *Out of Crisis* **(1986)**

The EC will appoint the Six Sigma Champion and Black Belts to lead the project, conduct periodic reviews of its progress, and make the required adjustments when the system is not as effective as it should be.

8

SIX SIGMA CHAMPION AND SIX SIGMA SPONSOR

The Six Sigma Champion is the Six Sigma project manager. The Champion provides the right people for the required time and ensures that the Six Sigma activities remain a top priority for the organization. The Champion also ensures that there are adequate funds in the annual budget to cover the cost of the Six Sigma process. Managers can't assign employees to Six Sigma activities without removing at least a portion of their workloads. Expecting employees to participate in Six Sigma projects in addition to their routine responsibilities is the major cause for Six Sigma and total quality management (TQM) failures around the world. A Green Belt will be expected to spend 20 to 60 percent of his or her time working on Six Sigma projects; a Yellow Belt will be expected to spend only slightly less time on Six Sigma projects.

The Champion is often a senior vice president of the organization and will work with the EC to define the improvement opportunities necessary for supporting the strategic plan. The Champion will approve all projects and set the goals and expectations for the SST. During the start-up phase of a Six Sigma project, a consultant is sometimes assigned to this position due to the amount of time and sophisticated problem-solving experience required to justify and organize early Six Sigma activities.

BUSINESS UNIT SPONSORS

Business unit sponsors (BUS) from different divisions, functions, and sectors will often be assigned to the Six Sigma process. BUSs provide a local view of the problems that are affecting the business unit's performance and can explain how their business units can react to support the strategic plan. He or she is often held accountable for the success of the Six Sigma system in the business unit. The BUS is responsible for ensuring that the business unit provides the required Six Sigma resources. He or she also provides input to the Champion related to the business unit's priority improvement needs. The BUS is typically a business unit executive.

MASTER BLACK BELTS

It's standard practice to have one Master Black Belt for every fifteen to twenty Black Belts or one per organization if it has less than 200 employees. A Master Black Belt is a highly skilled project manager who should be Project Management Institute-certified. Master Black Belts are experienced teachers and mentors, and they are the heart of the organization's Six Sigma process. Master Black Belts are responsible for:
- Certifying Black Belts and Green Belts
- Training Black Belts
- Developing new approaches
- Communicating best practices
- Helping Black Belts define root causes and implement changes
- Conducting long-term Six Sigma projects
- Identifying Six Sigma opportunities
- Reviewing and approving Green Belt and Black Belt project justifications and project plans

Typically, a Master Black Belt will interface with fifteen to twenty Black Belts to provide mentoring and development service in support of their problem-solving knowledge.

BLACK BELTS

"Black Belts are the workhorses of the Six Sigma system."
—HJH

Generally, organizations have one Black Belt for every 100 employees. Black Belts are highly skilled problem solvers who have thorough understandings of the most frequently used Six Sigma statistical tools. Their number one priority is to define and develop Green Belts to coordinate and lead Six Sigma projects. Black Belt candidates should be experienced professionals who are already highly respected throughout the organization. They should have experience as change agents and be very creative. Black Belts should generate a minimum of $1 million in savings per year as a result of their activities. Black Belts are not coaches, rather they are specialists who support Green Belts and Yellow Belts. They are also used as SST leaders of complex and important projects.

GREEN BELTS

There is usually one Green Belt for every twenty employees and five Green Belts for every Black Belt. A Green Belt is assigned to manage a project or work as a member of an SST by the Champion and his or her manager on a part-time basis. Green Belts should be candidates for future Black Belt assignments if they excel in project management.

A Green Belt works as a member of an SST that's led by Black Belts or other Green Belts; they can also form SSTs when projects are assigned to them. When a Six Sigma project is assigned to a Green Belt, his or her primary responsibility is to manage the SST for the entire project, usually with the help of Yellow Belts.

YELLOW BELTS

Yellow Belts are the process experts of an organization. There is usually one Yellow Belt for every five employees (or four Yellow Belts for every Green Belt).

To be a Yellow Belt, an individual must serve on an SST and complete one Six Sigma project and two or three days of Yellow Belt training. Yellow Belts have a practical understanding of some of the basic problem-solving tools and the define-measure-analyze-improve-control (DMAIC) process. They usually work part time on Six Sigma projects and retain responsibility for most of their normal work assignments, although they should have some of their routine workload reassigned to give them enough time to work on the SST. They usually serve as the expert and coordinator on the project for the area they are assigned to.

BLUE BELTS

"Blue Belts keep the Six Sigma culture alive in the organization year after year."
—HJH

All employees should be trained as Blue Belts as a standard practice. Blue Belts are an organization's regular work force; they may never be assigned to an SST, but they need to be part of the Six Sigma culture. They should be able to apply Six Sigma concepts to their day-to-day activities and will receive two to three days of training on the following subjects:

- How teams function
- What Six Sigma processes are about
- How Six Sigma applies to them
- How to define who their customers are
- The seven basic problem solving tools
- How to flowchart their processes
- Area activity analysis
- How to participate in the suggestion program
- How to participate in quick-and-easy *kaizen*

It's important to note that once the major problems and opportunities have been addressed by SSTs, the Six Sigma culture is sustained by the Blue Belts using area activity analysis, suggestion programs, and Fast Action Solution Teams (FAST) to attain continuous process improvements of between 5 to 15 percent annually. These efforts are the biggest benefits of Six Sigma, but they are often overlooked.

TRAINING THE SIX SIGMA TEAM

One of the basic Six Sigma tenets is that employees are an investment, not a cost. Measurement equipment must be regularly recalibrated, but when it comes to maintaining our most valuable assets (our people), managers are often misers. Training employees is required if they are going to perform at the Six Sigma level. Effective training is one of the most important investments that organizations can make. The Six Sigma system is based on providing the organization's employees and management with new skills that make the total organization more competitive and profitable. Without good training, Six Sigma will fail. The following are the typical training programs for the various Six Sigma assignments:

- Executive training: sixteen hours
- Sponsor/Champion training: two days
- Master Black Belt training: five days
- Black Belt training: ten to twenty days
- Green Belt training: five to ten days
- Yellow Belt training: two to three days
- Blue Belt training: two to three days

> "No company can escape the need to re-skill its people, reshape its product portfolio, redesign its processes, and redirect its resources. The real issue is whether transformation happens belatedly—in a crisis atmosphere—or with foresight in a calm and considered atmosphere . . . whether transformation is spasmodic and brutal or continuous and peaceful."
> —**Gary Hamel and C.K. Prahalad,** ***Competing for the Future***

SIX SIGMA CHALLENGES

To meet Six Sigma's quality challenges, an organization has only three options:
- Reduce the process variability.
- Center the mean of the population.
- Open the acceptable performance limit.

The first approach should always be to focus on centering the process mean and reducing the process breadth (width), using the following six steps:

1. Identify the product characteristics that are critical to satisfying the physical and functional requirements of internal and external customers.
2. Determine the specific product ingredients that contribute to achieving these critical characteristics.
3. Determine the process step or process choice that controls each critical characteristic.
4. Determine a nominal design value and the maximum allowable tolerance for each critical characteristic.
5. Determine the capability for the process elements that control critical characteristics.
6. If the process can't produce output with 99 percent of the product falling within 50 percent of the total tolerance, then change the design of the product and/or process. This will be explained in detail later in this book. Protect your customers by screening the errors out until this standard can be met.

To make Six Sigma more personal, a Six Sigma team member could prepare 1,000 250-word memos with no more than one spelling error. Certainly, this is very challenging based upon normal performance levels. It requires a radical new design to the way management functions. There are a number of points that need to be considered when you are using Six Sigma:

- Six Sigma works well when there are high production rates of the same or very similar parts.
- Six Sigma is very difficult to obtain in areas like administration, sales, and personnel.
- It's extremely difficult for management to perform at the Six Sigma level.
- It works well when variables data can be collected, but less so when attributes data are used.
- It's based on the use of normal distribution, not abnormal or skewed distributions.

Motorola defined a list of tools required to support Six Sigma. They are grouped into three categories: design, process, and material. These tools are:

- Design tools
  - ☐ Design to standard parts/materials
  - ☐ Design to standard processes
  - ☐ Design to known capabilities
  - ☐ Design for assembly
  - ☐ Design for simplicity
  - ☐ Design for robustness

- Process tools
  - ☐ Short-cycle manufacturing
  - ☐ Process characterization
  - ☐ Process standardization
  - ☐ Process optimization
  - ☐ Statistical process control

- Material tools
  - ☐ Parts standardization
  - ☐ Supplier SPC
  - ☐ Supplier certification
  - ☐ Material requirements planning

SIX SIGMA CORE PRINCIPLES

The eleven core Six Sigma principles are:
- Reducing variation improves customer satisfaction.
- Improve performance by reducing costs.
- Select projects that have a bottom-line effect.
- Prioritize projects based on their effect on the business and which results will have a positive effect on the customer.
- Focus on cross-functional processes.
- Pursue near-perfection.
- Analyze and solve problems using statistical techniques.
- Make judgments based on fact-based data.
- Use modifications of the plan-do-check-act (PDCA) cycle for controlling the problem-solving process.
- Respect and build on the knowledge, experience, and creativity of the people throughout the organization.
- Provide in-depth statistical training to key personnel.

SIX SIGMA KEY CONCEPTS
The following are the key concepts that Six Sigma is based upon:
- *Defect.* Anything delivered to an external customer that is not exactly what he or she wanted.
- *Process capability.* What the process can deliver compared to the internal or external customer requirements.
- *Variation.* The amount of drift between outputs from the process.
- *Stable operations.* Inserting constant, predictable processes to improve what customers perceive.
- *Critical-to-quality.* The attributes that are most important to external customers.
- *Design for Six Sigma.* Designing products to meet the customer's needs and process capabilities.
- *Yield.* This is calculated by dividing the number of good items that enter a process/activity into the number of good items that exit the process/activity. This includes reworked items.

YIELD

First-time yield (FTY) is calculated by dividing the number of items entering a process into the number of good items that successfully complete it without being reworked, multiplied by 100.

$$FTY = \frac{Quantity\ of\ good\ items\ that\ were\ not\ reworked/repaired \times 100}{Quantity\ of\ items\ entering\ the\ process}$$

Q_1 = Quantity of good items entering an activity = 900
Q_2 = Quantity of good items completing an activity without being reworked = 850

$$FTY = \frac{850 \times 100}{900} = 94.4\%$$

First-time reject rate = FTR
$$FTR = \frac{(Q_1 - Q_2) \times 100}{Q_1}$$

$$FTR = \frac{(900 - 850)}{900} \times 100 = 05.6\%$$

Rolled first-time yield (RFY) is the percent of items that complete a total series of activities (process) without being rejected. It's calculated by multiplying the first-time yield at each of the activities together. For example, if the FTY for five consecutive activities were:

■ Activity 1 = 98%
■ Activity 2 = 93%
■ Activity 3 = 85%
■ Activity 4 = 99%
■ Activity 5 = 95%

The RFY would be calculated as follows:
$$RFY = FTY1 \times FTY2 \times FTY3 \times FTY4 \times FTY5$$
$$RFY = 0.98 \times 0.93 \times 0.85 \times 0.90 \times 0.95 = 66.3\%$$

Figure 1.9 First-Time Yield vs. Number of Process Steps and Quality

Number of parts and/or process steps	3σ	4σ	5σ	6σ
1	93.32	99.379	99.9767	99.99966
2	87.09	98.76	99.95	99.99932
5	70.77	96.93	99.88	99.9983
10	50.09	93.96	99.77	99.9966
20	25.09	88.29	99.54	99.993
30	00.00	82.954	99.3	99.989
50	3.15	73.24	98.84	99.98
100	0.10	53.64	97.70	99.966
500	0	4.44	89.02	99.83
1,000	0	0.2	79.24	99.66
2,000	0	0	62.75	99.32

The same approach can be used when measuring a single item that has many error opportunities. If the item has ten error opportunities and each has an FTY of 69.15 percent, there would only be a 2.5 percent probability of an item being accepted at that activity (69.15^{10}). If there were twenty error opportunities, the probability of an item being accepted drops to 0.06 percent and to zero percent with thirty error opportunities.

Assume that a process is made up of fifty activities, each having ten error opportunities. This is a total of 500 error opportunities. If each error opportunity had an FTY of 93.32 percent, the RFY would be zero percent.

In other words, you have near-zero possibility of getting an acceptable product through the process without repair. This is assuming that all the parts or steps are in series with each other. Figure 1.9 illustrates this concept based on the number of steps or parts in the process and various sigma limits, assuming a 1.5 sigma shift.

ORGANIZATIONS EMBRACING SIX SIGMA CONCEPTS

Many organizations have embraced Six Sigma concepts:
■ IBM
■ Texas Instruments
■ Defense System Electronics Group (DSEG)
■ Asea-Brown Boveri

- Eli Lilly
- Foxboro
- Honeywell
- Lockheed Martin
- Raytheon
- Seagate
- General Electric

The health care industry has recently embraced Six Sigma as a way to reduce death rates, errors, and cost. Most quality-focused organizations performed at the 3 sigma level at the beginning of the 1990s in manufacturing areas and at 2 sigma in support areas. As of this date, we know of no organization that performs all of its measurements to Six Sigma requirements. Six Sigma and related methodologies are not implemented without difficulties. In their paper "A Benchmarking Framework for Quality Improvement," published by Marcel Dekker Inc. in 1993, authors G. Don Taylor and John R. English point out five problems related to the Six Sigma methodology:

- How to measure defects
- How to apply Six Sigma in nontraditional settings
- The problem of determining whether to relax specifications or to reduce the normal variability of the product
- The use of restrictive assumption
- The determination of appropriate tools to use to achieve Six Sigma goals

HOW SHOULD THE TOTAL SIX SIGMA SYSTEM BE MEASURED?

The focus of the Six Sigma system should be on the external customer. Therefore, its primary measure of success should be on improved customer satisfaction and market share, not on dollars saved. Too much attention is being placed on dollars saved that are not passed on to the external customer, but used to justify large retirement payments to top executives. Few organizations that use Six Sigma report how much their customer satisfaction or market share is improving.

SUMMARIES OF SUCCESSFUL SIX SIGMA PROJECTS

The following cases describe successful implementations of DMAIC. We recommend that the goal for improvement must be at least 50 percent for waste reduction. This will enable the Green Belts and team members to realize breakthrough improvement.

Case I: Improving a plating process

A plating process was having a random bubble problem on a high-yielding process. The process yield was about 98 percent. The objective was to reduce defect rate from 20,000 PPM to Six Sigma level.

Define

Problem was clearly stated as improving the process yield instead of reducing bubbles on the ceramic boards due to unavailability of defect samples for analysis. Process physics was studied, baseline process activities were established, and project scope was specified.

Measure

After process performance data was collected, basic statistics were used to describe them in terms of mean, standard deviation, and capability (Cp), which was slightly more than 1.0. This helped establish a clear goal of achieving a Cp of 2.0 or better.

Analyze

During the analyze phase, the process was modeled using an Ishikawa diagram and regression analysis. Its variation was studied with multi-vari charts. This helped to prioritize variation and identify the related causes of the problem. The cause turned out to be the improper position and spacing of electrodes in the plating tank, which caused significant reduction in process capability.

Improve

During the improve phase, process changes were made and verified to ensure improvement in process yield. Analysis of the changes showed that the process capability index Cp improved from 1.1 to 2.2.

Control

In the control phase, the inspection of boards was reduced and required process adjustments. As a result, the need for engineering support was reduced significantly and diverted to other process improvement activities.

Results

While attempting to fix the bubble problems on the plating surface, the entire process improved. This resulted in additional significant savings. Overall, the project saved about $250,000 annually.

Case II: Improving safety

Employee and other stakeholder safety is important on three levels—morally, legally, and economically. Safety in a small manufacturing business was becoming a major concern; it had suffered an average of four safety-related incidents per month.

Define

The organization wanted to reduce safety-related incidents by 50 percent with zero lost-time accidents. Existing safety-related processes such as training, auditing, incident reporting, and committee meetings were studied, baseline process performance was established, and the project scope was specified.

Measure

Process performance data were collected for incident type, task type, body part affected, and the department involved. A Pareto chart was used to identify the major contributors to the incidents.

Analyze

During the analyze phase, the process was modeled with an Ishikawa diagram and analyzed with failure mode and effects analysis. This helped in identifying related causes of the problem. The causes of the safety problems turned out to be noncompliance to personal protective equipment specifications and a lack of safety and safety monitoring by the line leaders and supervisors.

Improve

During the improve phase, changes to all the safety processes were made and action items with target dates were prepared for all stakeholders. Subsequent analysis of the changes identified a 50-percent reduction in safety incidents; the organization's insurance company later provided additional employee training that reduced its insurance premium.

Control

In the control phase, the company defined the continual monitoring of the safety critical parameters with measures and frequency of measurements.

Results

While attempting to fix the safety problems, the company improved its entire safety management process. A 50-percent decrease in accidents saved the organization about $70,000 annually.

Case III: Error reductions in a graphics department

To deploy Six Sigma in various departments, a graphics department chose to improve document quality. During the production of each report, errors were counted and tracked. The objective was to significantly reduce errors.

Define

In the define phase, a group of reports was selected in the printing area. The term "defect" was defined for editors and typists.

Measure

In the measure phase, the data were analyzed and baseline performance level was established in terms of defects per unit and sigma level. A trend chart along with a goal line was set up to monitor progress.

Analyze

In the analyze phase, defect types were analyzed and sources of errors were identified. For example, the department wanted to reduce typographical errors through higher performance visibility and raise awareness of the quality of the department's output for internal customers.

Improve

During the improve phase, internal procedures were modified to minimize errors and ensure effective verification of reports before being distributed.

Control

Weekly reporting of error rates was implemented. Trend charts were posted and discussed weekly to ensure that goals for error reduction were achieved.

Results

After several months, the error rate exceeded Six Sigma level, i.e., virtual perfection was achieved. The Six Sigma success was celebrated and recognized by the company's CEO.

Case IV: Improving pump performance

Machine productivity is vital to provide quality products on time to customers. Frequent pump failures in a small manufacturing business were becoming a major concern. The company had more than two dozen pump-related breakdowns in two months that resulted in excessive downtime and additional maintenance.

Define

The problem was defined as improving the pump failure rate by at least 50 percent. Existing pump-related processes such as maintenance and usage were studied, baseline process performance was established, and project scope was specified.

Measure

Process performance data were collected for frequency of various pump failures, machine downtime, and labor repair hours. A Pareto chart was used to identify the major contributors to the incidents.

Analyze

During the analyze phase, the process was modeled with an Ishikawa diagram and analyzed with failure mode and effects analysis. This helped in identifying related causes of the problem. The causes turned out to be the unavailability of work instructions for pump checks, pump troubleshooting, and pump rebuilding and assembly.

Improve

During the improve phase, work instructions were created and implemented. Pump failure rate was reduced by more than 50 percent.

Control

In the control phase, the organization scheduled training on work instructions and monitoring of pump performance by random audits.

Results

Pump failures were reduced by about 60 percent and resulted in direct savings of about $20,000 annually and improved production manufacturing capacity.

Case V: Surface spots

A tumbling process had poor yield and was producing cosmetic defects on well-machined parts, resulting in a production bottleneck and customer returns.

Define

During the define phase, the problem was clearly described, the process was mapped and understood, and stakeholders were identified. In this case, the process had five major steps; four of them were outsourced to external suppliers. Meetings with all vendors were held and agreement was reached on steps to follow for handling parts. The goal was set to double the process' first-time yield.

Measure

In the measure phase 100 parts with serial numbers were processed and inspected using vendor processes. Data were collected after each process step using new checklists and secured. Parts were inspected for observations and special conditions that couldn't be captured through the standard data-collection process.

Analyze

Data on the collected parts were analyzed for trends or patterns. Root cause analysis was done after each process to identify causes of variation. Just when the solution became impossible to find, correlation was observed between pattern of defects on the parts and process areas. Suddenly, the solution became clearer.

Improve

Three controlled evolutionary experiments were conducted to fine tune the process and increase the yield. Interestingly, there was minimal interaction among variables; thus with each planned experiment, the yield improved and finally exceeded 99 percent.

Control

During the control phase, the objective was to modify procedures for maintaining the redesigned process conditions and enforce compliance. The purchasing department was charged with continually monitoring supplier performance.

Results

The process yield improved dramatically and exceeded the project goal of doubling the yield.

Case VI: Inventory reduction

A small company had excessive inventory that affected its profitability. Its inventory management process had to be changed to improve its profitability.

Define

During the define phase, inventory issues were described and a project team was formed consisting of representatives from the quality, production, and purchasing departments. The goal was to reduce inventory by about 30 percent.

Measure

During the measure phase, inventory data were collected: quantities, age, parts, usage, incoming defect rate, and lead times.

Analyze

During the analyze phase, inventory was classified as dormant or active, part usage was analyzed, supplier management process was examined, and economic order quantity was examined for parts availability and quality.

Improve

During the improve phase, the purchasing processes were modified, most of the dormant inventory was labeled and saved as corporate assets, and long-lead time parts were identified and their ordering process managed. Internal communication and reporting methods were modified.

Control

During the control phase, inventory levels were monitored and new parts were ordered effectively. Instead of ordering parts freely, a new purchasing process was implemented with effective review of purchase orders.

Results

The inventory levels were significantly reduced and number of turns improved resulting in an improved profit margin. For a small company, such improvements have a big effect on profitability.

SUMMARY

Your Yellow Belt training provides you with the tools and methodologies to take advantage of 20 to 40 percent of the improvement opportunities that your organization faces. After you become competent in using these tools and methodologies, you should consider training at the next level of problem-solving maturity—the Green Belt level. At the Green Belt level you should be able to take advantage of 60 percent of the improvement opportunities.

The term "yellow" is often used to define a coward. In the case of Six Sigma, nothing could be further from the truth; they must be risk takers, Yellow Belts must be creative, and they must not be afraid of taking an unpopular stance. Becoming certified as a Yellow Belt is the start of a bright future.

"We cannot spell 'success' without a 'U'."

—HJH

CHAPTER 2

BEING A TEAM PLAYER

"The most basic need of an individual is to be part of a team.
Teamwork makes work fun."

—HJH

Problem solving is only a small part of Six Sigma. As a Yellow Belt, you play a very important role not only as a member of the Six Sigma team (SST) but also as a spokesperson for the organization's Six Sigma system. Six Sigma manages with statistics and facts; as a result, it's heavily statistically oriented, but there is another side to Six Sigma that's represented by an organizational attitude that each employee and manager can do near-perfect work.

This chapter will introduce you to some of the basic team-building tools that you will use as a Yellow Belt. Problem-solving tools will be covered in chapter 3. Although there are many tools in the Six Sigma toolbox, it's best if you concentrate on the ones that you are most apt to use. If you have a need for more advanced tools than the ones we have presented in this book, contact a Black Belt to provide training and direction.

It's important to remember that the average Six Sigma project lasts about three months and should yield at least $100,000 in savings, after the expenses of the SST and the implementation costs are subtracted. One of the big advantages of this training is that the tools can also be used in solving your day-to-day, less complex problems. What you learn as a Yellow Belt will benefit you in more ways than just the Six Sigma projects you work on.

KEYS TO TEAMWORK

The following are eight keys that can help teams work together:

- *Chemistry.* The "magic" when individuals unite to achieve something beyond the reach of a single person.
- *Recruiting.* Selecting people with specific knowledge, skills, education, and experience needed to excel in each role on the team.
- *Attitude.* This, more than aptitude, determines a team's final altitude.
- *Diversity.* Create and sustain an environment that values all individuals on the team and enables them to reach their full potential. The team benefits from exposure to other learning styles, social backgrounds, etc., by being more innovative with members' ideas and approaches to problem resolution.
- *Role acceptance.* Team members must be fully committed to their roles and the accompanying responsibilities.

- *Environment.* The team's work environment should provide direction and support.
- *Mission.* Team members must know what the organization expects from them.
- *Vision.* A compelling vision communicated in less than ten seconds can change the world.

TEAM ALIGNMENT

One of the major challenges for any team is to get everyone singing the same tune in the correct key. As the team comes together for its first meeting, each member has his or her own set of hopes, fears, beliefs, and strategies about what the project will accomplish for the organization and for him or herself personally. The following set of documents helps to transform the group into a team:
- Team charter
- Team objectives
- Team goals
- Team project plan

Team charter

A team charter is a written commitment or contract by management that states the purpose and objectives of the SST. It provides the team with clear direction from the Six Sigma leadership team. The team charter doesn't map the project's route; instead it provides its boundaries and destination. It includes project objectives, project process boundaries, limitations, key deliverables, outside resources, indicators, and targets.

The team charter should be prepared before the team is formed. It should reflect the proposed project's effect on quality, cost, schedule, and customer satisfaction. It approves the expenditure of funds to support the project and might be adjusted as the SST collects data. Management must approve all changes to the basic charter unless the proposed change is for a cost or schedule reduction. However, the SST should be allowed to autonomously make changes designed to improve the project's output without increasing cost and schedule, as long as the SST adheres to the basic parameters in the charter.

Team objectives

The team objectives set the direction for the team and are closely aligned with the team charter. A typical project objective would be to develop and implement changes that reduce customer complaints related to the product-delivery process by at least 50 percent over the next 120 days.

Team project goals

Goals should be quantifiable, measurable, time-related, and in tune with the project's charter. There are often several individual goals related to each project. For example:
- Reduce delivery-time variation by 50 percent.
- Reduce return rates by 25 percent.
- Reduce costs by 25 percent.
- Reduce response time by 30 percent.

Team project plan

A project plan is a formally approved document used to guide project execution and project control. It's primarily used to document assumptions and decisions to facilitate communications among stakeholders. It's also used to document approved scope, cost, and scheduled baseline. A project plan can be a summary or a detailed report.

The project plan provides a timeline of the strategies the SST will use to meet the team charter's requirements, project objectives, and project goals. This is called a work breakdown structure (WBS). The project plan is also used to define the interrelationships between individual activities and assignments.

DMAIC'S TWELVE TOLLGATES

There are typically twelve tollgates in a DMAIC project, as illustrated in figure 2.1. These tollgates provide the key points in the project's life cycle where management should review its status.

TEAM ROLES AND RESPONSIBILITIES

There are four key roles that help create a successful team: team sponsor, team leader, team facilitator, and team member. Each role carries specific responsibilities. Let's take a brief look at each team role.

The team sponsor

The sponsor initiates and guides the team. The sponsor isn't a member of the team but will be responsible for appointing the team leader. Together they will develop the team charter and select the team members. Your sponsor will be the team leader's primary point of communication outside the team.

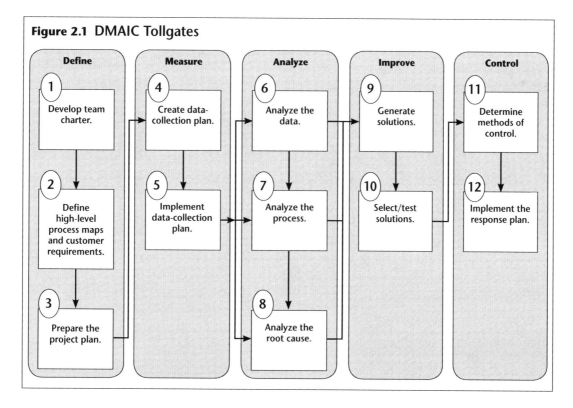

Figure 2.1 DMAIC Tollgates

Define	Measure	Analyze	Improve	Control
1 Develop team charter.	**4** Create data-collection plan.	**6** Analyze the data.	**9** Generate solutions.	**11** Determine methods of control.
2 Define high-level process maps and customer requirements.	**5** Implement data-collection plan.	**7** Analyze the process.	**10** Select/test solutions.	**12** Implement the response plan.
3 Prepare the project plan.		**8** Analyze the root cause.		

Some of the duties of the team sponsor are:

- Selects the team leader.
- Assists in developing the team charter.
- Helps the team leader select team members.
- Meets regularly with the team leader.
- Helps to remove obstacles.
- Provides additional resources.
- Champions the implementation of team solutions.
- Provides ongoing feedback.

The SST sponsor may either be the Six Sigma Champion or the Six Sigma sponsor; sometimes the Master Black Belt might take the role.

The team leader

The team leader may be elected by the team but is usually appointed by the team sponsor. The team leader usually has a deeper knowledge of the problem area than other team members, experience in the problem-solving process, and an excellent understanding of the team process. The team leader should also be a Green Belt, Black Belt, or Master Black Belt. Regardless of who the team leader is, he or she must be able to guide the team without dominating it and be an effective role model.

Some of the duties of the team leader are:

- Coordinates team meetings and activities.
- Teaches and trains team members.
- Promotes and sustains team synergy.
- Encourages individual member participation without coercing.
- Follows up on meeting action items.
- Assists the team in monitoring and measuring its progress.
- Ensures the team process is being followed.

The team facilitator

The team facilitator is a group process specialist and should be a Black Belt or Master Black Belt. The chief distinctions between the facilitator and the team leader are:

- The facilitator is adept at using a wide range of tools and techniques for decision making, problem solving, and process improvement.
- As the team's process expert, the facilitator focuses on the team's process; the team leader is primarily concerned with the project content.

Some of the duties of the team facilitator are:

- Coaching the team leader
- Helping the team stay on track
- Helping the team manage conflict effectively
- Coaching the team on how to use tools effectively

Team members

Team members are the lifeblood of the team. The idea of participative management is based on allowing employees to help management make better decisions. If the team leader guides effectively, the team members should assume responsibility for successfully completing the task.

Some team member responsibilities are:
- Willingness to express opinions or feelings
- Active participation
- Attentive listening
- Creative thinking
- Instructive communication
- Willingness to call a time-out when necessary
- Protecting the rights of other members

SST members are typically Yellow Belts or Green Belts, although occasionally they may have no Six Sigma training. Instead, these members usually have specific skills or knowledge related to the project or their manager wants them to gain the experience of participating on an SST. Black Belts will sometimes serve as members of a team that is led by another Black Belt or Master Black Belt.

TEAM GROUND RULES

The ground rules are a set of standards of behavior and attitudes that the team agrees to abide by. They should be established when the team is formed and should include expectations regarding:
- Punctuality
- Respect for team members
- Member responsibilities/commitments
- Meeting etiquette
- Juggling team tasks with routine work assignments
- Meeting agendas
- Communication
- Member participation
- Teamwork
- Follow up actions

The entire team is responsible for ensuring that the ground rules are established and followed. Figure 2.2 is a list of typical ground rules for the team leader. Figure 2.3 is a list of typical ground rules for all team members, including the team leader and the facilitator.

SUMMARY

The team is the heart of the problem-solution cycle. Without an excellent team, Six Sigma will fail. Bringing the team together is the most important part

Figure 2.2 Typical Ground Rules for the Team Leader

	Session leader
1	Start breaks on time (±10 minutes maximum).
2	Start session on time (±5 minutes maximum).
3	Follow the agenda.
4	End sessions on time (±15 minutes maximum).
5	Don't interrupt.
6	Keep accurate error-rate logs.
7	Send agendas out three days in advance.
8	Document meeting within forty-eight hours.

Figure 2.3 Typical Ground Rules for the SST

	Attendees
1	Arrive on time (±5 minutes maximum).
2	Back from breaks on time (±2 minutes maximum).
3	Back from lunch on time (±2 minutes maximum).
4	Ask one question or make one comment at each meeting.
5	Come to meetings with assignments completed and with copies of the results for the other members.
6	Encourage others to express their opinions.
7	Never belittle another team member's ideas. Build on them to make them better if you can.
8	Document meeting within forty-eight hours.
9	Stay to the end of the session.
10	Don't interrupt.
11	Don't monopolize the discussion.
12	Keep accurate error-rate logs.

of the system. Black Belts and Green Belts too often focus on Six Sigma's technical tools to the detriment of team building. Don't let that happen to you. As a Yellow Belt team member, you are responsible to help the team function. Do your part even if you're not the team leader.

"Yellow represents the gold in them thar hills. Go get it."

—HJH

CHAPTER 3

BASIC SIX SIGMA YELLOW BELT TOOLS

Ken Lomax assisted with the preparation of this chapter.

"Too many people only have a hammer and think everything is a nail."
—HJH

Yellow Belts are the problem solvers of Six Sigma teams (SST). This requires the Yellow Belt to have an excellent understanding of the basic problem-solving tools and know how SSTs work. This chapter is designed to provide the Yellow Belt with an understanding of the fifteen most used problem-solving tools:

- Affinity diagrams
- Brainstorming
- Cause-and-effect diagrams
- Checksheets
- Failure mode and effects analysis (FMEA)
- Flowcharts
- Force-field analysis
- Graphs
- Histograms
- Nominal group technique
- Pareto diagrams
- Root cause analysis
- Scatter diagrams
- Supplier, input, process, output, customer (SIPOC) diagrams
- 5Ws

Each tool has a description, an explanation of its use, examples, and where it is used during the design, measure, analyze, improve, and control (DMAIC) process. A list of Six Sigma definitions can be found in appendix A.

Many of the tools presented in this book require graphs and/or special forms. They can be generated by hand, but it's much faster, more accurate, and easier to use a computer program to do it for you. The software will also do all the statistical calculations for you. Although learning how to use these software programs is not part of Yellow Belt training, it is part of Green Belt training. If you are interested in learning about this software, ask a Green Belt or Black Belt to help you. The cost of the software runs from $140 to more than $1,000.

GRAPHS (CHARTS)

"It has been said, 'A picture is worth a thousand words.' I believe this
is conservative or the speaker never read a consultant's report."

—HJH

How to use graphs

Graphs (or charts, as the terms will be used here interchangeably) should present data as simply and clearly as possible. The comprehension and interpretation that graphs normally enhance are not ends in themselves. Graphs illustrate the current state and point out significant problems, causes of problems, or areas of potential difficulty so we can make the best-possible decisions.

Uses for graphs

Graphs are most often used to show trends, comparisons, progress, and controls. The following are typical applications:

- Rate of change in temperature, pressure, size, volume, weight, and other measurements
- Quality performance trends
- Process, procedure, and operating efficiency
- Distinguishing major and minor factors for setting priorities (Pareto diagrams)
- Distribution of variations in measurements of the same thing (histograms)
- Cost trends
- Records of attendance, turnover, training, and safety

There are many graphic ways to display facts and statistical data. The type of data and the ideas to be presented determine the most suitable method. Depending on their application, line graphs, bar and column graphs, area graphs, milestone/planning graphs, and pictorial graphs are all valuable tools.

The value of well-prepared graphs

The more significant values of well-prepared graphs are:

- In comparison with other types of presentations, properly designed graphs are more effective in creating interest and in attracting the attention of the reader.
- Visual relationships, as portrayed by charts and graphs, are clearly grasped and easily remembered.
- The use of graphs and charts saves time because the essential meaning of large masses of statistical data can be understood at a glance.
- Graphs and charts provide a comprehensive picture of a problem that provides a more thorough and better understanding than could be derived from less illustrative forms of presentation.
- Graphs and charts bring out hidden facts and relationships and can stimulate and aid analytical thinking and investigation.

Characteristics of graphs

A well-made graph has these characteristics:

- Summarizes data.
- Guides problem solving.
- Demonstrates a point.
- Doesn't mislead.
- Is visually interesting.

Figure 3.1 Three Different Graphs Showing the Same Data

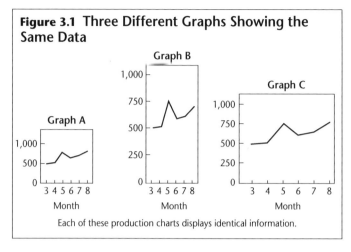

Each of these production charts displays identical information.

Take care to create simple graphs that aren't cluttered with too much information. The point must be clearly perceived. One necessity for ease of interpretation is a legend. The legend records what the graph covers, when and where the data were obtained, and who collected them. It also explains any special symbols used. These factors are relatively straightforward, requiring no more than accurately transcribing the data onto the graph.

The choice of numerical increments for the graph may require careful thinking. Different numerical increments will create different impressions, which can lead to data misinterpretation. Figure 3.1 shows three graphs displaying the same data on three different scales. Clearly, the choice of scale can distort and thus misrepresent the data.

For the sake of clarity, fractional increments should be avoided whenever possible. It's easier to read and interpret 2–4–6–8 than it is to read and interpret 2.5–5–7.5–9.

Multiple graphs

In analyzing problems (and certainly in presenting details about problems and possible solutions), a combination of graphs and charts is normally used. For example, data obtained from research into the major causes of a single problem can result in a cause-and-effect diagram or Pareto diagram, as well as the checksheet used to gather the data. Two Pareto diagrams can be used to show dollar-cost comparisons and also to show the frequency of occurrences. A line graph can illustrate different aspects of the same problem or summarize changes occurring over a period of time. Different aspects of the same problem are shown in figure 3.2.

Comprehension and interpretation of many facts—especially statistical data—are often best attained by analyzing graphs. Lengthy tabulations of data are the most difficult to understand. Data summaries make

Figure 3.2 Different Types of Graphs

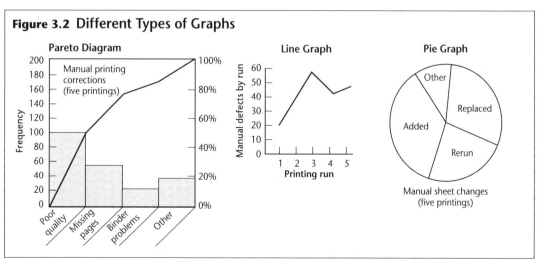

it easier, but graphic presentations are the best way to summarize complex information. In fact, numbers and data are often virtually meaningless until they're summarized graphically.

A graph that shows a single set of numbers is termed "one dimensional." This is a common graph, one that we view each time we look at the fuel gage in our cars or the temperature gage on a machine. (See figure 3.3.)

Multidimensional graphs depict the relationship between two or more sets of data. In almost all of the graphs to be explained here, the starting point of the graphic representation is the construction of the X and Y axes.

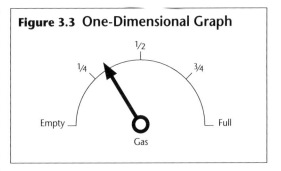

Figure 3.3 One-Dimensional Graph

X- and Y-axes graphs

An X- and Y-axes graph is a pictorial presentation of data on sets of horizontal and vertical lines called a grid. The data are plotted on the horizontal and vertical lines, which have been assigned specific numerical values corresponding to the data.

X axis is the name given to the horizontal line in a two-dimensional graph. The vertical line is called the Y axis. (See figure 3.4.)

The point where the two lines meet is called the zero point, point of origin, or origin. When numbers are used, their value is increased on both axes as they move away from the origin.

The horizontal X axis is most frequently used to record the time frame or cause of the data being plotted. Because of the fixed nature of the time frame or cause, they are also called independent variables.

The effect of the cause or the effect over a period of time is called the dependent variable and is almost always plotted on the vertical Y axis. (See figure 3.5.)

If two variables depend on each other or if they are affected by some other factor, they can be arbitrarily placed on either axis.

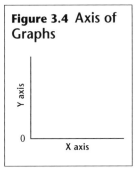

Figure 3.4 Axis of Graphs

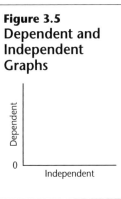

Figure 3.5 Dependent and Independent Graphs

Types of multidimensional graphs

Line graphs

Line graphs illustrate the relationship of one measurement to another over a period of time. They are the simplest graphs to prepare. They are often continually created as measurements are gathered. This procedure may allow the line graph to serve as a basis for projecting future relationships of the variables being measured. (See figure 3.6.)

Multiple-line graphs

Multiple-line graphs show the relationships of more than two sets of measurements on the same axes. (See figure 3.7.)

Area graphs

Area graphs are convenient methods of showing how 100 percent of something is apportioned. The most commonly used area graph is the pie chart. (See figure 3.8.)

Figure 3.6 Basic Line Graphs

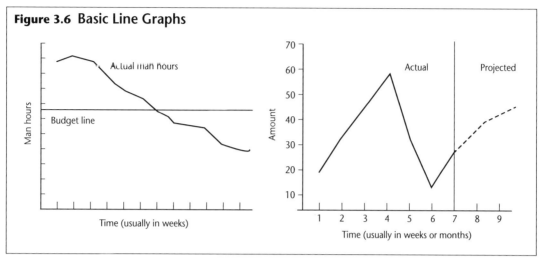

Figure 3.7 Multiple-Line Graph

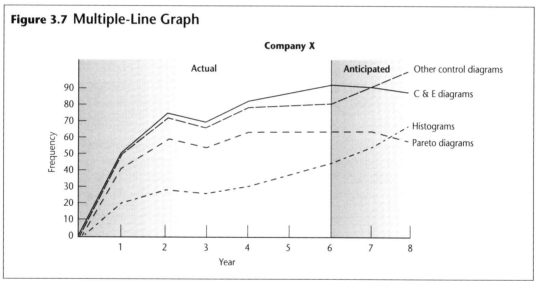

Figure 3.8 Area Graphs

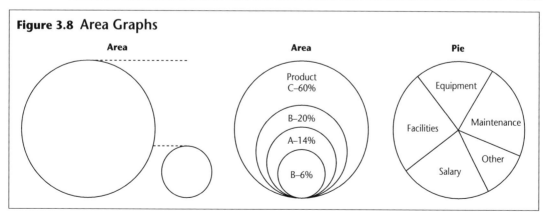

Bar and column graphs

Bar graphs have bands positioned horizontally (bars) or vertically (columns), which show variations in the magnitude of several measurements. There may be multiple bars or columns to show two or more related measurements in several situations.

Bar graphs have the bars originating from the Y axis. As a consequence, the normal location of dependent and independent variables is reversed. (See figure 3.9.)

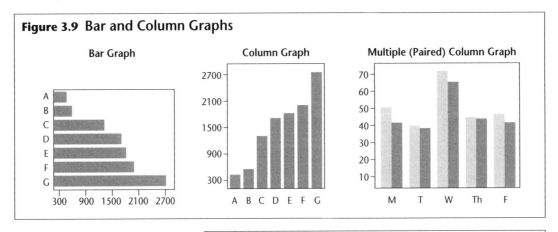

Figure 3.9 Bar and Column Graphs

Milestone or planning graphs

A milestone or planning graph shows the goals or target to be achieved by depicting the projected schedule of the process. Its primary purpose is to help organize projects and coordinate activities. (See figure 3.10.)

Figure 3.10 Milestone or Planning Graph

Activity code	Week																								
			5			10			15			20			25										

Pictorial graphs and pictograms

Pictorial graphs use pictures or drawings to represent data. Pictograms use symbols to represent a specific quantity of the item being plotted and are constructed and used like bar and column graphs. (See figure 3.11.)

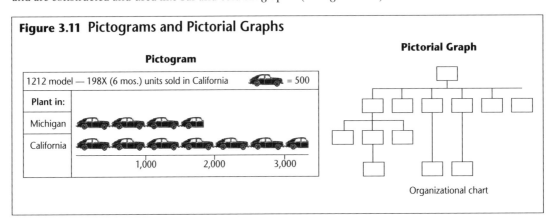

Figure 3.11 Pictograms and Pictorial Graphs

Many of the graphs represented in the previous figures are called "X-Y graphs," because they have an X axis and a Y axis. Although that's rather elementary, many of us have forgotten the basics when creating these graphs. Let's do a brief refresher.

Creating an X-Y axes graph

The creation of an X-Y axes graph is easy if the following process is used:

1. *Collect and list data.* No graph is possible without the collection of accurate data that are gathered in uniform time periods. When these are listed on some form of worksheet (such as a data analysis table, shown in figure 3.12), it's best to arrange the data in sequence using size or time. The information is thus organized to facilitate transfer onto the graph.

2. *Convert and round off data.* Raw data come in a variety of forms. One source may list a fraction (such as 2 ½ hours) and another may use decimals (2.5 hours). Whatever the system, the data must be displayed uniformly; this may require conversion.

   When numerical data appear in decimal form, you need use only the level of accuracy necessary to make your point clear.

Figure 3.12 Data Analysis Table

X Days	Y Units		
1	12		
2	9		
3	8		
4	11		
5	10		
6	11		
7	7		
8	6		
9	11		
10	14		
11	12		
12	10		

Data collection days are independent variables on the X-axis.
Units sold per day are dependent variables on the Y-axis.

Usually hundredths and thousandths can be rounded to tenths; sometimes tenths can be rounded to whole numbers. Certain circumstances will demand an accuracy that requires a more systematic rounding process. There are several methods available. The most common follows this rule:

1.1, 1.2, 1.3, and to 1.4 round down to 1
1.5, 1.6, 1.7, 1.8, and to 1.9 round up to 2

This method results in a number rounding down four times (0.1, 0.2, 0.3, and 0.4) and up five times (0.5, 0.6, 0.7, 0.8, and 0.9), thus introducing a statistical bias.

A preferred rule eliminates this bias by rounding 0.5 down half the time and up half the time. When an odd number precedes the 0.5, it rounds upward; when an even number precedes the 0.5, it rounds downward:

0.5 rounds down to 0
1.5 rounds up to 2
2.5 rounds down to 2
3.5 rounds up to 4

Because the number preceding the 0.5 has an equal chance of being odd or even, no statistical bias is introduced. This method can be used in rounding decimals of any length. For example, 8.075 become 8.08 and 14.3945 becomes 14.394.

3. *Select and scale the grid.* The next step is to determine the range of your data range for both axes. Examine the listed data, which are by now appropriately converted and/or rounded. The data's time span or number of causes and the smallest and largest numbers should be clear. You are now able to determine the major divisions necessary for the graph that will demonstrate your data clearly. (See figure 3.13.)

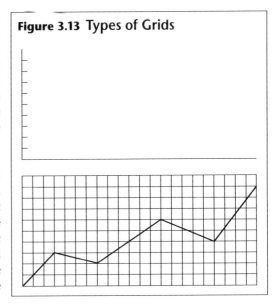

Figure 3.13 Types of Grids

Next you need to choose the type of graph that will be most appropriate for your data. Will a line graph or column graph best show the data and your intent in using this information? Do the data require single or multiple lines or columns? A question of basic format must also be answered. Will your completed graph show a two-dimensional grid or will the line or columns appear on a blank background within the X-Y axes?

A two-dimensional grid is made by drawing perpendicular lines from the X and Y axes to create a series of squares or rectangles. These lines are called divisions or scale lines. The lines must be uniformly scaled on an axis, though the mathematical progression need not be the same on both axes. If the data require it, accent lines can be added. For example, the X axis may have a series of divisions marking months with bolder accent lines demarking years.

The choice between grid and blank background may be determined by which of the two formats makes the data easier to read and understand. Sometimes the choice may be just a matter of preference. Ultimately, clarity is the main concern.

Scaling

Scaling the grid is important because you want to avoid visual distortion of the data's information. (See figure 3.14.)

The distortions in figure 3.14 are clear; unfortunately, there is no firm rule to follow to avoid such misrepresentation. The general practice is to place the lowest point on the Y axis within the bottom 20 percent of the graph and the highest point within the top 20 percent. A further aid to accurate representation is to use a square or rectangular proportion for the graph. The ratio between the sides should not exceed seven to ten; that is, neither side should be less than 70 percent or more than 140 percent of the length of the other side.

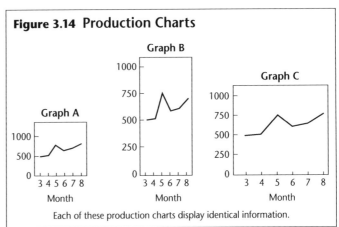

Figure 3.14 Production Charts

Each of these production charts display identical information.

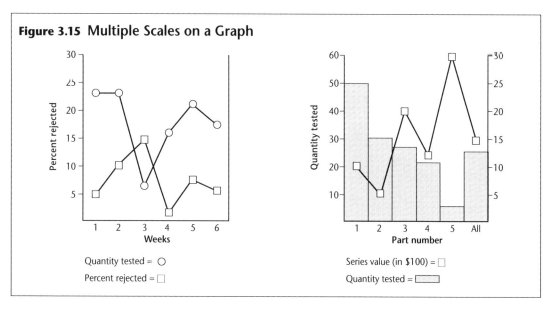

Figure 3.15 Multiple Scales on a Graph

Multiple scales

More than one scale will be needed on either the X or Y axis when you plot on the same graph multiple sets of data that use different units of measurement. Place the additional scales on either the same side or opposite sides of the graph, drawing an additional vertical line when necessary. (See figure 3.15.)

Multiple scales will always be used in creating a Pareto diagram—one for the percentage increments and the other to show frequency or cost. Other uses of multiple scales include such information as dollar sales and unit codes, or days, weeks, and months.

Break in the axis

Sometimes it's necessary to highlight small changes in data of large magnitude. Interrupting the axis and showing only the top portion of the data on a more refined scale can accent these changes.

Note that such a break distorts the amount of change because the graph will not give a true picture of the relation of the emphasized data to the base. To make it easy to see, it's best to extend the notion of the break across the entire graph. (See figure 3.16.)

4. *Label axes and title graph.* Every graph should have a full title. The title can be placed at the top or bottom of the graph or it may be boxed within the graph. A title is easier to read if it is parallel to the X axis. Each axis should be clearly labeled with its numerical values or categories and appropriate descriptions. Horizontal labels are easiest to read, but vertical or even top-to-bottom labels are acceptable. A graph should also contain a legend indicating the source of data, who collected the data, and the dates the data were gathered.

5. *Plot, connect, and identify data points.* Now that you have the framework to display your data, you're ready to plot them on the graph. Each data point

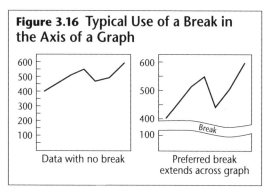

Figure 3.16 Typical Use of a Break in the Axis of a Graph

is plotted at its X and Y coordinates. It's always wise to double-check your points with the data to make sure there are no plotting errors. Note that when the X axis represents time, your data point is to be located in line with the mark or number which represents the end of the time period. (See figure 3.17.)

The process of connecting the plotted points will obviously vary according to whether you are making a line graph or a bar graph. In the latter case, construct the horizontal or vertical bars by drawing horizontal and vertical lines to depict the proper height and width.

Straight lines between the points on a line graph usually connect data points. One may also use a "French curve," which is a flat drafting instrument, usually made of plastic or celluloid with curved edges and scroll-shaped cutouts, that is used as a guide in connecting a set of individual points with a smooth curved line. (Note: A line connecting plotted points is called a curve even if it's a straight line. See figure 3.18.)

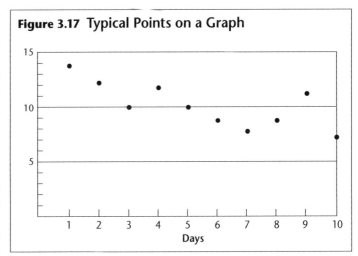

Figure 3.17 Typical Points on a Graph

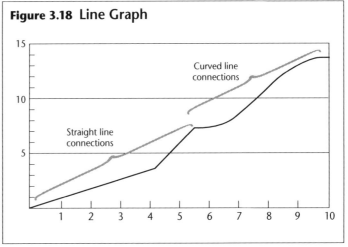

Figure 3.18 Line Graph

If more than one line is to be drawn on a graph, you can avoid confusion by plotting and connecting all the points of one line before moving along to the next. It's necessary to use different forms of lines in this case. For example:

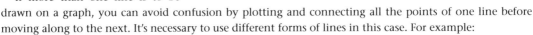

■ Primary data ——————

■ Secondary data ················

■ Tertiary data --------------

If more than three sets of data are presented, use combinations of these three types or clearly darker or lighter versions of them. For example, instead of one solid line (as used for the primary data), use a double solid line. The same applies for dotted and dashed lines.

In all cases where data are represented by a graph, the graph should have a legend that clearly identifies the type of data represented.

Identifying the value of each plotted point makes graphs easier to read. The value should be written in a place where it does not interfere with the line. (See figure 3.19.)

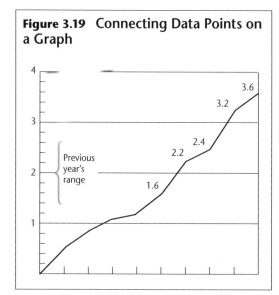

Figure 3.19 Connecting Data Points on a Graph

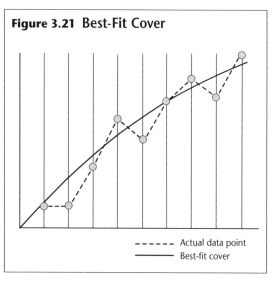

Figure 3.21 Best-Fit Cover

Actual data point
Best-fit cover

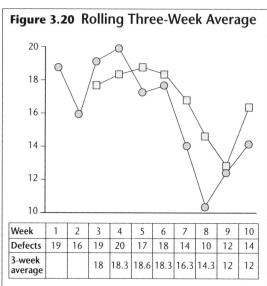

Figure 3.20 Rolling Three-Week Average

Week	1	2	3	4	5	6	7	8	9	10
Defects	19	16	19	20	17	18	14	10	12	14
3-week average			18	18.3	18.6	18.3	16.3	14.3	12	12

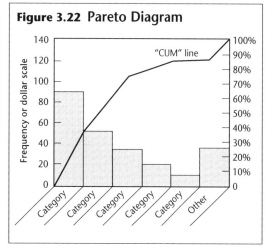

Figure 3.22 Pareto Diagram

"CUM" line

To show the range of the data that occurred in a period prior to that which the graph depicts, use a vertical bar inside the Y-axis and label it. Plotting a three-point average helps to "smooth" a graph. In this approach, three points are added together and divided by three to get the plot point, which is then plotted on the graph. (See figure 3.20.)

Another approach is plotting a best-fit cover between the points on the graph, as shown in figure 3.21.

Sometimes bar graphs and line graphs are plotted together, as in a Pareto diagram. (See figure 3.22.)

CHECKSHEETS

> "Make a list and check it twice. It's the best way to be sure you did not overlook something."
>
> —HJH

Definition

Checksheets, which are also sometimes called data tables, are basic but important tools for collecting and organizing facts and data. They are the foundation on which all of the more advanced data analysis techniques are built.

How to use checksheets

The key to successful problem solving is the use of facts and data, rather than opinion and guesswork. By collecting data, individuals and teams can identify problems more accurately and can effectively analyze causes and effects, thereby making better decisions, solving problems faster, and gaining management's support for their solutions.

Data are objective information; that is, information on which everyone can agree. An objective measurement of a piece of string could use a ruler as a tool to determine its length. If all their rulers are alike, the people measuring the string should have no difficulty agreeing on its length.

Data types

There are three primary types of data: counted, measured, and location.

■ Counted data (sometimes called attributes data) are noted as simply being present or absent. Counted data generally answer the questions "How many?" or "How often?" Examples include:

☐ How many of the final products are defective?

☐ How often are the machines repaired?

☐ How many people are absent each day?

☐ How many days did it rain last month?

■ Measured data (sometimes called variables data) answer questions such as "How long?," "What volume?," "How much time?," and "How far?" The key is that each datum is measured in some way by an instrument or device. Examples include:

☐ How long is each rod?

☐ How long does it take to complete this task?

☐ What is the weight of this material?

☐ What is the pH of this solution?

Measured data are generally regarded as being more useful than counted data, as they are more precise and carry more information. For example, you would probably have more useful information about the climate of an area if you knew how much it rained there in inches, rather than just how many days it rained. However, collecting measured data is frequently more time-consuming and expensive, so it's important to be very clear about the purpose of the data to be collected, to choose the right type of data, and to provide the right checksheet with which to collect and organize it.

attributes

variables

■ Location data, the third type covered here, answer the simple question "Where?" Examples include:

    ☐ Where are accidents occurring?

    ☐ What parts of the body are being injured?

    ☐ On what part of the product are defects occurring?

Construction and uses of checksheets

Two primary types of checksheets will be described here: recording checksheets for collecting counted or measured data, and location checksheets for collecting location data. A brief description of a third type, checklist checksheets, which serve as memory aids to ensure that all necessary tasks are accomplished, will conclude this chapter.

Consider the type of data to be collected when preparing a checksheet. What data will best meet your needs—counted, measured, or location? How much data do you need to collect? How long do you need to collect data to learn what you need to know? Do you need to record who collected the data, where it came from, or when it was collected? What about attributes such as size or color, or variables such as weight, length, and time period? When you have considered these questions, you are ready to design and construct the checksheet best suited to your data-collection needs.

Recording checksheets

Let's begin our look at some examples with a simple recording checksheet for counted (attributes) data about the frequency of defects on a production line. This is illustrated in figure 3.23.

Now look at figure 3.24. Notice that the addition of data regarding defects by shift, by day of the week, and with measured data provides even more useful information. Be sure to choose the data carefully and to provide sufficient room to enter the data.

Location checksheets

The second type of checksheet is the location checksheet, used to depict the location of problems and defects. These checksheets are pictures, illustrations, or maps on which the data are entered, rather than data tables. Entering data this way often simplifies the collection process and helps visualize the problem more clearly. Here are some examples of location checksheets:

■ *Defect location checksheet.* Defects on a part are checked off on a picture of that part, so that corrective or preventive action can be taken. (See figure 3.25.)

■ *Injury location checksheet.* This is often posted so that employees can see where injuries are likely to occur or what protective equipment is necessary. (See figure 3.26.)

■ *Accident location checksheet.* This can help in the analysis of risk areas or accident causes. Employees might then help make an area safer. (See figure 3.27.)

Figure 3.23 A Recording Checksheet with Counted Data

Problem	Place a mark each time it occurs
Failed test	ЖЖ ЖЖ ЖЖ l
Broken	ЖЖ ЖЖ ЖЖ
Lost	ЖЖ lll
. . . .	ЖЖ ЖЖ ЖЖ ЖЖ lll
. . . .	ЖЖ ЖЖ ll

Checklist checksheets

A third type of checksheet is the checklist checksheet, illustrated in figure 3.28. When there are several tasks to complete, or complex or critical tasks, we sometimes start by making a list. We can use the list as a memory aid and then check off each task as it's completed so we can be sure that nothing has been missed.

Figure 3.24 A Recording Checklist with Counted Data by Shift and Day of the Week (Measured Data)

Problem	Shift 1	Shift 1
Failed test	卌 l	卌 卌 卌 卌
Broken	卌 卌 卌	卌 ll
Lost	卌	ll
. . . .	卌 卌 卌	卌 卌 卌
. . . .	卌 lll	卌

Or your checksheet could look like this:

Problem	Shift 1					Shift 1				
	M	**T**	**W**	**T**	**F**	**M**	**T**	**W**	**T**	**F**
Failed test	l	lll		卌	卌 ll	lll	l	卌	ll	卌
Broken		卌	llll			卌	卌	l		ll
Lost	卌	ll	ll	lll	卌	llll	l	ll	卌	l
. . . .	l		lll	卌				ll	卌	lll

To collect measured data, be sure to leave enough room to write in each of your measurements.

Problem (liters)	Shift 1					Shift 1				
	M	**T**	**W**	**T**	**F**	**M**	**T**	**W**	**T**	**F**
High pH	372	9211								
Low pH	1219	1132								
Cloudy	482									
. . . .	1391									

Excellent examples of checklists for critical tasks are those used by pilots or astronauts before takeoff. At home, grocery lists are common examples of checklists. On the job, checklists may be useful for inspecting machinery or merchandise, or when setting up complex or delicate equipment. Supervisors frequently use checklists to be sure they have checked their entire areas. Workers can just as easily develop their own checklists to ensure thorough operations or inspections.

Figure 3.25 Defect Location Checksheet

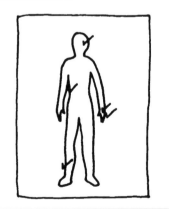

Figure 3.26 Injury Location Checksheet

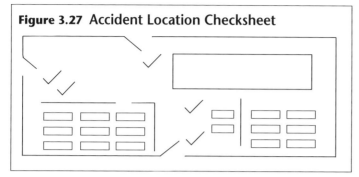

Figure 3.27 Accident Location Checksheet

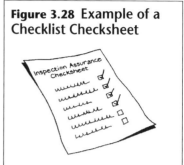

Figure 3.28 Example of a Checklist Checksheet

Checklist checksheet preparation

Now that you have studied some of the types and uses of checksheets, you are ready to prepare your own checksheet. To help you get started, you can use this checklist:

- Are the data historical or new?
- How much data will be involved? A hundred points? A thousand points? A million?
- What checksheet form should be used: recording, location, or checklist?
- Will an existing form do the job?
- Who will be responsible for the coordination?
- How can the tabulation best be done to avoid error?
- If the tabulation is interrupted, can it be restarted without errors?
- Is there an advantage to having several operators tabulate for a short time as opposed to one operator for a long time?
- What labels will be needed on the checksheet?
- Should copies be distributed? To whom?
- Is any training required?

SCATTER DIAGRAMS

"Data is often more confusing than helpful until it's organized."

—HJH

Scatter diagrams illustrate the relationship between two variables. The scatter diagram is used to test for possible cause-and-effect relationships. It doesn't prove that one variable causes the other, but it does show whether a relationship exists and reveals the character of that relationship.

How to use scatter diagrams

The relationship between the two sets of variables can be evaluated by analyzing the cluster patterns that appear on the graph when the two sets of data are plotted with each axis being used for one of the sets of data. The direction and tightness of the cluster gives an indication of the relationship between the two variables.

Steps to prepare a scatter diagram

1. Collect paired samples of data.
2. Construct the horizontal and vertical axes of the diagram. The vertical axis is usually used for the vari-

able that predicts or measures the possible effect. The horizontal axis is used for the variable being investigated as the possible cause of the other variable.

3. Plot the data on the diagram and circle the repeated data points.

4. Analyze the cluster pattern that appears.

Guidelines and tips

Although a scatter diagram is completed to study the cause-and-effect relationship between two variables, be careful about assuming that variable one causes variable two. There might be other reasons why two variables appear to be related, such as a third unrepresented variable that's related to both of the plotted variables.

Keep in mind that the full range over which variable one varies is sometimes key in detecting a correlation between two variables. For example, experimental studies are often done over a wider range than normal production.

Also note that correlations don't have to be linear. Notice in the last example that the two variables are correlated, but not in a linear fashion. Look for patterns that might indicate a relationship between two variables, as shown in figure 3.29.

Figure 3.29 Sample Scatter Diagrams

Weak positive correlation — Variable 1: Height vs. Variable 2: Weight

Strong positive correlation — Variable 1 vs. Variable 2

Weak negative correlation — Weight vs. Vertical leap

Strong negative correlation — Variable 1 vs. Variable 2

No correlation — Number of billing errors vs. Height

Non-linear correlation — Variable 1 vs. Variable 2

HISTOGRAMS

"There are no two things exactly alike. That adds variety in life, but it adds problems in business."

—HJH

Definition

A histogram is a visual representation of the spread or distribution represented by a series of rectangles or bars of equal class sizes or width. The height of the bars indicates the relative number of data points in each class.

How to use histograms

Data gathered about any set of events or series of occurrences will show variation. If the data are measurable, the numbers will vary because no two or more of the same item are identical. These fluctuations are caused by differences in the item or process being observed.

If the data are tabulated and arranged according to size, the result is called a frequency distribution. The frequency distribution will indicate where most of the data are grouped and show how much variation there is. The frequency distribution is a statistical tool for presenting facts to show the data dispersion along a measurement scale.

Description of a histogram

A histogram is a column graph depicting the frequency distribution of data collected on a given variable. It illustrates how the measurements vary around an average value. The frequency of occurrence of each given measurement is portrayed by the height of the columns on a graph.

The shape or curve formed by the tops of the columns has a special meaning. This curve can be associated with statistical distributions that can be mathematically analyzed. The various shapes are given names such as normal, bimodal (multi-peaked), or skewed. A special significance can sometimes be attached to the causes of these shapes. A normal distribution causes the distribution to have a bell shape and is often referred to as a bell-shaped curve, as shown in figure 3.30.

Normal distribution means that the frequency distribution's mean, or average, is symmetrical. To be technically correct, the bell-shaped curve would pass through the center point at the top of each of the bars. We have plotted it at the outside corner to make the histogram appear less complicated.

Uses of histograms

Histograms are effective tools because they show the presence or absence of normal distribution. The absence of normal distribution indicates an abnormality about the variable, which means that the population being measured is not under statistical control. When any process is not under statistical control, its conformance to any desired standard is unpredictable and should be corrected. A histogram is also useful in comparing actual measurements of a population against the desired standard or specification. These standards can be indicated by dotted vertical lines imposed over the histogram, as shown in figure 3.31.

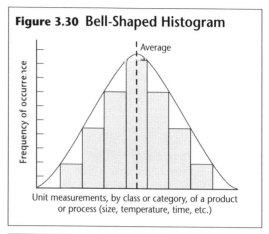

Figure 3.30 Bell-Shaped Histogram

Unit measurements, by class or category, of a product or process (size, temperature, time, etc.)

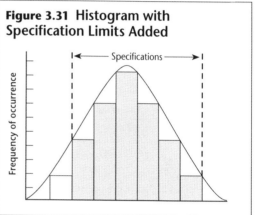

Figure 3.31 Histogram with Specification Limits Added

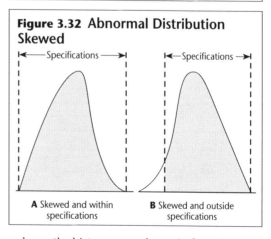

Figure 3.32 Abnormal Distribution Skewed

A Skewed and within specifications

B Skewed and outside specifications

Figure 3.31 indicates that although all the parts that were sampled met the specification requirements, they will need to be screened or a high percentage of defective products will be accepted. Consequently, histograms enable you to:

- Spot abnormalities in a product or process.
- Compare actual measurements with required standards.
- Identify sources of variation.

Abnormalities are indicated when the data don't form a bell-shaped curve (i.e., in the absence of normal distribution), as seen in figure 3.32.

Even when all samples fall within the specifications, a skewed histogram serves as a warning that the process is being affected by other than normal variations and is susceptible to drifting outside the standards, as is the case in figure 3.32.

Histograms can also be used to determine whether the process is producing units that fall within the established specifications or desired standards and, if not, to detect what's needed to fix the situation.

In figure 3.33, the histogram labeled "A" shows an excessive spread with both lower and upper limits being exceeded. This indicates that although the process is under control, its range of variability needs to be tightened up. The histogram labeled "B" shows a process that's also under control but whose average value is too far to the right side of the specifications. It needs a leftward population shift. The histogram labeled "C" has two problems: its spread is too wide, as is the spread in histogram A, and is biased to the right, as is the spread in histogram B. Both kinds of corrective actions are required to tighten and shift the spread.

The third use of histograms is to reveal the presence of more than one source of variation. This is shown when the data measurements form a multipeaked curve. Figure 3.34 illustrates a bimodal curve that contains data measurements from two sources.

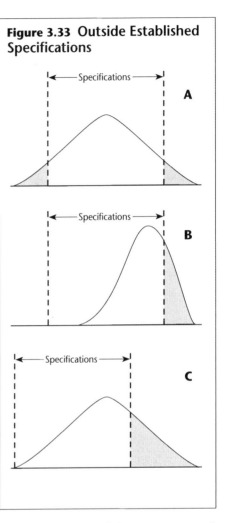

Figure 3.33 Outside Established Specifications

A histogram can be very distorted, as shown in figure 3.35. This type of distribution usually occurs when there is a natural barrier at one end of the measurement. A good example would be the following data from a phone call center:

- 34 percent of calls are answered on the first ring.
- 47 percent of calls are answered on the second ring.
- 8 percent of calls are answered on the third ring.
- 5 percent of calls are answered on the fourth ring or later.
- 6 percent of calls end in hang-ups.

The natural barrier in this case is the expectation that the call center staff will answer the phone as soon as it rings. There could be a natural barrier at the other end as well if the company installed a system that would transfer to voicemail all calls that remained unanswered after a certain number of rings.

Figure 3.34 Bimodal Curve Modeled from Data from Two Different Sources

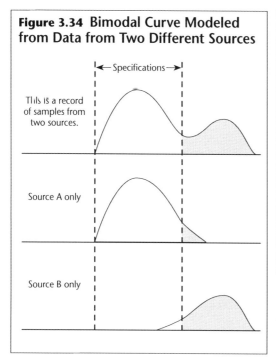

Figure 3.36 Data Table

Method A Length of processing time n = 50				
25	23	25.5	24	29
24	25	33	27	22.5
31	29	20.5	37	25.9
20	17	21	28.1	32.5
19	25.5	30.2	15	25
34	25	24	23.5	30
22	22.1	17.4	24.2	31
19.4	22	23	27	28
26.5	26	18	21.9	19.5
28.5	22	27.9	27.5	24

37 – 15 = 22 = Range
22 ÷ 10 = 2.2 = Width of each column

Constructing a histogram

The following example demonstrates the steps to be taken in constructing a histogram, using for our data the variations in time required to complete a single method, method A.

1. *Collect and organize data.* The more data you have, the more accurate your histogram will be. A minimum acceptable number of data is from thirty to fifty measurements; there is no maximum number. You need a certain type of data to properly construct a histogram. All of the measures must be of the same item or process, and measurements should be uniformly taken. The measure could be how much time it takes to do a certain thing, measured each of the fifty times it's done on a certain day. Another measure could be how many units were processed in an hour, with a simple count being taken for each hour in a forty-hour week. The measurements are of items or processes that should be approximately the same.

   Construct a data table to collect and record data. (See figure 3.36.) Find the range by subtracting the smallest measurement (fifteen) from the largest measurement (thirty-seven). In the example, the range is twenty-two. Divide the range by ten. This tells you the width of the intervals (columns) to be plotted on the histogram's horizontal X axis.

Figure 3.35 Distorted Histogram

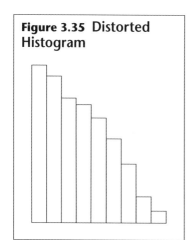

2. *Set histogram interval limits.* Put eleven marks along the X axis at equal intervals, take the largest measurement on the data table (37), and record it on the right end of the horizontal axis. (See figure 3.37.) Put the smallest measurement (15) on the left end of the horizontal axis and add to the smallest measurement the number you got when you divided the range by ten (2.2) to the smallest measurement. Place this new figure (17.2) by the first interval on the horizontal scale. Continue moving to the right so that each interval point is increased the same amount over the interval on the left.

The more data you have, the larger the number by which you should divide to determine the interval. Use the following as a guide.

Number of measures	Divided by
50–100	6–10
100–25	7–12
more than 250	10–20

3. *Set the scale for the Y axis.* Count the total number of measurements and divide this number by three. You may round off this answer. The number three is used as a general practice, as the probability that the highest frequency for any one interval is not likely to be more than 30 percent of your total measurements. This number—in our example, 50 (3 = 16.67, rounded off to 17)—is plotted at the top of the histogram's Y axis. (See figure 3.38.)

4. *Plot the data.* Count the number of measurements that fall between the first two numbers on the horizontal axis and mark the appropriate height. Do this for the remaining intervals along the horizontal line. In counting the number of measurements for each interval, a number that falls on the line between intervals is included in the column that begins with that number. For example, if you were plotting the data in figure 3.38 and the value of a specific measurement was 17.2, it would be plotted in the interval that's marked as 17.2 to 19.4. Then, draw and fill in the columns.

5. *Label the histogram.* Add a legend explaining what the data represent and where, when, and by whom they were collected. (See figure 3.39.)

Histograms are extremely valuable in presenting a picture of how well a product is being made or how well a process is working. This is not something that can be readily detected by a mere tabulation of data. The simplicity of their construction and interpretation make histograms effective tools for the analysis of data. Perhaps most important, histograms speak a common language. They tell whether a process is under statistical control and whether it's designed to meet its expected standard or specification.

The width of the histogram total population can be defined by calculating the standard deviation of the data. Standard deviation is an estimate of the spread of the total population based upon a sample of the population. Sigma is the Greek letter used to designate the estimated standard deviation.

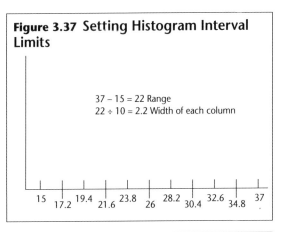

Figure 3.37 Setting Histogram Interval Limits

37 – 15 = 22 Range
22 ÷ 10 = 2.2 Width of each column

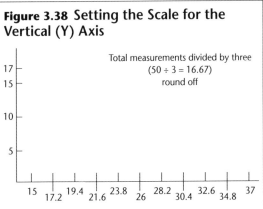

Figure 3.38 Setting the Scale for the Vertical (Y) Axis

Total measurements divided by three
(50 ÷ 3 = 16.67)
round off

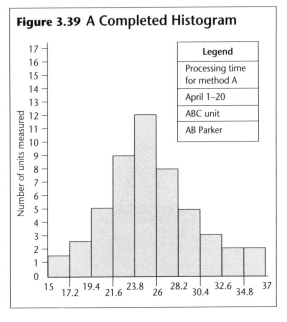

Figure 3.39 A Completed Histogram

Legend
Processing time for method A
April 1–20
ABC unit
AB Parker

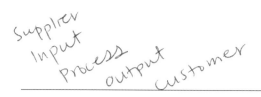

SIPOC DIAGRAMS

"Understand your suppliers and your customers
and you are 75 percent of the way to success."
—HJH

Definition

A supplier, input, process, output, and customer (SIPOC) diagram identifies all relevant elements of a process improvement project before work begins. It helps define a complex project that may not be well scoped and is typically employed in the measure phase of the Six Sigma DMAIC methodology. It's similar and related to process mapping and in/out-of-scope tools, but provides additional detail.

There are two approaches to understanding the present process: one is descriptive and the other is graphic. A good way to understand the process is to describe it. One benefit of describing the process is that it sometimes leads to the discovery of obvious problems and solutions that can be fixed quickly. A flowchart of the process is particularly helpful in obtaining an understanding of how the process works because it provides a visual picture. There are four types of flowcharts that are particularly useful:

- Top-down flowchart
- Deployment matrix flowchart
- Process map
- SIPOC diagram

Of the four types, the SIPOC diagramming method is the one that is most often used in the define phase. The SIPOC flowchart will assist with improvements and simplification by providing:

- A high-level description of the business process addressed by the project
- An accurate picture of how work is done to pinpoint the location or source of error
- Knowledge that will allow the problem solvers to narrow the range of potential causes to be investigated in the measurement and analysis phases

The team should ask and answer key questions such as:

- What does the process do?
- What are the stages of the process?
- What are the starting and finishing points of the process?
- What are the inputs and outputs from the process?
- Who are the suppliers and the customers of the process?
- Who uses the product and who pays for it?
- Are there obvious problems with the process?

A SIPOC flowchart shows only the essential steps in a process without detail. Because it focuses on the steps that provide real value, it's particularly useful in helping the team to focus on the steps that must be performed in the improved process. It allows people to focus on what *should* happen instead of what *does* happen. Usually, processes evolve in an ad hoc manner. When problems have occurred, the process has been fixed haphazardly. The end result is a complex process that was designed to be simple. A flowchart is a first step to simplify and standardize things.

SIPOC diagrams are impressively astute at identifying the part in the process that affects customer satisfaction the most. They illustrate the upstream inputs to the process, as well as the outputs and the customers served. This global view assists in identifying exactly where to make baseline measurements.

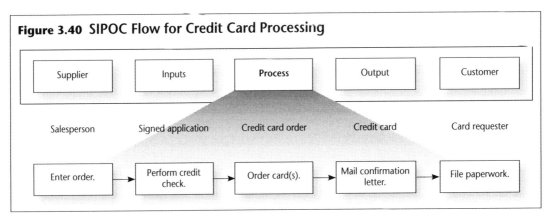

Figure 3.40 SIPOC Flow for Credit Card Processing

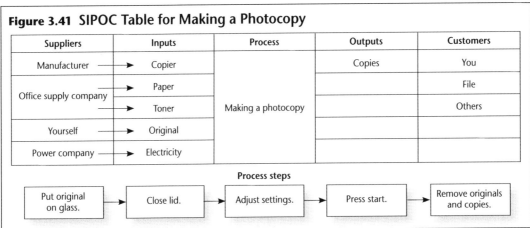

Figure 3.41 SIPOC Table for Making a Photocopy

Two examples illustrate how a SIPOC flowchart can keep the focus on the performance of the inputs and outputs so glaring problems can be identified. (See figures 3.40 and 3.41.)

This is useful because it shows who is responsible for each activity, how he or she fits into the workflow, and how the employee relates to others in accomplishing the overall job. To construct a SIPOC flowchart, list the major steps in the process vertically down the center of the page. List the suppliers and input groups on the left and the outputs and customers on the right.

Capturing the as-is picture of an organization's processes is important because it allows a company to be ready for project selection and the introduction of DMAIC tools and Six Sigma certification. If done correctly, defining the current state of a company's processes can help turn strategic focus areas into project ideas. In early Six Sigma deployments, project scopes are often too large, causing excessive cycle times and a loss of internal organizational support. The goal should be to identify high-value, well-scoped projects that are linked to the company's strategic objectives. This is also the importance of project identification and process mapping: It allows an organization to better understand all the steps, critical inputs, outputs, and product and information flows from supplier to customer. Armed with a detailed and shared visual understanding of how work actually occurs, the organization can more easily identify project ideas for improvement.

Once projects are identified, it's time to validate initial findings and prioritize projects. This healthy discussion with stakeholders allows everyone to come together and objectively discuss ongoing activities and gaps. This process also often produces new process improvement ideas. Team charters for the Six Sigma project ideas selected can then be drafted, providing a framework for the project. Baseline metrics are established at this point, allowing one to track project and process improvement performance. All of this starts with establishing the current state of the process.

The SIPOC approach expanded

As previously discussed, the purpose of mapping an organization's current process is to position it to quickly define, document, analyze, prioritize, and recommend solutions and follow-up plans to move the company toward its financial- and customer-focused goals. Any process mapping activity starts with a simple assessment that can be conducted by interviewing the key stakeholders of the processes. A key activity for this assessment is capturing the critical-to-quality (CTQ) factors of internal clients' processes and services. This lays the foundation for collecting data, developing metrics to measure success, and ultimately building value stream maps. Before a company can leverage the DMAIC process to identify and execute critical process improvement initiatives—let alone perform detailed mapping techniques such as value stream mapping—it needs to capture the basics from initial interviews and assessment. This is where one would use a SIPOC diagram. This initial phase of process mapping is the foundation leveraged throughout the initial phase of a Six Sigma deployment. Think of the SIPOC diagram as a simple process mapping tool used to map the entire chain of events—from trigger to delivery of the target process.

There are two ways to map a SIPOC diagram: swim lane or an unrelated method. A swim lane flowchart illustrates where and who is working on a particular activity or subset of the process, as shown in figure 3.42.

The swim lane flowchart differs from other flowcharts in that processes and decisions are grouped visually by placing them in lanes. Parallel lines divide the chart into lanes, with one lane for each person or group. Lanes are arranged horizontally or vertically and labeled to show how the chart is organized.

The unrelated method requires that the business unit capture all information without directly relating it to a certain process or output, similar to a brainstorming session. This vertical method works best with high-level mapping. The swim lane method is best suited for lower-detail level mapping. Swim lanes produce horizontal charts and allow the business unit to capture all information directly related to a specific process or output, etc. This method requires more space and several mapping sessions due to the amount of time required to map each process.

A team should initially avoid swim lanes unless the objective is detailed lower-level mapping, as this method takes many hours and sessions to complete. Part of the power of SIPOC diagrams is that they are simple to produce but full of helpful information. This enables the team to come to consensus not only about the SIPOC diagram itself, but also on the lessons learned and opportunities. Places in the processes for potential improvement can then be discussed and prioritized in a nonthreatening fashion. By having the business units participate in the session and rank/prioritize opportunities together, they tend to be clearer and more descriptive in a shorter period of time.

Figure 3.42 Swim Lane Flowchart

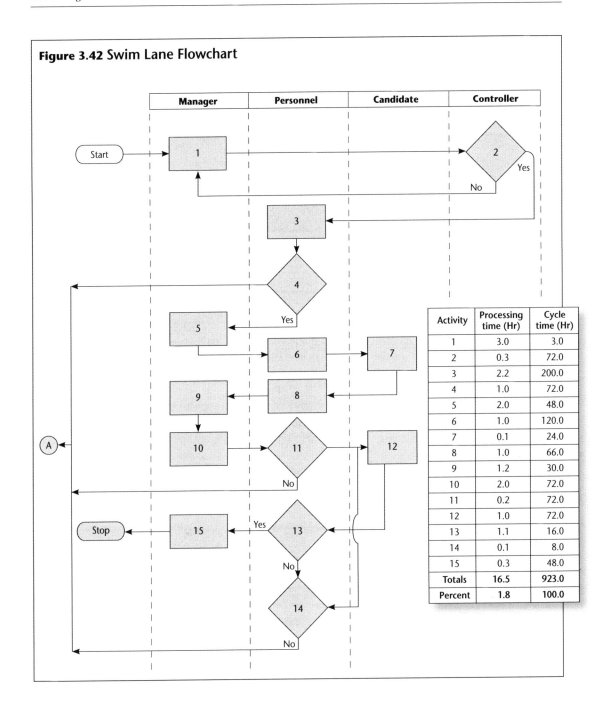

Mama Mia's customer requirements

One of our first steps was to go out and ask our customers what they liked and didn't like about Mama Mia's. Surveys, focus groups, and follow-up interviews with customers identified their most important requirements, which included fresh-tasting pizzas delivered on time. We subsequently interviewed internal customers, including the food preparation personnel, the vice president for procurement, the vice president for food and beverages, and delivery personnel. They indicated that having enough supplies on hand to fill orders and freshness were important requirements.

Mama Mia's Food Prep Chart

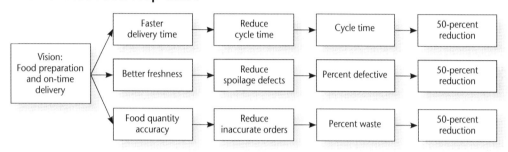

We also had to redefine our terms to clearly understand what a botched delivery meant. The company considered an order successfully delivered even if a pizza didn't get to the right house on the first delivery attempt. By our count, we were getting it right about 97 percent of the time—approximately 3.4 sigma. Mama Mia's customers, however, defined a botched delivery as receiving anything less than a perfect pizza the first time, on time. By their definition, we were only getting it right 87 percent of the time. We had a problem: How could we get the right pizza to the customers on time, every time?

Building a SIPOC diagram

When creating a SIPOC diagram, an SST doesn't necessarily begin at the beginning of the process. Instead, the team should start in the middle and ask questions about the process itself. It may label the process with the summaries of the most critical three or six steps. Next, it should document what is delivered to whom. The team can brainstorm and prioritize the most critical one to three customers and identify, prioritize, and align the outputs most significant to them. Later, the team can verify these initial assumptions with voice of the customer tools from the DMAIC process and/or designate them as critical to quality, speed, or cost. Finally, the team can identify what input or information is needed to perform the process and who provides the input. This brainstorming and prioritization of significant inputs finishes the activities around building a SIPOC.

The following are some definitions related to SIPOC diagrams:

- *Outputs:* Anything the business unit distributes. Frequency/timing is listed along with the output. Examples of outputs would be reports, ratings, products, and documents, etc.
- *Recipients (customers):* Anyone who receives outputs. It's important to note that the recipient must get the output directly from the business unit and doesn't necessarily have to be a user of the output. If the

output is received from a third party, the third party is not the recipient. Examples of recipients would be a manager, CEO, board of directors, or another department.

■ *Triggers:* Anything that starts the business unit's process. A trigger could be the receipt of a report or a certain day of the month, etc.

■ *Estimated time:* The estimated time is how long it takes to complete process steps. This can be continuous, days, weeks, or years, etc.

■ *Fail points:* Fail points are ranked/prioritized and then numbered based on their priority.

There are three reasons a Six Sigma engagement frequently begins with building a SIPOC diagram:

■ A SIPOC diagram quickly and easily captures the current state of the organization and processes in question.

■ The SIPOC exercise brings associates together in a nonthreatening way that builds teamwork and momentum to the Six Sigma cause.

■ The SIPOC exercise allows the team to objectively identify the most critical project opportunities.

Example: Mama Mia's SIPOC

The vice president of procurement creates and places a weekly order from Pizza Supplies R Us. She negotiates for price and quantity of the order. The order is scheduled for delivery to Mama Mia's warehouse. The order is tracked and received at the warehouse and is unloaded.

The vice president of food and beverage checks the order for completeness and freshness. The stock is put into inventory. The pizza supplies are inspected weekly for freshness. The vice president of food and beverage determines if the food is within its shelf life, disposes of spoiled food, and notifies the vice president of procurement of any items that spoil within their shelf lives.

The store manager orders supplies from the warehouse. The supplies are delivered and checked for completeness. The food preparation personnel stocks and refrigerates food supplies. Customers place their orders on the phone or in person and provide their addresses if needed. The food preparation person provides cost and estimated delivery time. The pizza is baked, boxed, and assigned to the delivery person, who scopes out the directions from an old plastic map. The pizza is delivered and money is collected. The delivery person returns to the store.

Order Procurement

Supplier	Input	Process	Output	Customer
Pizza Supplies R Us	Food	Order created	Food delivered	VP operations Food prep personnel
		Supplier contacted		VP procurement
		Order negotiated		VP food and beverage
		Orders placed		
		Delivery scheduled		
		Delivery tracked		
		Delivery occurs Truck unloaded		

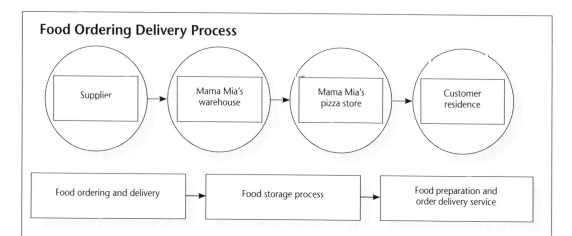

Food Ordering Delivery Process

Food Storage Flowchart

Supplier	Input	Process	Output	Customer
VP procurement	Crates of food from truck Delivery and unloaded	Check order for completeness and freshness.	Food stored	VP operations Food prep personnel
		Put stock into inventory.		VP food and beverage
		Inspect stock for freshness weekly.		
		Determine if food is within shelf life.		
		Dispose of spoiled food.		
		Notify VP procurement of spoiled items if within shelf life.		

FLOWCHARTS

"I document it to define it. I flowchart it to understand it."
—HJH

Flowcharting is a method of graphically describing an existing or proposed new process by using simple symbols, lines, and words to pictorially display its sequence of activities.

How to use flowcharts

Flowcharts have application in almost all parts of the problem-solving process. They are useful for identifying problems, defining measurement points for data collection, idea generation, and idea selection. The usefulness of flowcharts has been recognized to such an extent that structured flowcharts are increasingly used as the basis for Computer-Aided Software Engineering (CASE).

Seven types of flowcharts will be discussed below. The standard process flowchart is the most widely used, probably because it has the broadest applicability to problem solving and because it can be used as a baseline to create some of the other flowcharts that may better graphically represent a particular point. You should modify your use of flowcharts to your specific needs. Be creative.

An important part of flowcharts are the symbols used to represent various kinds of activities. The American National Standards Institute (ANSI) has developed a standard set of symbols for flowcharting. We have seen many modifications of the ANSI symbol set used effectively in organizations. It's important that there is consistency among documents and in the "symbology" used within the organization. The forms part of this section displays a list of some of the common ANSI symbols.

Steps

There is really no prescribed sequence for generating flowcharts. However, some common sense rules should apply. The following general steps have proven to be effective in most flowcharting activities:

1. Before beginning, define your objectives for flowcharting.
2. Determine the process boundaries:
   - What's included in the process?
   - What's not included?
   - What are the outputs from the process?
   - What are the inputs to the process?
   - What departments are involved in the process?

3. Select the most appropriate flowchart type(s) for your objectives.
4. Prepare a high-level block diagram of the process you wish to flowchart. Stretch the boundaries of the process to get the broadest view of the process possible. Prepare a block diagram regardless of if you will ultimately use it or a different flowchart type.
5. Determine what people or functional areas are involved in the process. Assemble the most appropriate team to flowchart the process.
6. Determine what tools and/or standard formats will be used if this has not already been established by a broader, perhaps companywide, initiative.
7. Begin flowcharting the process. Start at a high level and work toward more detail. Pay close attention to all interactions among people, departments, and functions. Using the guidelines and tips below, identify the suppliers of all process inputs and the customers of all process outputs.

8. Early in the creation of flowcharts, review the appropriateness of the process boundaries. Modify the process definition based on its boundaries as necessary. Also, modify the team members if necessary to reflect any changes in process definition.

9. Complete the flowcharts.

Guidelines and tips

The level of detail of your flowcharts is largely a matter of judgment and this will improve with experience. By fully understanding your objectives before starting to flowchart, you will have a better idea of the meaningful level of detail. Early in the flowcharting activity, it's often a good idea to take a small part of the process and dissect it with the team. Take it to a very fine level of detail and then agree with the team on the appropriate level of detail, based on the team's objectives.

There are two fundamentally different ways to create flowcharts. One way is to start at the beginning and define each step in great detail. Another way is to build a simple view of the process first and then add detail later. Although you should ultimately choose the method you're most comfortable with, it's generally easier to start simple and add detail.

It's very important to separate the flowcharting process from process improvements. Focus first on completing flowcharting. Create an issues list and defer judgment on this list until flowcharting is complete. Discussions on potential improvements can be a great distraction and delay the overall improvement process.

It's very important to flowchart processes in their current state or to flowchart the future desired state. It's crucial not to mix these in the same flowchart. Effective flowcharting, therefore, may require interviewing skills to uncover the current-state processes. Flowcharting may also be supplemented with process walkthroughs to ensure that current processes are accurately captured. Walkthroughs are a highly recommended part of the process. You will be surprised how many things you find during a walkthrough that are different from the way you have documented the process. The steps to a process walkthrough are:

1. Identify the scope of the process to be reviewed.
2. Develop the objectives of the walkthrough.
3. Determine the walkthrough method:
   - Interview
   - Observation
   - Sampling

4. Create the interview worksheet (who, what, when).
5. Conduct the walkthrough.
6. Update the flowchart.

Some common discoveries of process walkthroughs are:
- Differences between the documented process and present practice
- Differences among employees in the way they perform the activity
- Employees in need of retraining
- Suggested improvements to the process, identified by the people performing the process
- Activities that need to be documented/process problems, such as:
  - Duplication
  - Rework
  - Waste
  - Bureaucracy

- Roadblocks to process improvement
- New training programs required to support the present process

Date all flowcharts because flowcharting is an iterative process. Knowing which flowchart is the most recent version will save you many headaches.

Software tips

There are currently a number of software products on the market that can help you create process flowcharts. Some of them are generic tools, such as drawing programs, and others have been created specifically for flowcharting. One product we suggest is a software package produced by Edge Software Inc. called Work-Draw. This is an advanced process-modeling application that includes flowcharting capabilities. When using flowcharting software:

- Form a software users group and build a core of knowledge and skills with the software tool(s) you will use. These people can then teach others about the software.
- Flowchart the process on paper first. Try to get the flowchart near completion before using a software program.

There are basically seven types of flowcharts. Although there may be others, the seven shown in figure 3.43 are most often used by organizations to flowchart their processes.

Figure 3.43 Types of Flowcharts and Their Descriptions

Type	Description
1. Process blocks (block diagram)	Document what is done to illustrate a high-level flow of operations.
2. Process charts	Document how, by breaking down a process under study into activities chronologically.
3. Procedure charts	Document the detailed flow of activities in the process.
4. Functional flowcharts	Document the process, emphasizing responsibilities and interaction between departments.
5. Geographical flowcharts	Document the physical movement of people and/or materials.
6. Paperwork flowcharts	Document the detailed flow of paperwork within a process.
7. Informational flowcharts	Document office procedures (manual and automated) using standard symbols.

Figure 3.44 shows several interesting aspects of flowcharts as well as some of their characteristics.

Figure 3.44 Comparison of Flowcharts

Type	Level of detail	What is charted	What it includes
1. Process blocks	High	Activities	What
2. Process charts	Medium detail	Activities, tasks, decisions	What, how, where
3. Procedure charts	Detail	Tasks, material flow, individual actions	How, where, who
4. Functional flowcharts	Medium detail	Activities, tasks	What, who
5. Geographical flowcharts	Medium	Activities	What, where
6. Paperwork flowcharts	Detail	Documents	How, where, who
7. Informational flowcharts	Medium detail	Information, activities, decisions	What, how, who, where

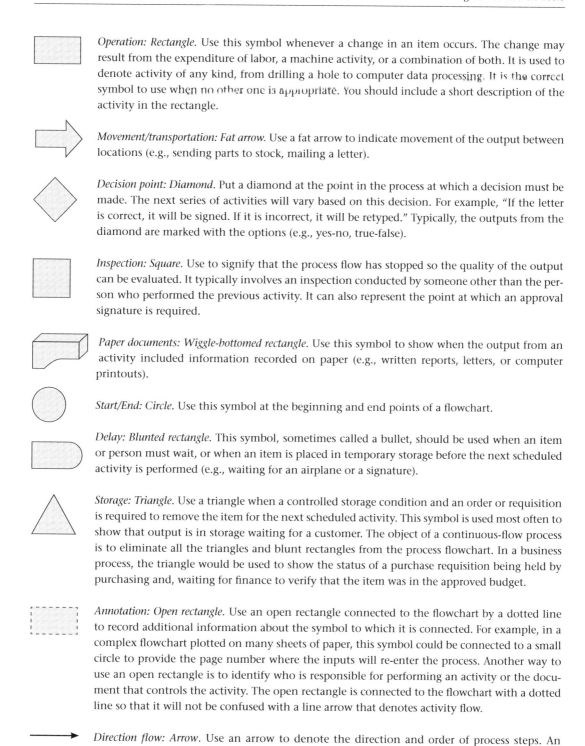

Operation: Rectangle. Use this symbol whenever a change in an item occurs. The change may result from the expenditure of labor, a machine activity, or a combination of both. It is used to denote activity of any kind, from drilling a hole to computer data processing. It is the correct symbol to use when no other one is appropriate. You should include a short description of the activity in the rectangle.

Movement/transportation: Fat arrow. Use a fat arrow to indicate movement of the output between locations (e.g., sending parts to stock, mailing a letter).

Decision point: Diamond. Put a diamond at the point in the process at which a decision must be made. The next series of activities will vary based on this decision. For example, "If the letter is correct, it will be signed. If it is incorrect, it will be retyped." Typically, the outputs from the diamond are marked with the options (e.g., yes-no, true-false).

Inspection: Square. Use to signify that the process flow has stopped so the quality of the output can be evaluated. It typically involves an inspection conducted by someone other than the person who performed the previous activity. It can also represent the point at which an approval signature is required.

Paper documents: Wiggle-bottomed rectangle. Use this symbol to show when the output from an activity included information recorded on paper (e.g., written reports, letters, or computer printouts).

Start/End: Circle. Use this symbol at the beginning and end points of a flowchart.

Delay: Blunted rectangle. This symbol, sometimes called a bullet, should be used when an item or person must wait, or when an item is placed in temporary storage before the next scheduled activity is performed (e.g., waiting for an airplane or a signature).

Storage: Triangle. Use a triangle when a controlled storage condition and an order or requisition is required to remove the item for the next scheduled activity. This symbol is used most often to show that output is in storage waiting for a customer. The object of a continuous-flow process is to eliminate all the triangles and blunt rectangles from the process flowchart. In a business process, the triangle would be used to show the status of a purchase requisition being held by purchasing and, waiting for finance to verify that the item was in the approved budget.

Annotation: Open rectangle. Use an open rectangle connected to the flowchart by a dotted line to record additional information about the symbol to which it is connected. For example, in a complex flowchart plotted on many sheets of paper, this symbol could be connected to a small circle to provide the page number where the inputs will re-enter the process. Another way to use an open rectangle is to identify who is responsible for performing an activity or the document that controls the activity. The open rectangle is connected to the flowchart with a dotted line so that it will not be confused with a line arrow that denotes activity flow.

Direction flow: Arrow. Use an arrow to denote the direction and order of process steps. An arrow is used for movement from one symbol to another. The arrow denotes direction—up, down, or sideways. ANSI indicates that the arrowhead is not necessary when the direction flow is from top to bottom or from left to right. However, to avoid misinterpretation by others who may not be as familiar with flowchart symbols, it is recommended that you always use arrowheads.

EXAMPLES

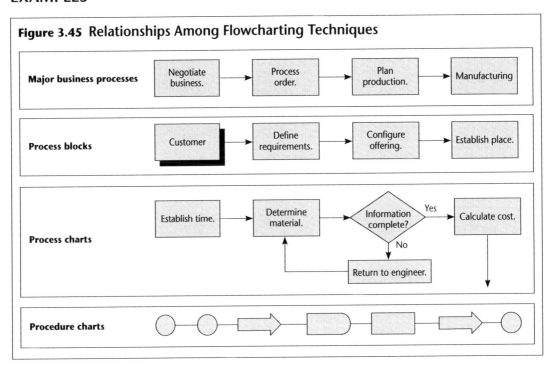

Figure 3.45 Relationships Among Flowcharting Techniques

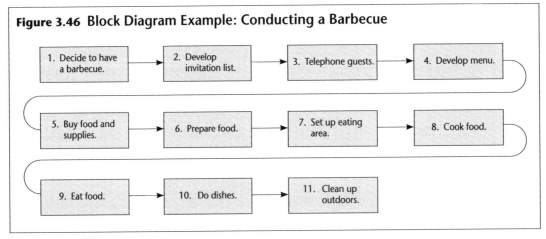

Figure 3.46 Block Diagram Example: Conducting a Barbecue

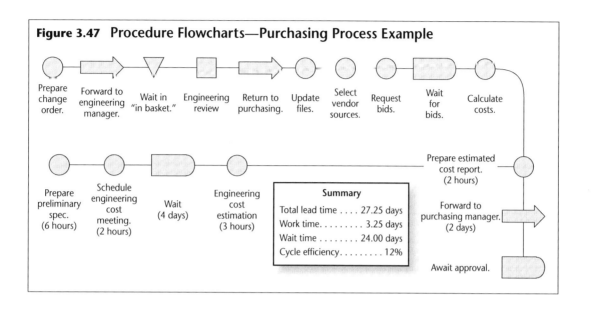

Figure 3.47 Procedure Flowcharts—Purchasing Process Example

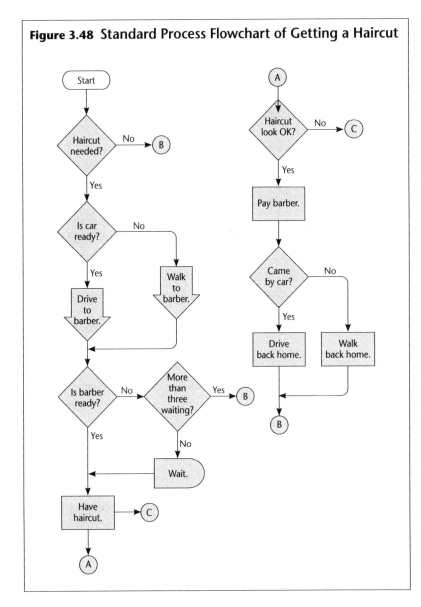

Figure 3.48 Standard Process Flowchart of Getting a Haircut

Figure 3.49 Standard Process Flowchart of Going Fishing

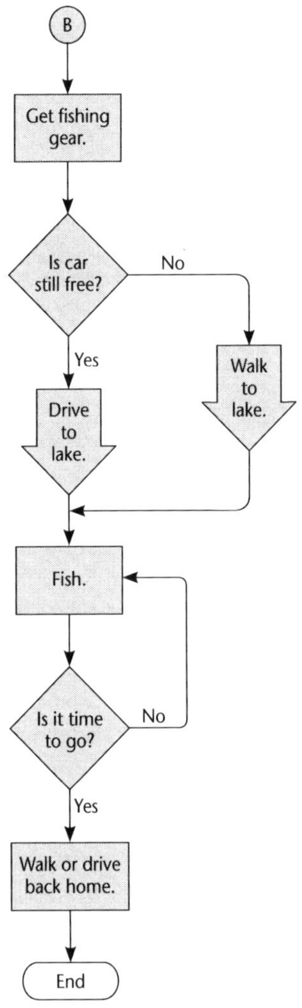

The following is an in-house procedure for conducting an internal job search and its related flowchart. This activity is then flowcharted in figure 3.50.

Conducting an Internal Job Search

Activity	Responsible area
1. Recognize need. Complete payback analysis. Prepare personnel requisition. Prepare budget request.	Manager
2. Evaluate budget. If yes, sign personnel requisition slip. If no, return total package with rejection letter to manager.	Controller
3. Conduct in-house search.	Personnel
4. If in-house candidates exist, provide list to management. If not, start outside hiring procedure.	Personnel
5. Review candidates' paperwork and prepare a list of candidates to be reviewed.	Manager
6. Have candidates' managers review job with the employees and determine which employees are interested in the position.	Personnel
7. Notify personnel of candidates interested in being interviewed.	Candidates
8. Set up meeting between manager and candidates.	Personnel
9. Interview candidates and review details of job.	Manager
10. Notify personnel of interview results.	Manager
11. If acceptable candidate is available, make job offer. If not, start outside hiring process.	Personnel
12. Evaluate job offer and notify personnel of candidate's decision.	Candidate
13. If yes, notify manager that the job has been filled. If no, go to activity 14.	Personnel
14. Were there other acceptable candidates? If yes, go to activity 12. If no, start outside hiring process.	Personnel
15. Have new manager contact candidate's present manager and arrange for the candidate to report to work.	Manager

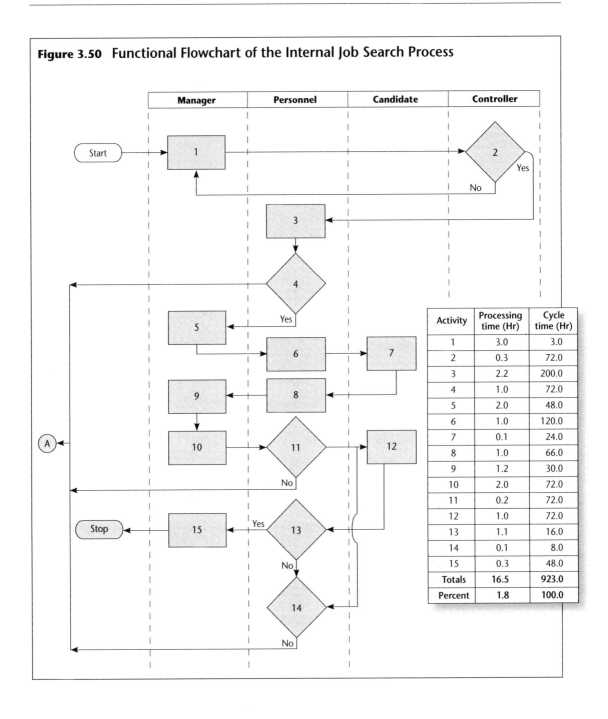

Figure 3.50 Functional Flowchart of the Internal Job Search Process

Activity	Processing time (Hr)	Cycle time (Hr)
1	3.0	3.0
2	0.3	72.0
3	2.2	200.0
4	1.0	72.0
5	2.0	48.0
6	1.0	120.0
7	0.1	24.0
8	1.0	66.0
9	1.2	30.0
10	2.0	72.0
11	0.2	72.0
12	1.0	72.0
13	1.1	16.0
14	0.1	8.0
15	0.3	48.0
Totals	16.5	923.0
Percent	1.8	100.0

Figure 3.51 Geographic Flowchart of a New Employee's First Day at XYZ Co.

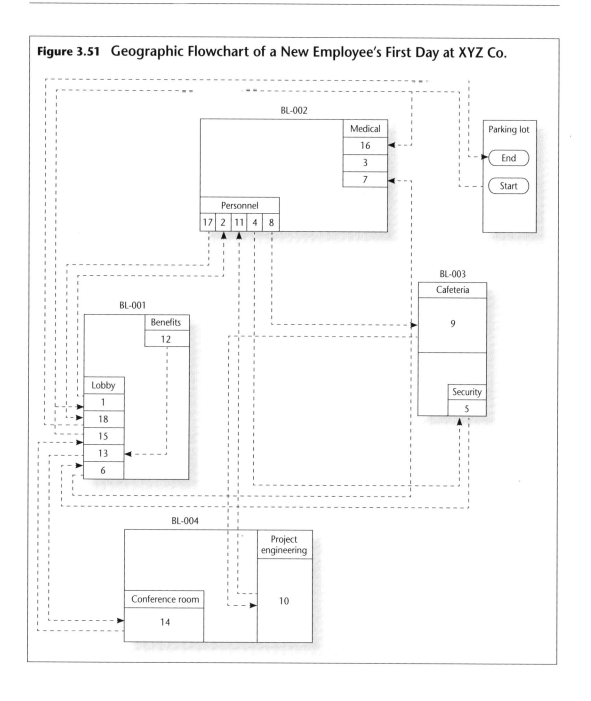

PARETO DIAGRAMS

"As good as you are, you can't do everything simultaneously.
So do the things with the big payback first."
—HJH

In a Pareto diagram, the bars are arranged in descending order from the left to the right. It's a way to highlight "the vital few" in contrast to "the trivial many."

How to use Pareto diagrams

A Pareto diagram presents data in a manner that allows comparison between a number of problems or causes. The comparison helps to set priorities. The Pareto diagram facilitates the process by graphically distinguishing the few significant problems or causes from the less significant many—a concept known as the Pareto principle.

The Pareto principle (80/20 rule)

The Pareto principle states a universal rule that's applicable to many fields: the phenomenon of the vital few and the trivial many. In our context, this means that a few significant problems or causes will be most important to the decision-making process.

This principle derives its name from Vilfredo Pareto, a 19th century economist, who applied the concept to income distribution. His observations led him to state that 80 percent of wealth is controlled by 20 percent of the people. (Hence, the principle is often referred to as the 80/20 rule.) The name "Pareto" and the universal applicability of the concept are credited to Joseph M. Juran, who applied the Lorenz curve to graphically depict it.

The Pareto diagram

In a Pareto diagram, the columns with the highest values are on the left and those with the lower values are on the right. (See figure 3.52.) The one exception to this rule is the diagram's "other" column, a collection of less-important factors. When it's included in the diagram, the "other" column is always the last column on the right. This makes it possible to include a cumulative or "cum" line (also called a Lorenz curve), which rises by steps according to the height of the columns to show the total of the percentages or the cumulative percentage. With the "cum" line, the Pareto diagram becomes a combined column and line graph.

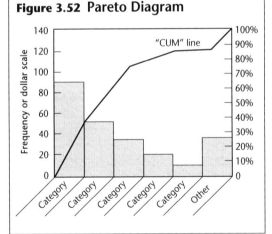

Figure 3.52 Pareto Diagram

Like other graphic representations, Pareto diagrams display data to assist investigation and analysis. They are employed to:

- *Establish priorities.* Problems and causes are identified through data comparison.
- *Show percentage of impact.* The "cum" line defines the proportionate importance of combined categories and indicates the likely effect of dealing with all of the categories up to that point in the diagram.
- *Show change over time.* Two or more diagrams can be used to demonstrate the result of decisions and actions by showing before and after data. (See figure 3.53.)

- *Aid communication.* The diagram should aid communication and be easily understood.
- *Demonstrate use of data.* This can be particularly helpful in management presentations to show the activities are solidly rooted in facts.

Data classifications

The data collected for transfer to a Pareto diagram are of three major types:

- Problems: Errors, defects, locations, processes, and procedures
- Causes: Materials, machines, equipment, employees, customers, operations, and standards
- Cost: For each data category

The purpose of using a Pareto diagram is to:

- Establish the biggest problem and rank the rest of the problems
- Establish the most important cause and rank the rest of the causes

The biggest and most important categories need to be measured not solely in terms of frequency but also in terms of cost. The number of occurrences may not be as significant as the cost of particular occurrences. Consequently, it's usually important to construct a Pareto diagram using cost data. Mere frequency can be misleading in judging significance.

Constructing a Pareto diagram

Before a Pareto diagram can be constructed, it's necessary to collect data according to the classifications or categories judged most suitable. With these data the diagram is constructed as follows:

1. *Summarize the data on a worksheet.*
   - Arrange the data in order of largest to smallest and total them. (See figure 3.54, "number" column.)
   - Calculate percentages. (See figure 3.54, "percent of total" column.)
   - Complete the cumulative percent column. (See figure 3.54, "cum percentage" column.)

2. *Draw the horizontal and two vertical axes.*
   - Divide the horizontal axis into equal segments, one for each category. (See figure 3.55.)
   - Scale the left-hand vertical axis so that the top figure on the axis is the sum of all the occurrences in the categories.

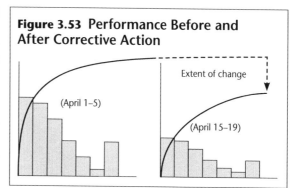

Figure 3.53 Performance Before and After Corrective Action

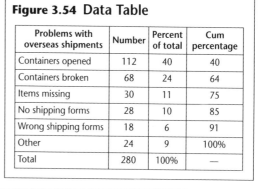

Figure 3.54 Data Table

Problems with overseas shipments	Number	Percent of total	Cum percentage
Containers opened	112	40	40
Containers broken	68	24	64
Items missing	30	11	75
No shipping forms	28	10	85
Wrong shipping forms	18	6	91
Other	24	9	100%
Total	280	100%	—

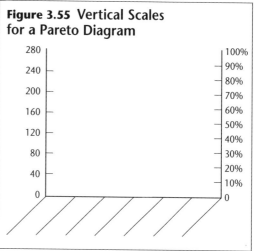

Figure 3.55 Vertical Scales for a Pareto Diagram

Figure 3.56 Plotted Pareto Diagram Without Cumulative Line

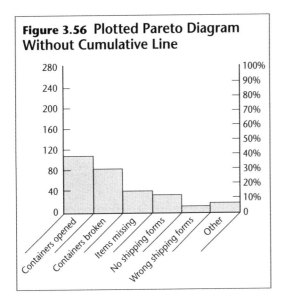

Figure 3.57 Pareto Diagram with Cumulative Line Plotted

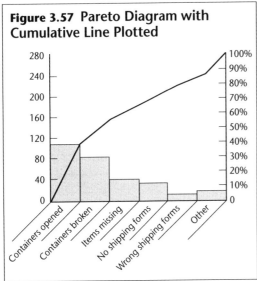

Figure 3.58 Completed Pareto Diagram

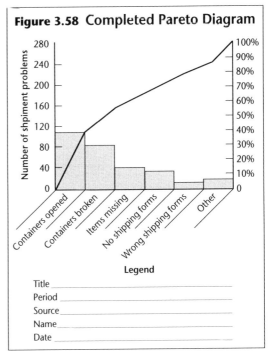

■ Scale the right-hand vertical axis so that 100 percent is directly opposite the total on the left-hand axis. The percent scale is normally in increments of 10 percent.

3. *Plot the data.* Construct a series of columns, putting the tallest column on the extreme left, then the next tallest, and so on. If several minor categories are consolidated into one "other" column, it is plotted on the extreme right, regardless of its height. (See figure 3.56.)

4. *Plot the cumulative line.*

■ Place a dot in line with the right side of each column at a height corresponding to the number in the cumulative percentage column on the worksheet. In the example shown in figure 3.57, the points would be at 40 percent, 64 percent, 75 percent, 85 percent, and 91 percent.

■ Beginning with the lower left corner of the diagram (the zero point of origin), connect the dots to the 100 percent point on the right vertical axis, as in figure 3.57.

5. *Add labels and the legend.*
■ Label each axis.
■ Add the legend. It should include the source of the data, date prepared, where collected, who collected them, period covered, and any other pertinent information. (See figure 3.58.)

BRAINSTORMING

"Together we are better than any one of us alone."
—HJH

Brainstorming is a technique used by groups to quickly generate large lists of ideas, problems, or issues. The emphasis is on quantity of ideas, not quality. Brainstorming is perhaps the most widely recognized technique used to encourage creative thinking. It's also one of the most important tools any individual can have in his or her improvement arsenal. Problem-solving groups can take advantage of brainstorming techniques during several different phases of their operation.

Brainstorming is an intentionally uninhibited technique for generating the greatest possible number of ideas. Group members suggest as many ideas as they can about a given subject. The quantity of ideas is more important than their quality; each idea will be evaluated later. Groups can use this idea-generating technique to identify work-related problems, their causes, and possible solutions.

A brainstorming group exhibits these characteristics:
- Has four to twelve members
- Determines the problem to be addressed
- Understands the problem
- Records all suggestions
- Gives each member the same opportunity to express opinions
- Encourages all ideas without criticism
- Has a leader who conducts the meeting and keeps the group focused on the selected problem

Brainstorming harnesses the resources of the entire problem-solving group. An SST can produce more ideas and more creative ideas than an individual could. The group should accept all ideas and write them all down—even the silly and frivolous ones. At the end of the session or later on in the problem-solving process, the group can screen the ideas for the good ones.

To determine the best solutions for important problems, assume that employees are conscientious, aware of problems affecting the quality of their work, and have considered solutions. Brainstorming is an opportunity to surface these ideas.

Using brainstorming

Groups use brainstorming to identify and analyze problems and to find solutions. Constant attention must be given to the essentials of brainstorming such as:
- Is everyone considering the same problem?
- Are all ideas encouraged and accepted without criticism?
- Are all ideas recorded?
- Do all of the group members have an equal chance to participate?

If all of these conditions are not satisfied, it's not a brainstorming session. Brainstorming is not a meeting in which everyone speaks simultaneously, nor is it an unorganized bull session.

Occasionally, SSTs are faced with unusual or difficult situations that can't be solved through experience, formula, or some other known method. In these cases, a stronger technique is needed. Brainstorming facilitates diversity in thinking and the production of many ideas. It's not used to produce a single line of thought, nor is it the answer to a problem that has only one solution. Brainstorming is a cooperative, creative technique to be used when individual efforts fail to yield satisfactory results.

Preparing for a brainstorming session

Brainstorming is worthwhile only when the problem to be solved can first be identified. All the members of the group should be aware of what the problem is and they need to see all of the data relating to it. Select a suitable meeting place for the occasion. The room needs to be just large enough to accommodate the group comfortably; too much room often leads to a loss of unity and makes it harder for the individual participants to coalesce into a group.

A relaxed atmosphere that accommodates laughter is best for a productive and creative session. It allows the participants to verbalize their offbeat ideas by presenting them tongue-in-cheek. Experience has proven that often in the resulting laughter a voice rises up to say, "You know, that's not such a crazy idea." Thus the unusual thought often leads to a viable avenue or idea.

Brainstorming techniques

There are several techniques that can be used to guide and expand brainstorming.

- *Idea-spurring.* The leader can ask questions like:
  - ☐ Can we make these smaller?
  - ☐ What can we add?
  - ☐ What can we combine or package with this idea?

These questions are designed to break down any mental barriers the group may have.

- *Participation in sequence.* It's a good idea to ask for ideas to be contributed in turn, beginning with one person and going all the way around the group. This technique can be used at the beginning of a session to ensure that everyone participates, even shy members. If a person can't think of anything to contribute, the appropriate response is "pass." A good idea may occur before the next turn.
- *Incubation.* Incubation is a process that occurs between brainstorming sessions. The initial brainstorming session gives the subconscious mind suggestions. The subconscious slowly works on these suggestions and sometimes generates very creative ideas.

Guidelines for brainstorming

- Generate a large number of ideas.
- Don't inhibit yourself or others, just let the ideas out. Say whatever comes into your mind and encourage others to do the same. The important thing is quantity.
- Encourage freewheeling.
- Even though an idea may be half-baked or silly, it has value. It may provoke thoughts from other members. Sometimes, making a silly suggestion can spur another idea you didn't know you had.
- Don't criticize. This is the most important guideline. There will be ample time later to sift through the ideas for the good ones. During the session, don't criticize ideas because you may inhibit other members. When you criticize the half-baked ideas, you throw away the building blocks for the great ones.
- Encourage everyone to participate. Everyone thinks and has ideas, so allow everyone to speak up.
- Record all ideas. Appoint a recorder to note everything suggested. The ideas should not be edited; rather, they should be jotted down just as they are mentioned. Keep a permanent record that can be read at future meetings. You may want to read through the list and take inventory of it a few times. This process sometimes stimulates more ideas.
- Let ideas incubate. Once you've started brainstorming, ideas will come more easily. Don't discontinue your brainstorming sessions too soon; let some time go by to allow those ideas to develop by themselves.
- Select an appropriate meeting place. A casual place that is comfortable and the right size will greatly enhance a brainstorming session.

Figure 3.59 A List of Brainstorming Ideas

• Hire freight carrier based on lowest rate available.	• Wrong count by operators on production floor
• Dock is overcrowded.	• Need classification by type of error
• Historical trends of errors	• Frequently change freight carriers
• What is a shipping error?	• Too slow getting replacement product or paperwork
• Time lag in order changes on computer	• Don't tell customer if shipping error is known but not detected by customer.
• When big customers push, switch labels and ship.	• Allow changes to orders over the phone
• Shipping errors only in certain product lines	• Sometimes substitute facsimile if product is unavailable
• Data entry complexity	• Computer system too slow — use handwritten forms instead
• Difficult to measure true cost of errors	• Labels fall off boxes.
• High turnover among shippers	• High turnover among data entry clerks
• New eleven-digit code too long	• No place to segregate customer returns
• Bar codes damaged/unreadable	• Some new, reusable packaging has wrong bar codes
• Dock used to store material for return to vendors	• Lack of training for data entry clerks
• How many are paperwork errors but the right product was shipped?	• Newest employees go to shipping
• Shipping sometimes contracted directly by sales representative to rush orders.	• Production bonus system encourages speed, not accuracy
• Old shipping boxes easily damaged, requiring replacement	• Dock is coldest place in winter, hottest place in summer.
• Customer orders still initially handwritten	• How many customers lost that we don't know about?

What inhibits effective brainstorming?

Although brainstorming is the most widely used process improvement tool, it's also the most misused. If the rules for brainstorming are not conscientiously followed, the quality of the session will suffer. Session leaders often allow criticism of suggestions during brainstorming, which turns off other members of the group and prevents the group's synergy from building. Brainstorming is not effective unless all members of the group participate. The leader should be especially careful to see that everyone is given the opportunity to contribute. It's the responsibility of the leader of the brainstorming group to encourage the members to comply with the rules for brainstorming.

NOMINAL GROUP TECHNIQUE

"Everyone has his or her own idea of what is most important.
The trick is to come to a common agreement on priorities."
—HJH

Nominal group technique (NGT) is a collaborative process that helps prioritize a list of problems, ideas, or issues. NGT is a special-purpose technique, useful for situations where individual judgments must be tapped and combined to arrive at decisions. It's best accomplished by all the people involved in the situation, and is a problem-solving or idea-generating strategy not typically used in routine meetings. Andre L. Delbecq and Andrew H. Van de Ven developed NGT in 1968. It was derived from social-psychological studies of decision conferences, management-science studies of aggregating group judgments, and social-work studies of problems surrounding citizen participation in program planning. Since that time, NGT has gained extensive recognition and has been widely applied.

NGT is a highly structured group process. It's best used when time is limited and when the resulting decision requires group ownership. It's also useful when multiple creative ideas are not necessarily critical to a problem's solution.

NGT is a seven-step process that works best in a group with seven to ten members. The participants should be physically present for sessions, and a leader or facilitator should control the meetings.

Steps for using NGT

1. Following an opening introduction in which the purposes of the session are outlined, participants are presented with a carefully worded task statement and NGT worksheet. (See figure 3.60.)

2. The group members are then instructed to provide their own ideas for the resolution to the problem statement on their worksheets. This is called silent generation and typically takes about ten minutes. No discussion should be allowed during this time.

3. Next comes the round-robin phase during which the facilitator calls on each participant to state one of the responses he or she has written. Participants may pass at any time and join in on a subsequent round. A participant should propose only one item at a time and each item should be recorded exactly as it's presented. The only discussion allowed is between the recorder and the participant who proposes the item, and this is limited to rephrasing suggestions if the recorder needs it. Participants are encouraged to add items to their personal list should new ones occur to them during the round robin. This continues until all ideas are recorded.

Figure 3.60 Example of a NGT Idea Worksheet

Problem: _____ Date: _____

_____

Individual ideas: _____

_____

_____

_____

_____

_____

Figure 3.61 Example of a NGT Ranking Worksheet

Problem Statement:_____   Date:_____

Idea		Ranking
A		
B		
C		
D		
E		

4. The fourth step is clarification. Once all items have been recorded, the facilitator or leader reviews them one at a time to ensure that all participants understand them. Duplicate ideas should be eliminated. New ideas might result from combining ideas. Participants may offer clarification, idea combinations, modifications, or deletions to the list. However, no evaluation is permitted. The final list of ideas should be assigned letters, A through Z, where Z depends on how many ideas were generated.
5. Next, each participant ranks the ideas. Use the form shown in figure 3.61.
6. The leader asks the participants to share their preferred ideas. As each one contributes an idea, the recorder makes a tick mark next to the idea on the flipchart. The idea with the most ticks is the one most favored by the group. This result will be very close to group consensus.
7. The final step is for the leader to verify the consensus of the group on the single idea preferred by the entire group and develop action plans based on the overall consensus.

The nominal group technique stimulates idea generation by keeping everyone involved in the problem-solving process. It prohibits strong personalities from dominating the group, allows ideas to be weighted for their relative worth, and encourages a shared commitment to solutions and implementation.

Example

A team is presented with the following task statement: "Our administrative group cannot keep pace with the required documentation generation." Each team member documents his or her response on his or her worksheet. Team member Bob shows the information shown in figure 3.62 on his worksheet:

Figure 3.62 Bob's Ideas Woksheet

Problem Statement: "Our administrative group cannot keep pace with the required documentation generation."   Date: August 5, 2008

Individual ideas: Hire more people.
Distribute the work more evenly.
Take on fewer new tasks.

In phase three each participant gives his or her own idea to the team. The facilitator has recorded all ideas on a flipchart. (See figure 3.63.)

After the idea list has been clarified and narrowed, it's time for Bob and the rest of the team to rank the remaining ideas. Bob's ranking form is presented in figure 3.64.

A new team list of preferred ideas is then generated. This often consists of each team members' first and second choices. (See figure 3.65.)

Figure 3.63 Team's Idea List

- Hire more people.
- Distribute the work more evenly.
- Take on fewer new tasks.
- Outsource some of the work.
- Change from word processors to computers.
- Hire part-time workers.
- Provide better training.
- Use first-in first-out system.
- Buy new word processors.

Figure 3.64 Bob's Ranking Worksheet

Problem Statement: "Our administrative group cannot keep pace with the required   Date: August 5, 2008
documentation generation."

Idea		Ranking
A	Hire more people.	7
B	Distribute the work more evenly.	8
C	Take on fewer new tasks.	9
D	Outsource some of the work.	6
E	Change from word processors to computers.	1
F	Hire part-time workers.	3
G	Provide better training.	4
H	Use first-in-first-out system.	5
I	Buy new word processors.	2

Summary

NGT uses several basic tools such as brainstorming, narrowing techniques, and consensus. This tool is very simple to use and produces dynamic results.

Figure 3.65 Team's Preferred Ideas

- Change from word processors to computers.
- Buy new word processors.

FIVE WHYS

"Why is the most valuable word in the problem-solving vocabulary."

—HJH

Five whys (5Ws) is a systematic technique used to search for and identify the root cause of a problem. This technique requires the team members to ask "Why?" at least five times. When the team is no longer able to answer the "Why?" the possible root cause has been identified.

Steps

1. *Start with a completed problem statement.* The problem statement should be as specific as possible:
   Incorrect: "The janitors are not emptying the trash in some rooms each night."
   Correct: "The janitors are not emptying the trash in the main conference room each night."

2. Ask "Why does this problem/situation exist?"
3. *Continue to ask "why" until the root cause has been identified.* In some cases it may not take five tries; in some cases it will take more. When the team can no longer answer the "Why?" it's time to consider if the root cause has been identified.
4. Once the root cause has been identified, move to the next step in the problem-solving process.
   Figure 3.66 compares the 5Ws approach to the 5Ws and 2Hs approach to problem analysis. Figure 3.67 shows an example of how the 5Ws is used to get to the root cause of the problem.

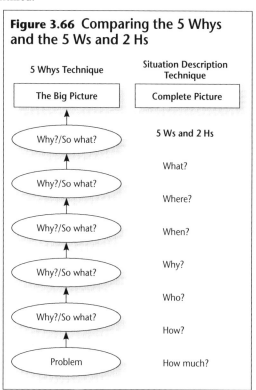

Figure 3.66 Comparing the 5 Whys and the 5 Ws and 2 Hs

73

Example

> **Figure 3.67 Example of an "Ask Why 5 Times" Form**
>
> **QC Team:** Day Shift Production   **Date:** 07/30/96
>
> **Problem statement:** "The janitors are not emptying the trash in the main conference room each night."
>
> | | |
> |---|---|
> | **Ask why?** | 1   Why are janitors not emptying the trash in the main conference room each night? |
> | **Response:** | The conference room has been locked after 5 p.m. for the last week. |
> | **Ask why?** | 2   Why is the conference room locked after 5 p.m.? |
> | **Response:** | Building maintenance was told to lock it at the end of the day shift. |
> | **Ask why?** | 3   Why was maintenance told to lock it? |
> | **Response:** | A special task team is working on a corporate issue and wants the door locked after the members leave. |
> | **Ask why?** | 4   Why do they want the door locked? |
> | **Response:** | They are leaving planning charts up on the wall and don't want them reviewed by the wrong parties or removed accidentally. |
> | **Ask why?** | 5   Why do they leave the charts on the wall? |
> | **Response:** | The charts are quite large they don't want to have to take them down and put them up each night. |
>
> **Has the root cause of the problem been identified?** ☐ Yes ☐ No
>
> If "no," continue asking "why."
>
> **State the root cause:** *The janitors cannot empty the trash because they temporarily don't have access to the room.*

FORCE-FIELD ANALYSIS

"There is a good and bad in all of us that we wrestle with all the time.
The same is true in the processes we design."

—HJH

Definition

Force-field analysis is a visual aid for pinpointing and analyzing elements that resist change (restraining forces) or push for change (driving forces). This technique helps drive improvement by developing plans to overcome the restrainers and make maximum use of the driving forces.

How to use force-field analysis

The force-field analysis technique has been used in a number of settings to do the following:

- Analyze a problem situation into its basic components.
- Identify key elements of the problem situation about which something can realistically be done.
- Develop a systematic and insightful strategy for problem solving that minimizes boomerang effects and irrelevant efforts.
- Create a guiding set of criteria for the evaluation of the action step.

The technique is an effective device for achieving each of these purposes when it is seriously employed. Kurt Lewin, who developed force-field analysis, has proposed that any problem situation—be it the behavior of an individual or group, the current state or condition of an organization, a particular set of attitudes, or frame of mind—may differ from the desired state. For example, smoking may become the basis for a problem when it occurs with greater intensity or at a higher level than one may desire. Quality, as another example, may become a problem when it isn't up to par. Depression or authoritarianism, as an example of an attitudinal activity level, can become a problem when it's too intense.

The level of the activity is the starting point in the problem identification and analysis. In order to constitute a problem, the current level typically departs from some implicit norm or goal. A particular activity level might result from a number of pressures and influences acting upon the individual, group, or organization in question. Lewin calls these numerous influences "forces," and they may be both external to and internal to the person or situation in question. Lewin identifies two kinds of forces:

■ Driving or facilitating forces that promote the occurrence of the particular activity of concern

■ Restraining or inhibiting forces that inhibit or oppose the occurrence of the same activity

An activity level is the result of the simultaneous operation of both facilitating and inhibiting forces. The two force fields push in opposite directions and although the stronger of the two will tend to characterize the problem situation, a point of balance is usually achieved that gives the appearance of habitual behavior or of a steady-state condition. Changes in the strength of either of the fields can cause a change in the activity level of concern. Thus, apparently habitual behaviors can be changed (and related problems solved) by shifting facilitation methods.

A force-field analysis can help you understand the influencers in a given situation. As a first step to a fuller understanding of the problem, the forces (both facilitating and inhibiting) should be identified as fully as possible. These should be listed and, as much as possible, their relative contributions or strengths noted.

Basic steps in force-field analysis

After the problem has been recognized and the appropriate stakeholders commit to change it, there are four basic steps used in force-field analysis to analyze the problem:

1. Define the problem and propose an ideal solution.
2. Identify and evaluate the forces acting on the problem situation.
3. Develop and implement a strategy for changing these forces.
4. Re-examine the situation to determine the effectiveness of the change and make further adjustments if necessary.

The first step is to define the problem and propose the ideal situation. It's important to be specific when stating the problem. To this end:

■ Propose an ideal situation in a goal statement. It can be prepared by answering the question: "What will the situation be like when the problem is solved?" The answer must be tested to determine if it gets to the root of the problem.

■ Another possible question is "What would the situation be like if everything were operating ideally?" Determining the precise goal statement is important because it guides the rest of the problem-solving steps. (See figure 3.68.)

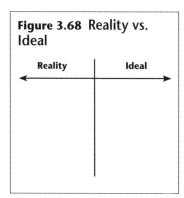

Figure 3.68 Reality vs. Ideal

Reality | Ideal

The second step is to evaluate the forces that act on the problem and goal, and to identify them as restraining or inhibiting forces. The facilitating forces tend to move the problem situation from reality toward the ideal. The restraining forces resist the movement toward the ideal state and counterbalance the facilitating forces. (See figure 3.69.)

You can visualize a problem situation by drawing a line down a sheet of paper and listing the facilitating forces on one side and restraining forces on the other side. Each of these forces has its own weight; taken together they keep the field in balance. (See figure 3.70.)

In addition to helping make the problem situation visual, force-field analysis provides a method for developing a solution. The most effective solution will involve reducing the restraining forces operating on the problem. (See figure 3.71.)

There are two reasons for reducing the restraining forces:

- To move the problem toward solution
- To avoid the effect of having too many facilitating forces

Because the forces on each side are balanced, removing or reducing the restraining forces will move the problem toward solution. On the other hand, adding facilitating forces without reducing restraining forces will likely lead to the appearance of new restrainers. Remember that although you may change the situation by changing a force, you may not have improved the situation. Some things to keep in mind during this process:

- An effective strategy cannot be planned without evaluating the restraining forces of two factors: First, whether and to what degree a restrainer is changeable, and second, to what degree changing a restrainer affects the problem.
- It's ineffective and a waste of energy to try to change an unchangeable force.
- One way to begin planning a strategy is to evaluate each force's flexibility. A simple three-point rating scale is sufficient:
  1. A fixed, unchanging force (i.e., a contractual item, a law, or fixed budget)
  2. A force changeable with moderate to extensive effort (i.e., an item that involves the efforts and cooperation of many departments)
  3. A change that can be readily performed, perhaps by revising a procedure which is within the control of the group

- The change or removal of some restrainers may have little or no effect. Accordingly, it's a good idea to rate the restrainers for their problem-solving effect.
- A three-point rating scale can be used to rate the effect a change will have on the problem:
  - ☐ No significant improvement will occur with the change.

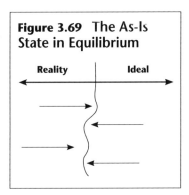

Figure 3.69 The As-Is State in Equilibrium

Figure 3.70 In Balance

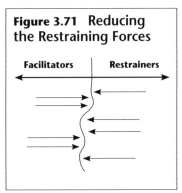

Figure 3.71 Reducing the Restraining Forces

☐ Some minor improvement will occur with the change, perhaps up to 20 percent of the improvement needed to solve the problem.

☐ A major improvement results from changing this force; that is, from 25 to 100 percent of the needed improvement.

■ After you have rated all of the forces operating on the problem situation, you can determine a priority for dealing with each force by adding together the numbers with which you rated each of the forces. The highest priority will be the restraining force, which will have the most effect and which is most changeable. Following will be the forces that you judge to have a large effect but are less changeable.

At this point in the force-field analysis, you are ready to begin the third step: developing and implementing a strategy for changing the forces affecting a situation. In deciding the priority, strive to balance the ease of change with its effect on the workplace. This will require creative thinking. The balance between the facilitators and the restrainers will help you decide which forces to change.

It might be a good idea remove the restraining forces to allow the point of equilibrium to shift. If the new point is not satisfactory, examine the driving forces and determine which ones you can successfully change. Next, examine the situation. If you are still not satisfied, determine which facilitating forces can be added.

Each time a change is planned, take the time to estimate and determine whether the change will be worth it. Ask:

■ Will it produce the desired results?

■ Which facilitating and restraining factors will be affected and by how much?

■ How will the equilibrium point be affected?

■ Is there a better way of getting the same results?

■ Does the change have a negative effect on other parts of the process?

■ What will be the return on investment?

Force-field analysis is a straightforward tool. Using it with diligence and in the ongoing evaluation of solutions will ensure that it can help achieve your desired goal. Force-field analysis is valuable because it goes beyond brainstorming by helping to develop plans and set priorities.

Example

Consider the example of starting a TQM project shown in figure 3.72. In this example the organization would have to consider if the restraining forces might be too great to overcome. If the organization decides to continue with starting a TQM, a great deal of effort must be expended to overcome the restraining forces.

Figure 3.72 Example of a Completed Force-Field Analysis Diagram

Facilitating force	Restraining force
• Customer-driven	• Management's buy-in
• Empowered employees	• Management's participation
• A team environment	• Potential of employee layoffs
• Quality improves	• Cost of additional resources
• Productivity improves	• Time commitment required
• Stakeholders are happy	• Management's long-term commitment
• Positive change occurs	• Managing the changes from TQM

CAUSE-AND-EFFECT DIAGRAMS

"Every negative effect is caused by something. The trick is to find the right cause so it can be corrected."

—HJH

Definition

Cause-and-effect diagrams visually represent the possible causes of a problem or condition. The effect is listed on the right side, and the causes are diagrammed in the shape of a fishbone. This is the reason they are sometimes called fishbone diagrams. They are also known as Ishikawa diagrams.

How to use cause-and-effect diagrams

Cause-and-effect analysis is a structured way to separate and define causes. The effects are the symptoms that illuminate the problem. The cause-and-effect diagram adapts well to repetitive processes. For this reason, most problems can be analyzed using cause-and-effect analysis. Processes under the control of one group or organization and for which responsibilities are clearly defined are also good candidates for cause-and-effect analysis.

Not only are there several types of cause-and-effect diagrams, but there are also several methods used to develop them. The "random" method is so called because members of the problem-solving group may suggest causes that apply to any of the major subdivisions of the diagram. Just as in brainstorming, a diagramming session has a leader. Scribes are appointed to record the contributions of the members of the group.

When developing a cause-and-effect diagram, the leader chooses one of the major subdivisions on which to focus the group's attention. The brainstorming process addresses the subdivision indicated by the leader. When that particular subdivision has been completed, the leader indicates the next one, and so on, until the cause-and-effect diagram is complete. Completed diagrams, whether generated by the random method or the systematic method, look alike.

The "process analysis" diagram is another type of cause-and-effect diagram. It looks much like a flow-chart. The "solution analysis" diagram, in some ways, is much like the cause-and-effect diagram except that it can be considered a backward fishbone.

Constructing a cause-and-effect diagram

Constructing a cause-and-effect diagram is a three-step process. It's demonstrated in figure 3.73.

Steps:

1. *Name the problem or "effect."* The effect is placed in a box on the right and a long process arrow is drawn pointing to the box.
2. *Decide on the major categories or subdivisions of causes.* These major categories are placed parallel to and some distance from the main process arrow. Arrows slanting toward the main arrow connect the boxes.

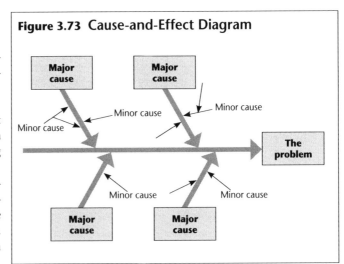

Figure 3.73 Cause-and-Effect Diagram

3. *Brainstorm for causes.* The causes are written on the chart and clustered around the major category or subdivision that they influence. Arrows pointing to the main process arrow connect them. The causes should be divided and subdivided to show, as accurately as possible, how they interact.

To have a little fun, use the cause-and-effect diagram shown in figure 3.74 to perform the same analysis.

Remember that either the random method or systematic method may be used to generate the cause-and-effect diagram.

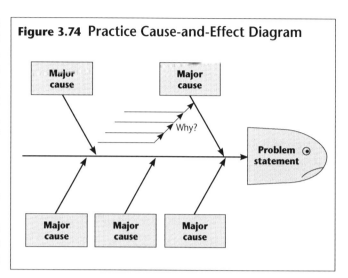

Figure 3.74 Practice Cause-and-Effect Diagram

Constructing a process-analysis diagram

To construct the process-analysis diagram such as the one illustrated in figure 3.75, you must first list the series of tasks you wish to analyze in the order in which they are performed. Next, place each of these in boxes and in sequential order, connecting the boxes with arrows to indicate the process' progress. The third step is to brainstorm—using either the random or systematic method—all of the causes that contribute to each step. These are listed on the chart and connected by arrows to the box containing the step to which they refer.

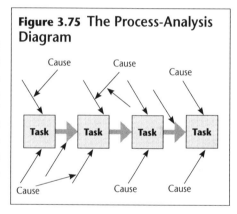

Figure 3.75 The Process-Analysis Diagram

Constructing a solution-analysis diagram

Using the cause-and-effect diagram and process-analysis diagram, we start with the effect (the problem) and analyze it for causes. In a solution-analysis diagram, (illustrated in figure 3.76) we do the reverse: start with a single cause (a proposed solution) and analyze it for all of the possible effects. To best determine all the effects of a possible solution, use a solution-analysis type of cause-and-effect diagram. It will help to make better solution choices and to answer questions about your activities.

The first step is to name the proposed solution and enclose it in a box.

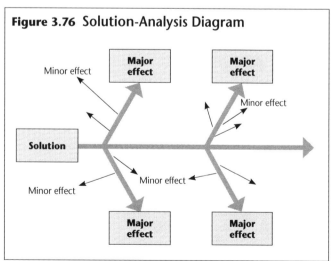

Figure 3.76 Solution-Analysis Diagram

The box is placed on the left side with a process arrow leading away from it. This arrow shows the direction of influence. Next, decide on the major categories or subdivisions of effects. These are the areas the proposed solution is likely to influence. The third step is to brainstorm—using either the systematic or random method—the likely effects (good and bad) of the proposed solution. These effects are clustered around the major categories with smaller arrows leading away from the arrows indicating major categories. After this step has been completed, list the positive outcomes in one column and the negative in another. Compare the positive and negative results of the proposed solution. Use this information in deciding which solution to employ.

Use of cause-and-effect diagrams
Cause-and-effect diagrams can be used to:
- Assist individual and group ideation.
- Record ideas.
- Reveal undetected relationships.
- Investigate the origin of a problem.
- Investigate expected results of a course of action.
- Illustrate important relationships.

Diagramming causes and their effects quickly indicates whether the problem has been thoroughly investigated. A cause-and-effect diagram with a lot of detail shows how deeply a group has investigated a process. On the other hand, a cause-and-effect diagram without a lot of detail might indicate that the problem was not significant, or that the problem solvers were not very thorough. Likewise, a complete solution-analysis diagram shows the group's careful consideration of a proposed solution.

Constructing cause-and-effect diagrams
When constructing a cause-and-effect diagram, pay attention to a few essentials that will provide a more accurate and usable result.
- All members must feel free to express their ideas. The more ideas considered, the more accurate the diagram will be.
- Don't criticize any ideas. To encourage a free exchange, write down all ideas just as they are mentioned in the appropriate place on the diagram.

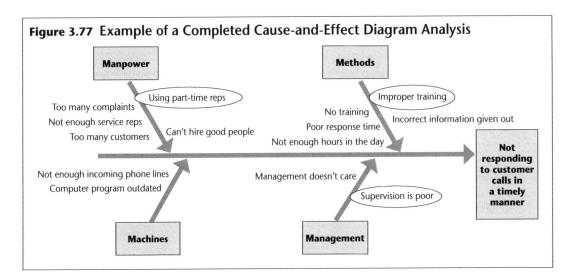

Figure 3.77 Example of a Completed Cause-and-Effect Diagram Analysis

- Visibility encourages participation. Everyone in the group must be able to see the diagram. Use large charts with large printing and conduct diagram sessions in a well-lit area.
- Connect related causes as they are mentioned so the relationships are illustrated as the diagram develops.
- Don't overload the diagram. As a group of causes begins to dominate the diagram, that group should be isolated and a separate diagram made for it.
- Construct a separate diagram for each problem. If your problem is not specific enough, some major categories of the diagram will become overloaded. This indicates the need for additional diagrams.
- Circle the most-likely causes. This is usually done after all possible ideas have been posted on the cause-and-effect diagram. Only then is each idea critically evaluated.
- Create a solution-oriented atmosphere in each session. Focus on solving problems rather than on how problems started. The past cannot be changed, but the group can improve the future state by eliminating causes of undesired effects.
- Understand where each cause is to be placed on the diagram.

AFFINITY DIAGRAMS

"Ideas are like bricks. They just lay around until someone picks them up and builds a cathedral out of them."

—HJH

Definition

An affinity diagram organizes a variety of subjective data (such as options) into categories based on the intuitive relationships among individual pieces of information. It is often used to find commonalties among concerns and ideas.

How to use affinity diagrams

The affinity diagram organizes ideas based on their natural relationships. It's particularly useful for organizing thoughts after a brainstorming session that has generated a lot of ideas. If used effectively, it's a creative process that lets new patterns and relationships between ideas be discovered, leading to more creative solutions. The technique is usually used in group problem solving, but it can also be used by individuals for the same objective.

How to do it

1. State the problem in broad terms. Avoid detailed problem statements.
2. Brainstorm ideas on how to solve the problem. Record the responses on 3 in. × 5 in. index cards.
3. Shuffle the cards and place them randomly in the middle of a table.
4. The group should silently sort the cards into piles of related ideas. Limit the number of piles to between five and ten. Team members should do this exercise quickly, relying more on their first impressions than logical thought.
5. For each pile of cards, pick a card that best represents the theme in the pile. Put that card on top. If no card clearly stands out as representative of the whole group, and if another idea comes to mind which does summarize the theme, then create a new card for that theme and put it on top of the pile.
6. Using the card groupings, record the grouped ideas on paper. Draw lines around each grouping.

Guidelines and tips

■ This technique works best with groups of six to eight people.

■ Short brainstorming statements are best. Statements should be as concise as possible, and include a noun and a verb.

■ The recommendation to sort cards quickly cannot be stressed enough. By using intuitive processes instead of logic in grouping the cards, new patterns and relationships can be found between elements of a problem. This can lead to more creative solutions.

■ If using this technique as an individual, take some time off in between idea generation and using the affinity diagram to organize them. Going from idea generation directly into organizing thoughts will not be as creative, since the associations that led from one idea to another in idea generation will result in established patterns of thought.

■ One way to do it is to record the responses on small Post-it notes and attach them to a whiteboard as the ideas are generated. This makes it easy to move them around into groupings.

Examples

For the ABC Manufacturing Co., what are the issues involved in missing promised delivery dates?

■ Figure 3.78 lists ideas generated in a brainstorming meeting on this problem.

■ Figure 3.79 shows the same brainstorming ideas organized in an affinity diagram.

Figure 3.78 A List of Brainstorming Ideas

• Hire freight carrier based on lowest rate available.	• Wrong count by operators on production floor
• Dock is overcrowded.	• Need classification by type of error
• Historical trends of errors	• Frequently change freight carriers
• What is a shipping error?	• Too slow getting replacement product or paperwork
• Time lag in order changes on computer	• Don't tell customer if shipping error is known but not detected by customer.
• When big customers push, switch labels and ship.	• Allow changes to orders over the phone.
• Shipping errors only in certain product lines	• Sometimes substitute facsimile if product is unavailable.
• Data entry complexity	• Computer system too slow — use handwritten forms instead.
• Difficult to measure true cost of errors	• Labels fall off boxes.
• High turnover among shippers	• High turnover among data entry clerks.
• New eleven-digit code too long	• No place to segregate customer returns.
• Bar codes damaged/unreadable	• Some new, reusable packaging has wrong bar codes.
• Dock used to store material for return to vendors	• Lack of training for data entry clerks
• How many are paperwork errors but the right product was shipped?	• Newest employees go to shipping.
• Shipping sometimes contracted directly by sales representative to rush orders.	• Production bonus system encourages speed, not accuracy.
• Old shipping boxes easily damaged, requiring replacement	• Dock is coldest place in winter, hottest place in summer.
• Customer orders still initially handwritten	• How many customers lost that we don't know about?

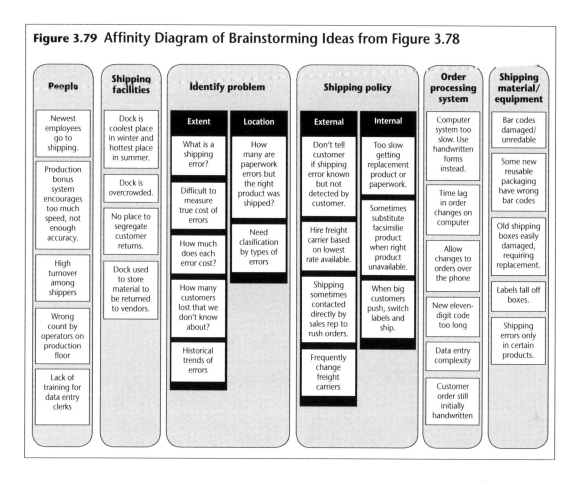

Figure 3.79 Affinity Diagram of Brainstorming Ideas from Figure 3.78

People	Shipping facilities	Identify problem		Shipping policy		Order processing system	Shipping material/ equipment
		Extent	**Location**	**External**	**Internal**		
Newest employees go to shipping.	Dock is coolest place in winter and hottest place in summer.	What is a shipping error?	How many are paperwork errors but the right product was shipped?	Don't tell customer if shipping error known but not detected by customer.	Too slow getting replacement product or paperwork.	Computer system too slow. Use handwritten forms instead.	Bar codes damaged/ unredable
Production bonus system encourages too much speed, not enough accuracy.	Dock is overcrowded.	Difficult to measure true cost of errors	Need clasification by types of errors	Hire freight carrier based on lowest rate available.	Sometimes substitute facsimilie product when right product unavailable.	Time lag in order changes on computer	Some new reusable packaging have wrong bar codes
High turnover among shippers	No place to segregate customer returns.	How much does each error cost?		Shipping sometimes contacted directly by sales rep to rush orders.	When big customers push, switch labels and ship.	Allow changes to orders over the phone	Old shipping boxes easily damaged, requiring replacement.
Wrong count by operators on production floor	Dock used to store material to be returned to vendors.	How many customers lost that we don't know about?		Frequently change freight carriers		New eleven-digit code too long	Labels fall off boxes.
Lack of training for data entry clerks		Historical trends of errors				Data entry complexity	Shipping errors only in certain products.
						Customer order still initially handwritten	

ROOT CAUSE ANALYSIS

"Treating the symptoms often will not correct the problem."
—HJH

    Root cause analysis is the process of identifying the various causes affecting a particular problem, process, or issue and determining the real reasons that caused the condition.

How to use root cause analysis

    There are many books about root cause analysis and although their approaches differ, they all advise against treating symptoms; rather, the goal is to define problems' root causes so they can be corrected. It sounds so simple, but most books never tell you exactly how to find the root cause. Why do they avoid giving details about this crucial activity? The reason is simple: Defining the root cause is often very difficult and complex and there is no one right way that works all the time. The practitioner must be skilled at selecting the most effective approach.

There are a number of ways to get to the root of a problem. A good failure analysis laboratory can provide the insight necessary to understand how a failure, such as a broken bolt, occurred. Duplicating the failure under laboratory conditions has also proven to be an effective way to define the root cause of problems. You know you've found the root cause when you can cause the problem to occur and stop at will. Either of these approaches works well, but they require expensive laboratories and highly trained personnel.

Excessive variation is at the heart of most problems—at least the difficult ones. Variation is part of life. No two items or acts are exactly identical. Even identical twins have very different fingerprints, voice patterns, and personal values. No two screws made on the same machine are exactly the same. Equipment may not be sensitive enough to measure this variation, but it nonetheless exists. To make matters even more confusing, some variation is good. It keeps our lives from being monotonous.

Variation that's within specific limits has little or no effect on output. Uncontrolled, variation can cause an entire plant to come to a halt. The variation we're concerned about here is the variation that causes waste. There is no such thing as a random problem—only problems whose occurrence can be infrequent, meaning that the combination of variables that sparks the problem variation occurs more or less infrequently. The art of defining the root cause is the art of variables analysis and isolation.

The root cause of a problem has been found when the key variables that caused the problem have been isolated. Over the years, there have been many methods developed to isolate key variables. Design of experiments and Taguchi methods are popular today, but the difficulties and effort required to prepare and conduct these studies cause them to be used on only a small fraction of the problems. Engineers, managers, production employees, and sales personnel solve most of their problems by brute force and a lot of luck. Even then, most of the time, the answer that is implemented is often not the best solution to the problem.

By studying different types of variation, the source of the variation can be identified. Then the problem solver can quickly and effectively reduce the many potential sources to a critical few and often to a single factor, thereby greatly simplifying the problem evaluation cycle and reducing the amount of data for collection. The results can be profound:

- Problems can be solved faster.
- Fewer samples are required.
- Less-skilled people can solve very complex problems.
- Preventive and corrective action plans can be evaluated quickly.
- Nontechnical people can easily understand the results of a technical evaluation.

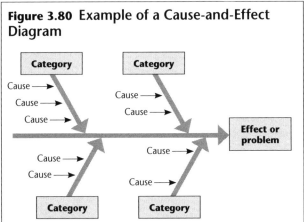

Figure 3.80 Example of a Cause-and-Effect Diagram

How to perform a root cause analysis in six steps

1. *Identify the potential root cause of the problem.* The most effective method of root cause analysis is to determine how the root cause will be identified or what approach will be used. One of the most frequently used tools for identifying root cause is the cause-and-effect or "fishbone" diagram. Its primary function is to provide the user with a picture of all the possible causes of a specific problem or condition. (See figure 3.80.)

2. *Gather data on the frequency of the problem.* Use checksheets or other approaches to track occurrences of problems and to identify their causes. Figure 3.81 shows how a checksheet can be used for several problems that may result from one or more causes.

3. *Determine the effect of the problem.* Use a scatter diagram, such as the one in figure 3.82, or a similar tool.

4. *Summarize all major root causes and relate them back to the major opportunity areas.* The purpose of this is to:
   - ■ Identify root causes that affect several problems.
   - ■ Ensure that the major root causes are identified in all opportunity areas.
   - ■ Aid in selection of the key root cause to eliminate.

Figure 3.81 Example of a Checksheet

Checksheet for Identifying Defective Copies

Machine No.:_____ Operator's name: _____ Date:_____

	Missing pages	Muddy copies	Showthrough	Pages out of sequence	Total
Machine jams	|||			||||	7
Paper weight	||				6
Humidity		||				3
Toner		|||			4
Condition of original	||||	||||	||	||||	14
Other (specify)					
				Total	34

Comments

5. *Prioritize the root causes.* Use a prioritization matrix, as shown in figure 3.83. This procedure consists of the following four steps:
   I. List the criteria to be used to evaluate the causes.
   II. Weight each criterion according to its relative importance. Put the weight for each criterion in that column heading.
   III. Using one criterion at a time, rank the causes, with "one" being the least important. Enter the ranking in the column under the criterion in question.
   IV. Multiply each rank order figure by the weight of each of the criteria to arrive at a total for each cause. Enter these totals in the final column of each row.

6. *Select the key root cause to eliminate.* This decision should be based on the analysis of all available data. If you use a prioritization matrix, you may simply decide according to the totals in the final column.

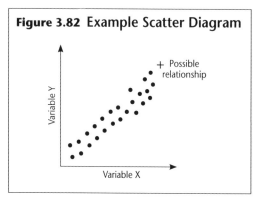

Figure 3.82 Example Scatter Diagram

+ Possible relationship

Variable Y

Variable X

Figure 3.83 Example of a Prioritization Matrix

Root causes \ Criteria	Criteria 1	Criteria 2	Criteria 3	Criteria 4	Totals
Root cause 1					
Root cause 2					
Root cause 3					
Root cause 4					
Root cause 5					
Root cause 6					
Root cause 7					
Root cause 8					

Example

The fault-tree analysis is another alternative and sometimes is more effective than the approach just described. (See figure 3.84.) This can be considered the "What could cause this?" approach.

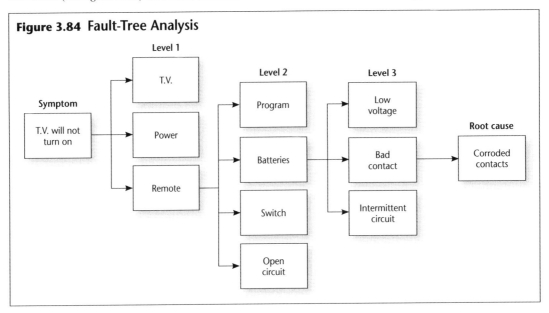

Figure 3.84 Fault-Tree Analysis

Symptom: Television will not turn on
What could cause this? (Level 1)

■ Television is defective
■ Electrical power is out
■ Remote control is defective

Investigation: Television turns on when the "on" button is pushed, but not when the "on" button on the remote control is pushed. What could cause this? (Level 2)

■ Not programmed to the television
■ Discharged batteries
■ Defective "on" switch
■ Open circuit

Investigation: Replaced batteries. Remote control now turns on the television. Put back in the old batteries and the remote turned on the television.
What could cause this? (Level 3)

■ Batteries' voltage is low so the remote control works intermittently
■ Bad contact
■ Intermittent circuit

Investigation: Inspected battery terminals and found that they were corroded. Cleaned terminals. Checked the age of the batteries; they were less than two months old. Checked the voltage and current of the batteries; they were fine. Put the old batteries in the remote control and it turned on the television at a distance of two times the normal usage.
Root cause of failure: Corroded terminals

FAILURE MODE AND EFFECTS ANALYSIS (FMEA)

"Prevention is defining how an error could occur and then changing the process so that it can't occur."

—HJH

Definition

FMEA identifies potential failures or causes of failures that may occur as a result of process design weaknesses.

How to use FMEA

This preventive technique provides the process owner or product designer with a method of studying the causes and effects of failures before the design is finalized. The three types of FMEA applications are:

■ *Design FMEA.* Covers new designs and major design changes to an existing product, service, or process before rollout to understand how it could fail once released. It exposes problems that may result in safety hazards, malfunctions, shortened product life, or decreased customer satisfaction.

■ *Process FMEA.* Used to improve existing transactional and operational processes to understand how people, materials, equipment, methods, and the environment can cause process problems. It exposes process problems that may result in safety hazards, defects in product, service errors, or reduced process efficiency.

■ *System FMEA.* Used to analyze systems and subsystems in the early stages of concept design.

FMEA should be used when:

■ Designing a new product, service, or process.

■ Changing an existing produce, service, or process.

■ The new or revised product, service, or process design concept is completed but before starting the detailed design.

As it's not normally economically feasible to conduct FMEA for each component, those deemed most critical to the product are selected for review. A deeper analysis will be required if the reviewer finds he or she doesn't have enough information for some of the failure modes as the analysis proceeds. The process steps for this are as follows:

1. The product components are studied for all known ways in which they may fail.

2. An estimate is made of the effect on the product (or process, system, etc.) and its severity for each potential failure mode.

3. A review is made of the planned action for each component under consideration. This review is to help minimize the probability for failure and/or to minimize the effect of the component failure.

FMEA is also used in Six Sigma applications:

■ In the define phase to understand the project risk

■ In the measure phase to understand how KPIs relate to risk, and to help with prioritization of the measurements

■ In the improve phase to understand the risk related to the corrective action and to error-proof the process

■ In the control phase to help define the needed controls

Example

Figure 3.85 shows an example of a completed analysis on a laser printer design. The component system under review is the path the paper takes through the unit. The concern is potential paper jams. For each component there are many possible failures, but for this example we will list only one to keep the sample from being too long.

Figure 3.85 FMEA Example

Product: Laser printer   Date: 10/5/93

Concern: Paper jams   Review team: Paper flow

Component No. Part Nos.	Possible failure	Cause of failure (failure mechanism)	P	D	S	Effect of failure on the system	How can failure be reduced or eliminated
Face down tray	Rough surface	Excessive wear	1	1	3	Uneven paper feed	Change to another plastic
Fuser assembly	Fuser cleaner Not snug in slot	Improper install Bad molding	3	3	4	Paper won't print Could cause fire	Close QC on case vendor
Paper feed guide	Wrong size	Bad selection	2	1	3	Uneven paper feed	Install SPC at supplier
Registration roller	Gears worn Rough/warped roller(s)	Poor maintenance High heat	3	2	2	Paper won't move	Vendor surveillance Stiffen roller guides
Paper cassette	Not in slot all the way	Improper install Molding tabs	3	1	4	Unit shut down	Redesign molding tabs
Paper feed roller	Gears worn Rough/warped roller(s)	Excessive wear High heat Roller binding	3	2	2	Paper won't move	Vendor surveillance Stiffen roller guides
Multipurpose tray	Not in slot all the way	Improper install	1	1	3	Paper will not feed	Redesign tray to click in place
EP cartridge	Worn mating gear(s) Not in slot	Alignment molding Excessive wear Gear selection	3	1	1	Unit shut down	Redesign molding slot Vendor surveillance Gear design

P = Probability of occurrence
D = Likelihood of damage to other components
S = Seriousness of failure to system

1 = Very low or none (<1 in 10)
2 = low or minor (3 in 10)
3 = Medium (50/50)

4 = High (7–10)
5 = Very high or failure (>9–10)

SUMMARY OF BASIC TOOLS

In this chapter we presented the most-used Yellow Belt nonstatistical problem solving tools. Chapter 4 will present the most used basic statistical tools used by Yellow Belts. If you would like to learn more about other nonstatistical problem-solving tools, the next most-used tools are:

- Calibration
- Communication techniques
- Conflict resolution
- Critical path methods
- Error proofing
- Fast Action Solution Teams (FAST)
- General surveys
- Interviewing techniques
- Key performance indicators (KPI)
- Measurement error
- Measurement tools
- Negotiation techniques
- Organization change management
- Prioritization concepts
- Prioritization plots
- Simplification approaches
- Types of data

**"The time to repair the roof is
when the sun is shining."
—John F. Kennedy**

"A real professional always knows and has
the right tool for the job at hand."

—HJH

CHAPTER 4

STATISTICAL TOOLS FOR YELLOW BELTS

Praveen Gupta assisted with the preparation of this chapter.

Yellow Belts must be familiar with statistics because statistical tools are an essential part of each phase of the Six Sigma define-measure-analyze-improve-control (DMAIC) model. This chapter focuses on those statistical tools that are most important for Yellow Belts.

PROCESS ELEMENTS, VARIABLES, AND OBSERVATIONS CONCEPTS

Elements are the process steps, objects, or parameters on which information is collected. For example, in a study of the airline industry one can identify the top ten airlines that become the elements in the data set. A variable is a measure of interest, which is normally a process input, in-process, or output parameter that needs to be studied and analyzed. In the airline example, the process inputs might be customer satisfaction, performance, take-off times, departure times, arrival times, in-flight service, and flight load. Each piece of information collected for a variable of a process element is called an observation. The observations for a process constitute data.

DATA, SCALE, AND SOURCES

Data are the first set of information that need be collected to learn about process performance. The data can be classified as attributes or variables. Attributes data represent performance levels, such as pass or fail, go and no-go, OK or not OK, and accept or reject. Attributes data are analyzed for their frequency distribution and prioritization for more data collection. Variables data include actual measurements, such as current, voltage, speed, RPM, length, height, width, depth, distance, thickness, and many more. Variables data represent a specific value with or without decimals and are analyzed for their distributions and related probabilities.

Attributes data provide information primarily about the problem, and variables data show the size or magnitude of the problem. Generally, simple and stable processes use more attributes data, and new or dynamic processes must collect more variables data.

Scales of measurement represent the categories of information of data. There are four scales of measurement:

- Nominal
- Ordinal
- Interval
- Ratio

A nominal scale applies a label or the name of the data that can only be categorized for analysis based upon their frequency of occurrence. Such data include Social Security numbers, names, or problem categories. In our airline example, the names of the airlines will represent the nominal scale data. The nominal data could be alpha, alpha-numeric, or numeric.

Ordinal scale data exhibit the properties of nominal data that can be used for ranking of the process elements. For example, information collected through passenger surveys would allow you to rank airlines. Employee performance appraisal, on a scale of one to five, or A, B, C, and D corresponding to the performance rating, would also represent ordinal scale. The ordinal data are either alpha or numeric with a relative value.

Interval scale data represent an additional dimension to the ordinal data when the interval between data correlates to the process performance. Interval data are always numeric. For example, GMAT scores of 600, 580, 640, and 700 for four students can be ranked from low to high, and the differences between the scores are meaningful.

The ratio scale represents the data where interval and ratios are meaningful. For example, consider the following on-time performance data of four airlines: 60, 70, 80, and 90 percent. Both the difference (30) between 60 and 90 percent, and the ratio (1.5) of these figures provide meaningful information. The variable data are of ratio scale. Figure 4.1 shows an overview of various scales of measurement.

The nominal scale represents attributes data; the ratio scale represents variables data. The nominal scale, or ordinal scale, data are typically the qualitative data representing limited opportunity for statistical analysis. The qualitative data can be chiefly summarized as the count or proportion of observations in each category. When data represent a count or a specific amount of something, the data are discrete in nature.

The interval and ratio measurement scales represent quantitative data. These are numeric values that indicate amount. Quantitative data allow more opportunities for statistical analysis and mathematical operations. Typically, quantitative data are continuous on a scale where one can specify a value or quantity. They are also called continuous data.

Figure 4.1 Overview of Various Scales of Measurement

Scale of measurement	Description	Example	Type of data
Nominal scale	Data collected are names or labels.	Names of airlines that are operating in the United States	Qualitative data
Ordinal scale	Data exhibit the properties of nominal data and the rank of the data is meaningful.	Survey results of the airline	Qualitative data
Interval scale	Data have the properties of ordinal data and the interval between observations is meaningful.	Customer satisfaction score	Quantitative data
Ratio scale	Data have the properties of interval data and the ratio of observations is meaningful.	Customer service time at the airline check-in counter	Quantitative data

Source: *The Six Sigma Performance Handbook* (Gupta, 2004)

Sources of data are critical aspects of process improvement. Because collecting good data is important to problem solving, this activity requires careful planning about what data are needed, for how long they need to be collected, and from where they can be obtained. Sometimes data are available from a routine process, and sometimes data are collected when necessary. Sometimes part and process-performance data are collected from external resources.

DATA ACCURACY

People often complain that data used for analysis were not accurate, or because data were not believable, no analysis was performed. The data may be inaccurate due to data entry, recording error, or a faulty measuring device. In other words, data inaccuracy occurs due to either malfunctioning equipment or operator error. An uncalibrated measuring device won't provide accurate measurements. The operator may not be consistent in gathering data due to lack of training or inability to function well due to lack of sleep. Sometimes data are inaccurate because nobody bothered to look at them for so long that the operators decided to enter expected numbers.

In any case, data-entry errors are easiest to find when they look excessive. One can find the data-error entry either through sorting or evaluating minimum and maximum values. Sometimes zero or decimal points are misplaced. Measurement device errors will be somewhat more difficult to determine unless multiple devices are involved. By reviewing the data, you can often isolate data associated with the erroneous measuring device.

In the case of fake data entered by the operator, the data can be isolated because the data look too good. Their variation will be excessively minimal. Regardless of the reason for the data inaccuracy, we can pinpoint the causes and take necessary remedial actions to improve them. The Six Sigma team (SST) must be aware of the data errors before analyzing the data.

STATISTICAL THINKING

If you are a Six Sigma practitioner at an airline and you have been assigned the task of reducing customer service time at the ticket counter, the first thing you would want to know is the current length of time it takes to issue a ticket. To acquire this data, you may decide to measure the ticketing time for fifty customers using a stopwatch over several days, randomly picking different ticketing counters throughout the day to represent the customer base. (See figure 4.2.)

Now that you have the data, you need to analyze them. Begin by summarizing the data and calculating basic statistics such as the average time to issue a ticket and the variation in these times. After the analysis, you would make recommendations to reduce the average time to issue a ticket. As an approach, you would group the data in different ranges in minutes, construct a frequency distribution as shown in figure 4.3, and then determine the mean value and variation.

There are two types of data variation: those that occur randomly and those that occur rarely. The variation that occurs randomly is called "random variation" and the variation that occurs rarely is called "assignable

Figure 4.2 Time in Seconds for Passengers at Airline Ticket Counters

175	198	168
185	160	175
183	166	176
189	167	177
173	159	178
172	212	178
171	161	179
169	186	162
177	172	178
180	174	178
180	188	178
181	187	213
184	200	168
188	150	163
170	199	155
165	196	181
191	163	

variation." It disturbs the normal bell-shaped curve and makes it look like a different-looking distribution. Statistical thinking requires a clear understanding of the difference between random and assignable variation. Random variation occurs due to uncontrolled variables or circumstances that exist in the environment around the process. There are many of these uncontrolled variables that contribute to the process variation. They are always present in the process and are difficult to pinpoint and resolve.

Assignable variation normally doesn't exist, occurs rarely for a specific reason, and is easy to pinpoint for removal. For example, in case of the length of time to issue an airline ticket, the random variation could be due to slight variation in passenger situations, such

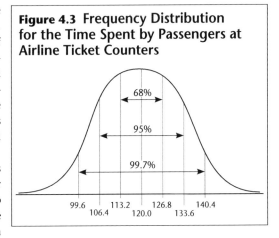

Figure 4.3 Frequency Distribution for the Time Spent by Passengers at Airline Ticket Counters

as someone having lost his or her ticket or forgetting his or her driver's license. Other variations could be caused by such events as an untrained ticket agent or a faulty computer. Such circumstances cause unexpected delays that can irritate customers. If the extended delays were included in the sample data, it would show excessive variation and thus would be considered an assignable variation.

Similarly, fluctuation in temperature, relative humidity, or variations in commute time would be examples of random variation. Arriving home late by an hour or so may occur due to a traffic jam or accident.

BASIC STATISTICAL CONCEPTS

Basic statistics includes a group of commonly used statistical tools that are used to establish statistical performance levels for a process. These measurements include mean, range or standard deviation, scatter plot, and histograms. These measures also are used to construct a bell-shaped curve or normal distribution curve that can be used to visualize and predict process performance.

Summation (Σ = taking the sum of)

The summation is the addition of a set of numbers; the result is their sum. The numbers to be summed (*n*) may be natural numbers, complex numbers, matrices, or more complicated fractions.

Because it's necessary to add numbers frequently in statistics, the symbol Σ is used to indicate "take the sum of." If there is a set of *n* values for a variable labeled X (*n* = any number of items that will be summed together), the expression $\sum_{i=1}^{n} x_i$ indicates that these *n* values are to be added together from the first value to the last (*n*th) value. Thus:

$$\sum_{i=1}^{n} X_i = X_1 + X_2 + X_3 + \ldots + Xn$$

To illustrate summation notation, suppose there are five values for a variable X:

$X_1 = 5, X_2 = 0, X_3 = -1, X_4 = -4,$ and $X_5 = 6$

For these data,

$$\sum_{i=1}^{n} X_i = X_1 + X_2 + X_3 + X_4 + X_5 = 5 + 0 + (-1) + (-4) + 6 = 6$$

The following is the calculation of a second set of numbers labeled *Y*

$$\sum_{i=1}^{n} Y_i = Y_1 + Y_2 + Y_3 + \ldots + Y_n$$

$Y_1 = 1$, $Y_2 = 3$, $Y_3 = -2$, $Y_4 = 4$, and $Y_5 = 3$

$$\sum_{i=1}^{n} Y_i = 9$$

Sometimes you need to sum the squared values of a variable. The sum of the squared *X*s is written as:

$$\sum_{i=1}^{n} X_i^2 = X_1^2 + X_2^2 + X_3^2 + X_4^2 \ldots + X_n^2$$

$$\sum_{i=1}^{n} X_i^2 = (5)^2 + (0)^2 + (-1)^2 + (-4)^2 + (6)^2 = 68$$

Note that the only thing that's different is the number two, which indicates that *X* squared is added to each *X* value using the preceding data:

$$\left(\sum_{i=1}^{n} x_i \right) \left(\sum_{i=1}^{n} Y_i \right) = (6)(9) = 54$$

This is not the same as $\sum_{i=1}^{n} X_i Y_i$ which equals nine.

Mean

Process mean is the most familiar and used statistical measure. The mean typifies the expected or most-likely value of a parameter. Thus, it's also most important to understand that most of the measurements cluster around the mean. The mean is calculated by adding all the data points and dividing the sum by the number of data points.

The mean for data from a sample is denoted by $\bar{X}$, and the data from a population are denoted by the Greek letter μ. Each data point is represented by X_i.

Sample mean: $\bar{X} = \Sigma X_i / n$, for "i" = 1 to *n*

Where $\Sigma X_i = x_1 + x_2 + x_3 + x_4 + \ldots + x_n$
n = sample size

Population mean: $\mu = \Sigma X_i / N$, for i = 1 to N, and
Where $\Sigma X_i = x_1 + x_2 + x_3 + x_4 + \ldots + x_N$
N = population size

Consider the data for our airline's time to issue a ticket: The mean can be calculated using Excel or any other statistical software. For an Excel worksheet, one uses the formula as "=AVERAGE (data cell range for variable *x*)," for example: "=AVERAGE (A2:A52)." In our airline ticketing process example, the mean value would be 177.6 seconds.

Median

Median is another measure of centrality. The mean sums the data points and divides the result by the number of observations; the median counts data points and determines the data set's middle point. For an odd number of observations, the middle value is obtained by sorting observations in an ascending or descending order and locating the middle value. For an even number of observations, the median is the average of the two middle values. Median is used when data are less variable in nature or contain extreme values.

It provides an indication of the distribution of data points. The command in Excel is "=MEDIAN (data cell range for variable X)." In our airline ticketing process example, the median value would be 177.5 seconds.

Mode

The mode is the value that occurs with greatest frequency. You may encounter situations with two or more different values with the greatest frequency. In these instances, more than one mode can exist. If the data have exactly two modes, they are "bimodal." The command in Excel is "=MODE (data cell range for variable X)."

In our airline ticketing process example, the mode value would be 178 seconds.

Range

The range is simplest measure of variability. It's the difference between the largest and the smallest value in the data set. It has limitations because it's calculated using two values irrespective of the size of the data. The range can be calculated by finding the maximum value ("=MAX (data cell range for variable X)"), the minimum value ("=MIN (data cell range for variable X)") and then finding the difference between the two.

In our airline ticketing process example, the range would be sixty-three seconds.

Variance

Variance is a measure of inconsistency in a set of values or in process performance. It uses all data values instead of the two values used in calculating the range. The variation is the average of the squared deviations, where deviations are the difference between the value of each observation (x_i) and the mean.

Population (all data points) variance is denoted by Greek symbol σ^2.

$$\sigma^2 = \Sigma\,(x_i\text{-}\mu)^2/N$$

Sample (a subset of larger dataset or population) variance is denoted by s^2.

$$s^2 = \Sigma\,(x_i\text{-}\bar{X})^2/(n\text{-}1)$$

If the sample mean is divided by n-1 and not n, the resulting sample variance provides an unbiased estimate of the population variance. Using Excel, variance is determined with the command "=VAR (data cell range for variable x)."

In our airline ticketing process example, the variance would be 178.6 seconds.

Standard deviation

Standard deviation is the square root of the variance. Thus:
- Sample standard deviation: $s = \sqrt{s^2}$
- Population standard deviation: $\sigma = \sqrt{\sigma^2}$

The command for calculating standard deviation using Excel is "=STDEV (data cell range for variable x)." In our airline ticketing process example, the standard deviation would be 13.4 seconds.

Correlation coefficient

A scatter plot represents the relationship between two variables, such as experience of employees and passenger time spent at the ticket counter, as shown in figure 4.4. The correlation coefficient is a statistical measurement of the relationship between two variables. Depending on the relationship of data for two variables, the correlation and the correlation coefficient can be negative or positive. The value of correlation coefficient lies between 0 and ±1. A correlation coefficient of +1 indicates a direct positive relationship and a value of −1 indicates a direct negative relationship. A zero value of correlation coefficient implies no correlation, thus two independent variables.

The command for calculating correlation coefficient using Excel is "=CORREL (data cell range for variable *x*, data cell range for variable *y*)."

In our airline ticketing process example, the correlation coefficient would be −0.75, which is expected because experienced employees would be able to help passengers faster than their less experienced colleagues.

Histograms

A histogram is a graphical representation of the frequency distribution of data. In a histogram, the horizontal axis (*X*) represents measurement range and the vertical axis (*Y*) represents the frequency of occurrence. The histogram is one of the most frequently used graphical tools for analyzing variable data. A histogram is like a bar chart except that it has a continuous *X*-scale opposite separate and unrelated bars.

Histograms display central tendency and dispersion of the data set. By plotting the limits around the process mean, one can tell what percent of the

Figure 4.4 Scatter Plot of the Time at Airline Ticket Counters vs. Employee Experience

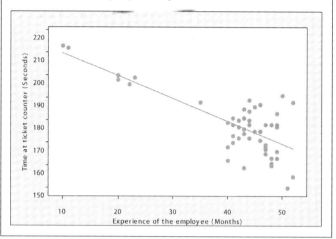

Figure 4.5 Histogram of Time Spent by Passengers at Ticket Counter

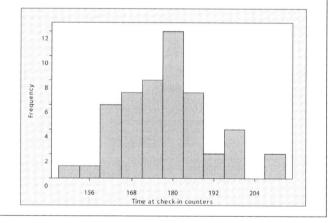

data is beyond the limits. This is useful to determine acceptable and reject rates of a process. By including known distributions or using software, it's also possible to estimate the probability of producing good products or bad products. This allows organizations to determine expected process performance and initiate preventive action, if necessary.

Figure 4.5 shows the histogram with central tendency and the dispersion for the time spent by the passengers at the airline ticket counter.

BASIC PROBABILITY CONCEPTS

Probability is a measure of the likelihood that some event will occur. The probability of the occurrence of any event (A) is defined as:

$$P\,(A)\;=\;\frac{\textit{Number of times event "A" occurs or could occur}}{\textit{Number of times the experiment was conducted/total possibilities}}$$

The probability of any event's occurrence ranges from zero to one. For example, to calculate the probability of finding a three when we toss a fair die once, we know we can get six different values and a three can come only once. Hence the probability of finding it in the random toss of a die would be:

$P\,(3) = 1/6 \text{ or } 0.17$

PROBABILITY THEORY

Most statistical concepts are based upon probability theory, so Yellow Belts should understand it. One of the ways to demonstrate probability theory is through the games we play, such as dice or cards. Let's start with the dice example. A single die specification is:

- Has only six sides.
- Only one side can be up at a time.
- Each of the six sides have the same probability of occurrence.
- The probability of any one side coming up is one in six, or 0.1667.
- Each of the six sides has a different number on it that ranges from one to six.

The probability of a single event (in the case of a die the same number) is $P\,(A)$ if A is independent of any other event. (Example: $P\,(A)$ could be the probability (P) of a one (A) coming up on one die, or 16.67 percent.)

If you add a second die (B), its probability of throwing a one is the same as die (A). But if you throw the two die together, the sum of the numbers is dependent on the probability of a specific number coming up on die A or $P\,(A)$ and a specific number coming up on die B or $P\,(B)$. This is the probability of both occurring at the same

Figure 4.6 Dice Combinations

	1	2	3	4	5	6
1	2	3	4	5	σ	7
2	3	4	5	σ	7	8
3	4	5	σ	7	8	9
4	5	σ	7	8	9	10
5	σ	7	8	9	10	11
6	7	8	9	10	11	12

time. This joint probability of A and B occurring at the same time is multiplicative by nature and is equal to $P\,(A) \times P\,(B)$, or the probability of rolling any given combination with two die is $1/6 \times 1/6 = 16.67 \times 0.1667 = 0.0278$, or 2.7896 percent.

There is only one combination that can produce a two (i.e., both dice come up with ones) or twelve (i.e., both dice come up with sixes). As a result, we can say they are mutually exclusive. When two events are mutually exclusive, the probability of the event occurring is calculated by adding their individual probabilities $P\,(A \text{ or } B) = P\,(A) + P\,(B)$ or $0.0278 + 0.278 = 0.0556$, or 6.56 percent. In other words, the probability of rolling a number from three to eleven will be 94.44 percent every time you throw the dice. Figure 4.6 shows the total combinations of rolling two dice.

There is a possibility of rolling thirty-six different combinations, each of them have a probability of occurrence of $P\,(A) \times P\,(B) = 0.1667 \times 0.1667 = 0.0278$. By analyzing figure 4.7 we can see that there are five combinations that can result in a total of six. (See figure 4.7.)

Because all five events are mutually exclusive, their total effect is the sum of all five individual probabilities, or 13.9 percent. Figure 4.8 illustrates the probability of rolling any specific number with two dice.

Now let's look at a deck of fifty-two playing cards. The probability of selecting a specific card out of the deck without looking is 1/52, or 0.0192. To calculate the probability of being dealt a royal flush (the ace, king, queen, jack, and ten cards in one suit) is as follows:

In this case, the events are not mutually exclusive because to have a royal flush, all cards have to be the same suit and be from an ace to ten with no one value duplicated. Therefore, the total probability of being dealt a royal flush is calculated by multiplying the probability of the value of the five individual cards together or:

$P(1) \times P(2) \times P(3) \times P(4) \times P(5) = 0.3846 \times 0.0784 \times 0.06 \times 0.0408 \times 0.0208 = 0.000154\%$

The probability of being dealt a royal flush is 649,739 to one. You will note that the probability for the first card is 5/13 (0.3846) because it can come from any of the four suits and can be any of the five required cards. After the first card, the other four cards must come from the same suit that the first card came from.

MUTUALLY EXCLUSIVE EVENTS

Two events are mutually exclusive when they cannot happen at the same time. For example, being twenty-five years old and becoming president of the United States are mutually exclusive because the U.S. Constitution requires that the president be at least thirty-five years old. When the two events (A and B) are mutually exclusive, the probability of occurrence of either of the events is:

$P(A \cup B) = P(A) + P(B)$

For example, to know the probability of rolling a one or two when we toss the die twice, we would use the formula:

$P(1 \cup 2) = P(1) + P(2)$

We know from the earlier example that the probability of finding any one number in the toss of a single die is 1/6, therefore:

$P(1 \cup 2) = 1/6 + 1/6$, or 1/3 or 0.33

Complementary events

When events have only two possible outcomes, they are called complementary events. For example, when we toss a fair coin, the two possible outcomes are heads or tails.

The probability of occurrence of a complementary event is calculated with the formula = $1 - P(A)$.

Figure 4.7 Probability of Rolling a Six

Dice 1 + Dice 2	Sum	Probability of Occurrence
5 + 1	6	0.0278
4 + 2	6	0.0278
3 + 3	6	0.0278
2 + 4	6	0.0278
1 + 5	6	0.0278
Total		0.139

Figure 4.8 Two-Dice Combination Probabilities

Value	Combinations	Probability
1	0	0.0000
2	1	0.0278
3	2	0.0556
4	3	0.0833
5	4	0.1111
6	5	0.1389
7	6	0.1667
8	5	0.1389
9	4	0.1111
10	3	0.0833
11	2	0.0556
12	11	0.0278
Total		1.0000

Card Probability

Card	Probability
1st card — 5/13	0.3846
2nd card — 4/51	0.0784
3rd card — 3/50	0.0600
4th card — 2/49	0.0408
5th card — 1/48	0.0208

Independent events

Two events are independent if the outcome of one event doesn't depend on the outcome of the other event. For example, if we toss a coin twice, the second toss doesn't depend on the first toss. If we get heads in the first toss, we may get heads again in the second toss.

Conditional events

A conditional event is when two events depend on each other. For example, if we draw two cards from a deck of fifty-two and want to know the probability of finding an ace with the second draw, it depends on what was found in the first card drawn.

The conditional probability of an event (A) given that event B has occurred is expressed as:

P *(A/B) = P (A∩B)*
$\quad$ *P (B)*

Let's apply this concept to the problem of drawing the cards:
- The probability of finding the first card to be an ace can be calculated by computing *P (ace 1) = 4/52.*
- The probability of finding the first two cards to be aces can be determined with the formula *P (ace 1 and ace 2) = 4/52 × 3/51.*
- The probability of finding the second card to be an ace if the first card was an ace can be expressed as: *P (ace 1/ace 2) = P (ace 1 and ace 2)/P (ace 1) = (4/52) × 3/51)/(4/51) = 3/51,* or 0.06.

SAMPLING

A sample is a subset of a population that's expected to represent the entire population. It's also called random sampling. Due to economic and practical reasons, it's not possible to collect and analyze the data for an entire population. However, an analysis of a sample can produce inferences about the population. The sample should be an unbiased representation of the population; all members of the population should have an equal chance of being picked to be in the sample.

Sample size depends on the confidence interval and the population size.

SIX SIGMA MEASURES

The basic tenet of Six Sigma is "measure what we value." It's understood that if a process adds value but has waste, it must be measurable. The initial measure of waste is the defect per unit (DPU) at the product or the process output level, the defects per million opportunities (DPMO) at the process level, and sigma level at business level for benchmarking. DPU is typically measured first because it's easier and affects the process customer directly. The higher the DPU at a process, the more likely it is to cause customer dissatisfaction and to produce waste. Once the DPU is known, DPMO is needed to relate to the opportunities for mistakes to occur.

The DPMO figure is also used for benchmarking various processes in an organization in dealing with variety of products. Thus, the complexity of the product and process affects the number of opportunities for things to go wrong. Monitoring the DPMO is a way to normalize the DPU measure based on the complexity of the operation. The probability of producing defects is directly related to the number of opportunities in the process. Thus, the higher the number of opportunities, the more defects are likely to occur.

To reduce number of defects in a process or product, we must try to reduce the number of opportunities for error by simplifying it. Devices and products that are simply made are more reliable and less likely to fail.

Unit: A discrete output of a process is called a unit. The unit represents the deliverable of a service, the output of a process, or a product.

Defect: Any attribute of a unit that fails to meet the target is a defect. A defect can be caused by excessive variation in the process or customer expectations that the resulting product fails to meet.

Opportunity for error: An activity, task, component, item, piece of information, or event that presents an opportunity for making mistakes or producing a defect.

To illustrate opportunities for error, consider the following example: A ticket agent must gather passengers' possessions, verify their identities, use the airline's reservation system (this may have some critical entries), print the ticket, weigh the luggage, check the baggage, attach a tag to the baggage, put the baggage on the conveyor belt, and deliver the boarding pass and baggage tags to the passenger. These steps provide ten opportunities for making an error.

Opportunities for error can be identified through process inputs, outputs, in-process activities, and variables. The number of components in a product can constitute the number of opportunities for error in it. When counting opportunities for error, count only the steps that matter, not those that never go wrong. For example, in mechanical assembly, counting every washer may increase the number of opportunities for error. However, depending on the application, some washers could become a critical opportunity for a defect to occur, such as in case of airplanes or space vehicles.

To determine sigma level, one first needs to know the process' performance in terms of defects, errors, or yield. DPU is used to measure process performance:

- *DPU* = total number of defects or errors/total number of units verified
- *DPMO* = DPU × 1,000,000/number of opportunities for error in a unit

To determine the first-pass yield, i.e., the yield of a process without any repair or rework, the following formula is used:

First pass yield (FPY) = e^{-DPU}

The command for calculating FPY using Excel is "= EXP (–DPU)."

To calculate the DPU for our airline ticket counter example, let's assume that the ticket agents serve 250 customers in a day. Fifteen of these customers left the counter very dissatisfied. Of those, the ticket agents made twenty-five mistakes or could not address the customer's issues.

DPU = 25 mistakes/250 = 0.1
DPMO = (0.1 (DPU)/10 opportunities) × 1,000,000 = 100,000

One can also determine the sigma level from a conversion table or using a software program. Because a 3 sigma level corresponds to 66,810 PPM, it's safe to say that the sigma level for the ticket agents is less than 3 sigma. Specifically, the sigma level is 2.78.

Although it's critical to measure defects, companies often don't have the right measurements to track them. However, it's possible to use the process yield to calculate DPU and the corresponding sigma level. The formula for calculating DPU from process yield is:

Calculated DPU = – (LN (yield%/100)), where LN represents natural logarithm.

The command for using Excel is "= (–(LN (Yield/100)))."

PROCESS CAPABILITY STUDIES

When it comes to process capability, you have three options:
1. Design the process so that it produces good output.
2. Try to inspect quality into the output.
3. Go out of business.

> "I like option No. one."
> —HJH

Definition

A process capability study is a statistical comparison of a measurement pattern or distribution to specification limits that determines if a process can consistently deliver products within those limits.

How to use process capability studies

Before trying to understand this approach, the reader should read the about histograms and standard deviation, which are described in chapter 3.

Process capability indices

You will find that different statisticians, companies, and/or quality control texts vary in their notation of the formulas used to derive the process capability indices. This is not important as long as you understand what's being conveyed. All of these formulas have as their basis the conventional statistical theory about probability distributions (frequency distributions); that is, with a process under statistical control and exhibiting a normal distribution pattern, 99.73 percent of the output will fall within ±3 standard deviations of the mean of the distribution. The common base for computing the various indices is six standard deviations (six sigma) width. (See figure 4.9.)

Cp-inherent capability of the process

The baseline index (Cp) is the ratio of the tolerance width to the calculated ±3 standard deviation width. The formula is

$$C_p = \frac{Tolerance}{\pm 3\ \sigma}$$

Therefore, if the tolerance width is the same as the ±3 standard deviation width, the Cp index is equal to 1.0.

Since the ±3 standard deviation limit only encompasses 99.73 percent of the output—even if the process is operated at the mid-point of the tolerance—most companies establish a requirement that the Cp = 1.33 (±4 sigma) before the process is considered capable.

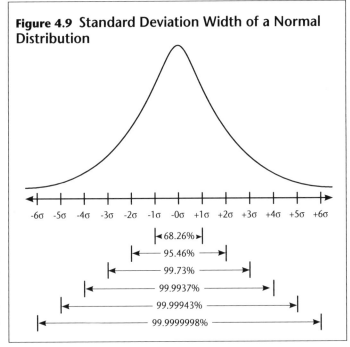

Figure 4.9 Standard Deviation Width of a Normal Distribution

Relating Cp location to a specification limit

As stated above, the Cp index is useful only to compare the spread of the process with the spread of the specification limits, or tolerance. It doesn't address the comparison of the locations of these two spreads. Therefore, although a process might be inherently capable (Cp = 1.0 or higher), it might be operated off-center from the specification at midpoint. (See figure 4.12.)

Another index, Cpk, compares the width and location of the distribution to the specification limits. Two methods are used to derive a Cpk index. One makes a comparison between the process mean and the specification mid-point as a ratio of half of the tolerance. This method is called the K factor and is used by the Japanese. The other (used by Ford Motor Co.) makes a measurement between the process mean and the nearest specification limit using a standard deviation as the unit of measurement (called Z_{min}).

In the first method, the centers are used for comparison; the second method uses the distance to the nearest specification limit. We prefer the Z_{min} method because it depicts both the location and the spread of a process in a single index that can be used directly with a Z table to estimate the proportion of output that will be beyond the specification limit and, therefore, be defective. (See figure 4.15.) However, for those wishing to use the K factor method, it, too, will be explained.

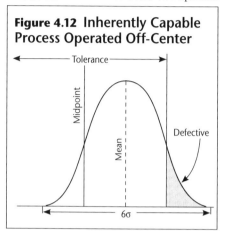

Figure 4.12 Inherently Capable Process Operated Off-Center

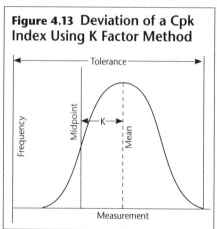

Figure 4.13 Deviation of a Cpk Index Using K Factor Method

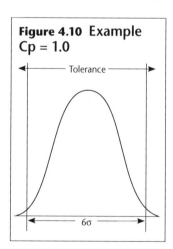

Figure 4.10 Example Cp = 1.0

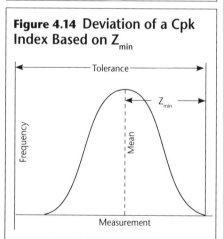

Figure 4.14 Deviation of a Cpk Index Based on Z_{min}

Figure 4.11 Cp Decision Table

Cp value	Decision
Greater than 1.33	Process is capable.
Between 1.0 and 1.33	Process is capable, but should be monitored as Cp approaches 1.0.
Less than 1.0	Process not capable.

Figure 4.15 Z Table

Entries in the body of the table represent areas under the curve between $-\infty$ and z.

z	0.00	0.01	0.02	0.03	0.04	0.05	0.06	0.07	0.08	0.09
0.0	0.5000	0.5040	0.5080	0.5120	0.5160	0.5199	0.5239	0.5279	0.5319	0.5359
0.1	0.5398	0.5438	0.5478	0.5517	0.5557	0.5596	0.5636	0.5675	0.5714	0.5753
0.2	0.5793	0.5832	0.5871	0.5910	0.5948	0.5987	0.6026	0.6064	0.6103	0.6141
0.3	0.6179	0.6217	0.6255	0.6293	0.6331	0.6368	0.6406	0.6443	0.6480	0.6517
0.4	0.6554	0.6591	0.6628	0.6664	0.6700	0.6736	0.6772	0.6808	0.6844	0.6879
0.5	0.6915	0.6950	0.6985	0.7019	0.7054	0.7088	0.7123	0.7157	0.7190	0.7224
0.6	0.7257	0.7291	0.7324	0.7357	0.7389	0.7422	0.7454	0.7486	0.7517	0.7549
0.7	0.7580	0.7611	0.7642	0.7673	0.7704	0.7734	0.7764	0.7794	0.7823	0.7852
0.8	0.7881	0.7910	0.7939	0.7967	0.7995	0.8023	0.8051	0.8078	0.8106	0.8133
0.9	0.8159	0.8186	0.8212	0.8238	0.8264	0.8289	0.8315	0.8340	0.8365	0.8389
1.0	0.8413	0.8438	0.8461	0.8485	0.8508	0.8531	0.8554	0.8577	0.8599	0.8621
1.1	0.8643	0.8665	0.8686	0.8708	0.8729	0.8749	0.8770	0.8790	0.8810	0.8830
1.2	0.8849	0.8869	0.8888	0.8907	0.8925	0.8944	0.8962	0.8980	0.8997	0.9015
1.3	0.9032	0.9049	0.9066	0.9082	0.9099	0.9115	0.9131	0.9147	0.9162	0.9177
1.4	0.9192	0.9207	0.9222	0.9236	0.9251	0.9265	0.9279	0.9292	0.9306	0.9319
1.5	0.9332	0.9345	0.9357	0.9370	0.9382	0.9394	0.9406	0.9418	0.9429	0.9441
1.6	0.9452	0.9463	0.9474	0.9484	**0.9495**	**0.9505**	0.9515	0.9525	0.9535	0.9545
1.7	0.9554	0.9564	0.9573	0.9582	0.9591	0.9599	0.9608	0.9616	0.9625	0.9633
1.8	0.9641	0.9649	0.9656	0.9664	0.9671	0.9678	0.9686	0.9693	0.9699	0.9706
1.9	0.9713	0.9719	0.9726	0.9732	0.9738	0.9744	**0.9750**	0.9756	0.9761	0.9767
2.0	0.9772	0.9778	0.9783	0.9788	0.9793	0.9798	0.9803	0.9808	0.9812	0.9817
2.1	0.9821	0.9826	0.9830	0.9834	0.9838	0.9842	0.9846	0.9850	0.9854	0.9857
2.2	0.9861	0.9864	0.9868	0.9871	0.9875	0.9878	0.9881	0.9884	0.9887	0.9890
2.3	0.9893	0.9896	0.9898	0.9901	0.9904	0.9906	0.9909	0.9911	0.9913	0.9916
2.4	0.9918	0.9920	0.9922	0.9925	0.9927	0.9929	0.9931	0.9932	0.9934	0.9936
2.5	0.9938	0.9940	0.9941	0.9943	0.9945	0.9946	0.9948	0.9949	0.9951	0.9952
2.6	0.9953	0.9955	0.9956	0.9957	0.9959	0.9960	0.9961	0.9962	0.9963	0.9964
2.7	0.9965	0.9966	0.9967	0.9968	0.9969	0.9970	0.9971	0.9972	0.9973	0.9974
2.8	0.9974	0.9975	0.9976	0.9977	0.9977	0.9978	0.9979	0.9979	0.9980	0.9981
2.9	0.9981	0.9982	0.9982	0.9983	0.9984	0.9984	0.9985	0.9985	0.9986	0.9986
3.0	0.9987	0.9987	0.9987	0.9988	0.9988	0.9989	0.9989	0.9989	0.9990	0.9990

Definition of Z_{min} standard deviations from process mean to nearest specification limit

Z_{min} is the distance between the process mean and the nearest specification limit (upper or lower) measured in standard deviation (sigma) units. The effect is to provide an index value in Z units that conveys the capability of the process, keeping in mind that ±3 standard deviations encompasses 99.73 percent of the output of a process that's in a state of statistical control. Its calculation can be stated as follows:

$Z = \sigma$ *(standard deviation)*

Z_{min} = *minimum of* Z_U *or* Z_L

where U and L = upper and lower specification limits, respectively. It's graphically portrayed in figures 4.16 and 4.17.

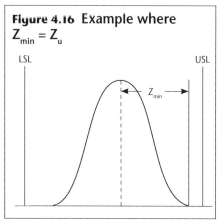

Figure 4.16 Example where $Z_{min} = Z_u$

Cpk—OPERATIONAL (LONG-TERM) PROCESS CAPABILITY

The Cpk index combines a measure of the inherent capability of the process with where it's operating in relation to its specification(s). It converts the Z_{min} into units of three standard deviations. Since Z_{min} is expressed in Z units, and equals standard deviation units, convert Z_{min} to Cpk with the following formula:

$$C_{pk} = Z_{min}/3 = minimum\ of\ \frac{(USL-\bar{X})/3\sigma}{3\sigma\ \bar{X}\text{-}LSL}$$

If Z_{min} equals three, by the formula $Z_{min}/3$, we obtain a Cpk index of 1.0 when the minimum capability is three standard deviations. Because the Cp index of 1.0 also connotes a ±3 standard deviation capability when a process is centered, then Cpk = Cp. However, figure 4.19 shows a condition where Cpk = 1.0 even when Cp = 1.2. This is caused by the process being off-center. Thus, a Cpk that is lower than Cp indicates a process that is off-center.

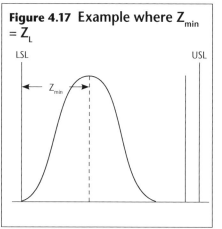

Figure 4.17 Example where $Z_{min} = Z_L$

CPU AND CPL—UPPER AND LOWER PROCESS CAPABILITY INDICES

$Z_{min} = 3.0$

$C_{pk} = \dfrac{Z_{min}}{3} = 1.0$

$\dfrac{Z_{min} = 1.0}{3}$

$C_p = \dfrac{tolerance}{6\sigma} = \dfrac{3.0''}{2.5''} = 1.2$

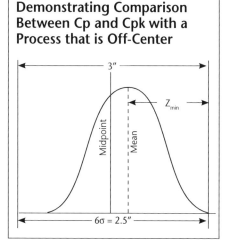

Figure 4.18 Example Demonstrating Comparison Between Cp and Cpk with a Process that is Off-Center

A process that is off-center will have different Z values (standard deviation units) for the upper and lower specification limits. As a result, it will have a different capability index value. In addition, there are times when only one tolerance applies. The CPU and CPL indices are designed to provide for these situations. The formulas are the same as for Cpk but for one specification limit only:

$CPU = (USL–\bar{X})/3\sigma$

$3\sigma =$

$CPL = X–LSL/3\sigma$

The computation of CPU and CPL is illustrated in the example below, where:

$X = 4.68$
$\sigma = 0.33$
$USL = 5.68$
$LSL = 3.0$
Thus, $CPL = 4.68–3.0 = 1.68$ and $CPU = 5.68–4.68 = 1.0$

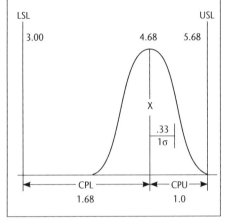

Figure 4.19 Example of Off-Center Process Showing CPL and CPU Indices. For Centered Process, CPU and CPL are Equal to Cp.

This process is marginally capable with 0.135 percent of the output expected to be outside the upper specification limit.

It should be noted that Ford and its suppliers use a notation of Z_U and Z_L for this purpose. Because a Z unit is one standard deviation (not in three standard deviation units as are CPL and CPU), Z_U and Z_L will be three times the number of the CPL and/or CPU index.

One of the most valuable uses for a capability index is to determine the proportion of the output that will be beyond either specification limit. In using the standard normal distribution (Z table) in figure 4.16, both sides of the distribution need to be considered in estimating the proportion of defectives from the process.

CPK—USING THE K FACTOR METHOD

To determine Cp using the K factor, first find K, which is the proportion of half of the tolerance that the process mean varies from the specification mean.

The formula is:

$$K = \frac{process\ mean–specification\ midpoint}{Tolerance/2}$$

The best value is zero, because a zero value means that the process is being operated exactly at the midpoint of the tolerance. If K is positive, the process mean is off-center toward the upper specification limit (USL). Conversely, if K is negative, it's off-center toward the lower specification limit (LSL).

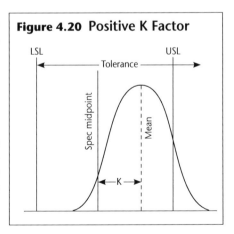

Figure 4.20 Positive K Factor

Although the K factor is helpful in portraying the centering of the process relative to the spec, it tells nothing about the relationship between the process spread versus the tolerance spread. To overcome this deficiency, the K factor is combined with the Cp index and converted to three standard deviation values by the following formula;

$$C_{pk} = C_p \ (1\!-\!K)$$

To illustrate, figure 4.19, shown earlier to portray Cpk based on Z_{min}, is repeated below and used to calculate Cpk using the K factor method.

$$C_p = \frac{tolerance}{6\sigma} = \frac{3.0''}{2.5''} = 1.2$$

$$K = \frac{(process\ mean\!-\!midpoint)}{Tolerance/2}$$

$$\frac{Mean\!-\!midpoint}{Tolerance/2} = \frac{4.75''\!-\!4.5''}{3''/2} \ 0.167$$

$$C_{pk} = C_p \ (1\!-\!K) = 1.2(1\!-\!.0167) = 1.0$$

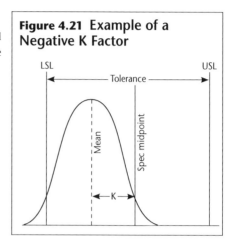

Figure 4.21 Example of a Negative K Factor

Note that both methods produce the same Cpk result.

Using process capability indices

Knowing the capability of a process provides answers to two questions: Can a process—as currently designed, equipped, and operated—meet its requirements? If not, what proportion of the output is expected to be defective?

A process goes through a variety of stages as it moves from design to full production; accordingly, there are a variety of analyses that may be applied to it. A number of different terms are used to identify a given stage of a process, including process capability studies, process performance evaluations, process improvement programs, and process optimization. The name is not important; what is important is to realize that nothing is constant. Even if a process is capable today, it may not be tomorrow. Therefore, there needs to be a never-ending effort to maintain whatever level of proficiency has been achieved and to continuously strive to reduce the natural variation of all processes.

It's important to understand that process capability as expressed by some index is not an absolute but rather an attempt to quantify and compare the degree to which various processes can be expected to meet their requirements. For instance, the numerical value of a process capability index can differ for a number of reasons. If the index was derived from past control chart samples, it might not be the same as one derived from current samples. If the sample sizes and frequency of samples were to be changed, one might get a different value of the standard deviation of the process, thus changing the process capability index. To be more specific, if samples within a subgroup are taken very closely together, the R value will tend to be smaller than if the samples in the subgroup are taken over a longer period. The latter will increase the value of R, thus increasing the size of estimated standard deviation. This broadens the control limits and decreases the process capability index.

Process capability indices are valuable tools, but they must be used with judgment and an understanding of the conditions under which they were obtained.

PROCESS CAPABILITY ANALYSIS

Process capability analyses have a variety of applications. Manufacturing processes typically undergo several stages of development before they are ready for full production, so it's important to determine the capability of the processes during these development stages. Unfortunately, the earlier the stage, the less hard data are available. During the design stage any attempt to ensure process capability will need to be performed with estimates. This increases the margin for error, so it's a good idea to use a target of CP = 1.67 ($\pm 5\sigma$).

As the process moves into pilot line production, it's important to be cognizant of the process capability's effect on elements such as an organization's tools, machines, set-ups, and operators. Although capability analysis during this stage can be computed from hard data, it's still difficult to predict what the production capability will be.

Process capability measurements and indices are most often used for ongoing processes. The need for the study may be brought about by customer complaints, poor yields, design and/or production method changes, or in a quest for constant quality improvement.

Process capability study steps

The following are steps that can be used when undertaking a process capability study:

1. *Preparation.* Become familiar with the process to be studied. What physical shop conditions exist (tools, machines, materials, labor, etc.)? What are the specification limits? What variables are to be studied? What historical data exist? What data need to be collected?

2. *Data collection.* Select the size and sequence of the subgroups to be measured. Typically a rational subgroup of four or five pieces is sufficient. These should be sequential and from a single stream of production over a short interval. They should represent, as nearly as possible, production under similar conditions. Next, decide the frequency of subgroups to be chosen. Subgroups taken very frequently will reflect variations that occur with little external influence; those taken over a twenty-four-hour period will reflect the effect that operator change, tool wear, etc., have on production. The objective is to detect all the changes the process will normally undergo.

Figure 4.22 Example of Completed Study

Condition	No. 1	No. 2
USL 46		
MID 43		
LSL 40		
Index		
Z	3/3 = 1.0	2/3 = .67
Z_{min}	$\frac{46-43}{1}$ or $\frac{43-40}{1}$ = 3.0	$\frac{46-43}{.67}$ or $\frac{43-40}{.67}$ = 4.5
C_p	6/6 = 1.0	6/4 = 1.5
C_{pk}	3/3 = 1.0	4 5/3 = 1.5
CPU	$\frac{46-43}{3}$ = 1.0	$\frac{46-43}{2}$ = 1.5
CPL	$\frac{43-40}{3}$ = 1.0	$\frac{43-40}{2}$ = 1.5
Analysis		
Center condition	Centered	Centered
Inherent capability	Capable	Capable
Operational capability	Minimally capable	Capable
Action	Improve system to add margin of safety.	None

Figure 4.23 Example of Completed Study

Condition	No. 3	No. 4
USL 46		
MID 43		
LSL 40		
Index		
Z	$2/3 = .67$	$4/3 = 1.33$
Z_{min}	$\dfrac{46-45}{.67}$ or $\dfrac{45-40}{.67} = 1.5$	$\dfrac{46-42}{1.33}$ or $\dfrac{42-40}{1.33} = 1.5$
C_p	$6/4 = 1.5$	$6/8 = .75$
C_{pk}	$1.5/3 = .5$ $1.5/3 = .5$	
CPU	$\dfrac{46-45}{2} = .5$ 4	$\dfrac{46-42}{2} = 1.0$
CPL	$\dfrac{45-40}{2} = 2.5$ $\dfrac{43-40}{4} = .5$	
Analysis		
Center condition	High	Low
Inherent capability	Capable	Incapable
Operational capability	Incapable	Incapable
Action	Center the process	Improve system

(The No. 3 column shows a distribution curve with value 45; the No. 4 column shows a distribution curve with value 42.)

Examples

Figures 4.22 and 4.23 recap all the indices we've covered with examples of their calculations and interpretation of their results. A similar portrayal could be made using the K factor method.

STATISTICAL PROCESS CONTROL

"Statistical process control is prevention in action."
—HJH

Definition

Statistical process control (SPC) is using data for controlling processes and for making outputs of products or services predictable. It's a mathematical approach to understanding and managing activities. It includes three of the basic statistical quality tools: design of experiments, control charts, and characterization.

How to use SPC

The goal of SPC is defect or error prevention. It uses statistical probability analyses to evaluate and monitor process performance. These techniques help in the identification of special and common causes that affect process performance. Common causes are inherent to the process and are caused by variations and interactions of the people, machines, and raw materials that make up the process. Special causes are due to an abnormality that prevents operational stability.

Understanding this distinction and how to apply the principles of SPC make it possible to remove special causes to achieve a stable condition and to determine ways to continue to reduce variation. SPC helps organizations understand their processes and obtain predictable performance levels.

SPC is most effective when used as part of a total quality management system, but it can be used in conjunction with or separately from almost any organizational improvement process.

To understand SPC, there are ten essential tools an individual or team should become familiar with:

- Data collection
- Sampling
- Frequency distribution
- Stratification
- Variables control charts
- Attributes control charts
- Scatter diagrams

- Process capability
- Characterization
- Design of experiments (Design of experiments is a Black Belt tool and will not be covered in this book.)

Laying the foundations for SPC is a management task that includes establishing quality awareness throughout the entire organization. W. Edwards Deming stated:

> *"Everyone in the company must learn the rudiments of the statistical control of quality, not just to solve a problem, but as a plan of knowledge by which to find problems and the causes thereof. It will not suffice to have some brilliant successes here and there."*

SPC is a term generally used to describe a concept and methodology using proven statistical analyses to:
- Determine whether a repetitive activity is in a predictable state.
- Enhance the ability to manage the activity in the predictable state once it's attained.

SPC should operate holistically and involve each person in the organization. Understanding how a system works allows us to deal with reality and to make changes in the system to optimize it.

Because management usually controls systems, management must develop and espouse the critical concepts required for statistical methods to be useful and to maximize organizational performance. These critical concepts are outlined below. Without these, there can be no effective process or system approach to quality control.

- Management must strive for the *prevention* of defects, not the *detection* of defects.
- There is no such thing as unchanging operational performance. There are only two natural states: operational performance improvement and operational performance deterioration.
- A continual and determined effort to improve quality must be incorporated into management practices. The mentality of an acceptable quality level (AQL) can no longer be accepted.
- AQL quantifies the percentage or proportion of defects considered satisfactory quality performance for a process or product. However, making decisions on quality using attribute sampling and AQL has a tendency to maximize cost in the long run and is therefore not recommended.
- The importance of quality cannot be delegated, understated, or assumed. It requires the training of all employees.
- Process or system control is the only way in which quality can be predictably defined. Samples taken from lots or batches produced under unknown conditions cannot provide accurate, predictable information about quality.
- All resources used in systems or processes must come from stable sources. Statistical evidence of quality must be provided with each resource to have confidence in the quality of the process output.
- Only statistical analysis that uses proven statistical techniques can provide evidence of the quality that's acceptable by customers. Successful data analysis uses graphical techniques to establish whether the process output comes from a stable source and whether it's within specification requirements.
- Special or assignable causes are responsible for unstable conditions. These causes are usually operation-oriented and can be corrected at the operator level. Deming estimated that 15 percent of all causes are special causes.
- Common or chance causes are the result of process variations. Corrections or reduction in process variation require physical changes to the process or system. Deming estimated that 85 percent of all causes are common causes.
- Customers' demand for quality requires that no defective products be delivered and only statistical evidence accepted as proof of the quality delivered.

■ Internal and external vendors and suppliers will need to implement process control programs. The responsibility for educating vendors and suppliers is that of the customer. Only if vendors are trained can they be expected to learn what quality and supporting evidence is required.

Let's elaborate on these points. The basic concept of SPC is almost universal. It can be applied to any area where outputs exhibit variation and where there is a desire to make improvements.

The desire for improvement goes hand-in-hand with a strategy that emphasizes prevention rather than detection. After-the-fact inspection is unreliable and inefficient because it detects existing wasteful, unreliable production. It's much more effective to adopt a prevention strategy by not producing goods that will be unusable in the first place. This strategy is exemplified in the slogan "Do it right every time."

To effectively use SPC, keep in mind that:

■ A process control system is essentially a feedback system with several elements.
■ The process is the aggregate of the people, equipment, materials, methods, and environment that work together to produce goods or services (the output).
■ The ultimate performance of the process depends on how it has been designed, constructed, and operated.
■ The system is useful only if feedback from it is used to improve its performance.

Feedback or information on the output from the process—when gathered and correctly interpreted—indicates whether the process or its output needs to be changed. Any action must be appropriate and timely to take full advantage of the feedback data. Keep in mind that there is a difference between action on the process and action on the output.

Action on the process is future-oriented; that is, appropriate and timely actions prevent the production of output that is not within specification. This type of action could theoretically be taken on any of the components integral to the system. The effects of any action taken should be monitored and further actions taken if analysis of feedback indicates that a further change in the process is required.

■ Action on the process prevents the production of out-of-specification output. It could be taken on any of the components integral to the system. The effects of any action should be monitored and further actions taken if feedback analysis indicates that a further change in the process is required.
■ Action on the output detects already-produced out-of-specification products and services. Acceptance sampling is too late to have any effect on the inherent quality of products already produced. If output doesn't consistently meet customer requirements, it may be necessary to institute a costly sorting, reworking, and/or scrapping operation for out-of-specification items. This damaging effort to a quality and productivity program must continue until the process has been corrected or until requirement specifications for the product have been modified. Obviously, inspection of output only is a poor substitute for doing it right the first time.

Variation

To effectively use the data generated from observing a process, you must understand the concept of variability. Variation is a part of nature. No two things, products, or characteristics are exactly alike. Uniformity doesn't exist because all processes contain many sources of variability. As the tolerance requirements of a process get more stringent, the harder it is to control the variation that exists naturally within it.

There are three types of variation: periodic, trend, and independent. In addition, there can be combinations of these three types. Consequently, time periods and conditions for which feedback (data and measurements) is obtained affect the amount of total variation that is represented in the feedback. Examples of causes of variation that occur over long periods are tool/machine wear, changes in environment, aging materials, and changes in methods or procedures.

Reducing a process' variation requires tracking it back to its sources and treating the variation there. To do this requires an understanding of the differences between special (assignable and operational) causes and common (system and natural) causes.

- Special or assignable causes of variation are not inherent in the system; rather they occur as a result of operating the system. These operational causes are usually a result of the skill level of the operators, the source of materials they use, the tools used, the procedures followed, the operating condition of the equipment or machines, or the physical environment when the process is operated. Operational causes of variation usually require some local action. Unless and until the operational causes of variation are identified and corrected, they will continue to have an unpredictable effect on the process output, thereby preventing the process from being brought into a state of statistical control.

- Common causes refer to the sources of variation within a process that is in statistical control. These causes occur randomly during the operation of the process and cannot be isolated as unique, definable causes. Simple statistical techniques will indicate the extent of the common causes of variation. It's usually management's job to improve common causes, although other people directly connected with the process are in a better position to identify them and alert management. Improving common causes requires deliberate, planned actions to physically change the process by altering the resources used to establish or operate the process.

The majority of correctable causes can only be corrected by management action on the system. Joseph M. Juran and Deming observed that the proportion of problems correctable by line workers is approximately 15 percent. They estimated that management action is required to correct the other 85 percent. This, of course, varies with the nature of the process and the degree of responsibility for the system that is allocated to the line workers. Only by statistical analysis can systemic problems be sorted out and appropriate action taken.

These systemic causes of variation result in defects when variation exceeds the required tolerances. Correction of these defects requires continued refinement of the physical operating nature of the process. This could result from refinements in technological precision, reduction in variation of materials used, the enhancement of operator skills through training, the description of operating procedures in clear, accurate language, and control of environmental conditions.

Measuring process outputs

The measurement of process output is also a possible source of error in describing process behavior. Measuring device calibration must be checked to prevent biases in describing process behavior. Measurement procedures must also be verified for consistency. Measurement errors are special causes that can mislead the portrayal of process behavior.

The goal of a statistical process control system is the ability to make sound decisions about actions affecting the process. Be careful that you aren't requiring such close tolerances that meeting them costs more than it's worth. A process is considered to be in statistical control when the only sources of variation are common causes. Deming stated that:

> *"A state of statistical control is not a natural state for a manufacturing process. It is instead an achievement, arrived at by elimination, one by one, by determined effort, of special causes of excessive variation."*

The first function of a process control system is to provide feedback on the behavior of a process. Process behavior is the description of a process where a sequence of samples is taken and a particular characteristic (attribute or variable) is measured and plotted on an appropriate statistical chart. This feedback provides information leading to inferences about process stability and capability.

- Process stability exists when a predictable pattern of statistically stable behavior is demonstrated by a sequence of observations made and plotted on appropriate charts with all interpretation rules being satisfied.
- Inherent process capability is the range of variation that will occur from the predictable pattern of a stable process.
- Operational process capability is determined by the manner in which the process is operated in respect to how this predictable pattern meets specification requirements.

Summary

To attain SPC, the process must first achieve process stability by identifying and eliminating all operational causes of variation. This allows prediction of the performance of the process. The next step is to assess the output to determine process capability. Then, take actions necessary on the system's causes of

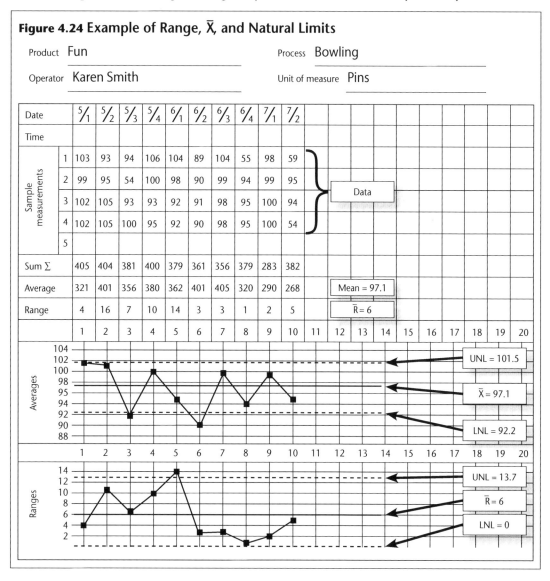

Figure 4.24 Example of Range, X̄, and Natural Limits

Product	Fun								Process	Bowling											
Operator	Karen Smith								Unit of measure	Pins											

Date		$\frac{5}{1}$	$\frac{5}{2}$	$\frac{5}{3}$	$\frac{5}{4}$	$\frac{6}{1}$	$\frac{6}{2}$	$\frac{6}{3}$	$\frac{6}{4}$	$\frac{7}{1}$	$\frac{7}{2}$									
Time																				
Sample measurements	1	103	93	94	106	104	89	104	55	98	59									
	2	99	95	54	100	98	90	99	94	99	95		Data							
	3	102	105	93	93	92	91	98	95	100	94									
	4	102	105	100	95	92	90	98	95	100	54									
	5																			
Sum Σ		405	404	381	400	379	361	356	379	283	382									
Average		321	401	356	380	362	401	405	320	290	268		Mean = 97.1							
Range		4	16	7	10	14	3	3	1	2	5		R̄ = 6							

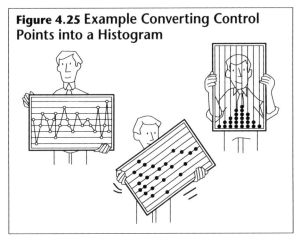

Figure 4.25 Example Converting Control Points into a Histogram

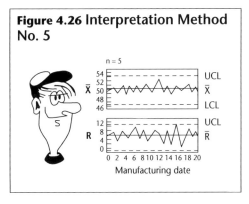

Figure 4.26 Interpretation Method No. 5

variation to eliminate all system-caused defects. This drives a never-ending search for improvements to decrease the range of variation while maintaining or monitoring the process to ensure that it stays in a state of statistical control.

The mathematical and probability laws that form the basis of SPC need to be thoroughly understood by the individuals using SPC tools. These tools include such analytical techniques as sampling, frequency distributions, stratification, control charts, and scatter diagrams. Of these, control charts are the workhorse of SPC. Walter A. Shewhart developed this simple, powerful tool to identify common causes and special causes.

Although there are several types of control charts, they all have the same basic uses: as a judgment, to give evidence whether a process has been operating in statistical control and to signal the presence of special causes so that corrective action can be taken; and as an operation, to maintain statistical control by monitoring current output as a basis for preventive measures.

VARIABLES CONTROL CHARTS

> "Variables data results in more precise controls."
> —HJH

Definition

A variables control chart is a plot of parameter variables data of a process' performance. It's usually determined by regular sampling of the product, service, or process as a function of time, unit numbers, or other chronological attribute. This is a frequency distribution plotted continuously over time that gives immediate feedback about the behavior of a process. A control chart will have the following elements:

- Centerline (CL)
- Upper control limit (UCL)
- Lower control limit (LCL)

How to use variables control charts

Variables control charts are the most frequently used SPC technique. They are used to monitor counted data or the trend of a specific measurement of a product or process. Here are some helpful definitions:

■ *Variables data.* The kind of data that are always measured in units, such as inches, feet, volts, amps, ohms, centimeters, etc. Measured data give you detailed knowledge of the system and allows for small, frequent sampling.

One of the most powerful tools for controlling quality is to provide operators with the means to know whether or not a process is under control. This is what control charts are all about. They let us know if the process is under statistical control or if the variations that are occurring indicate that the process is out of control.

A control chart is nothing more complicated than a basic line graph. The only addition is the central, upper, and lower control limit lines. Control charts are time-plotted frequency distributions with limits to indicate whether the process variations are under statistical control. (See figure 4.27.)

The three most commonly used types are:

■ Control charts that record defective parts or units
■ Control charts that record the number of defects
■ Control charts that record measurements or variables

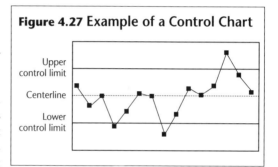

Figure 4.27 Example of a Control Chart

Control charts that count defective units are called attributes control charts and are divided into p charts and pn charts. The difference between the two is that p charts are plotted in percentage of defective units and are used when the sample size varies. A pn chart is used when the sample size is constant and is plotted in the number of defective units.

Attributes control charts that count defects are also divided into two types: c charts and u charts. A c chart plots the number of defects per sample with a constant sample size and u charts plot the number of defects per unit with a varying sample size.

Control charts that plot measurements of variables data are called variables control charts. Variables control charts that plot averages and range are called $\bar{X}$ bar charts and R (range) charts. Usually, these are used simultaneously and are plotted one over the other.

Figure 4.28 Simple Line Graph Showing Defective Units

■ *Range.* The difference between the highest and lowest measurement is the range. $\bar{X}$-R-$\bar{X}$ control charts are the most difficult and costly charts to obtain data for, but they are also the most useful in analyzing problems. The underlying concept of control charts is that with the use of control limit lines, one is able to decide when to make adjustments to the process and when to leave things alone. The basic idea of using control limit lines is to statistically signal when something abnormal is occurring and needs investigation.

Let's examine why a control chart is more useful than a line graph. The person in figure 4.28 doesn't know whether he's doing a reasonably good job or not. He knows it's better to have fewer defective parts, but how can he tell whether the day-to-day variations are normal?

With the central line (see figure 4.29) and the upper and lower control limit lines added, it's clear that the day-to-day variations are under statistical control. To significantly reduce defective units will require that some action be taken on the system.

Figure 4.29 pn Control Chart Showing Defective Units

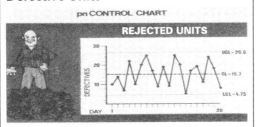

Figure 4.30 How Histograms and Control Charts are Related

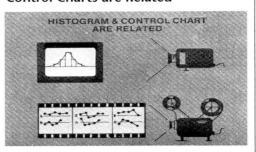

Figure 4.31 Variables Control Chart

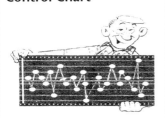

Figure 4.32 Grouping the Points on a Control Chart Together

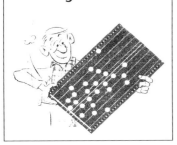

Figure 4.33 The Control Chart Converted Into a Histogram

Figure 4.34 Control Chart Showing Out-Of-Control Points

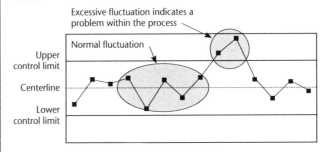

Figure 4.35 Control Chart Showing Abnormality

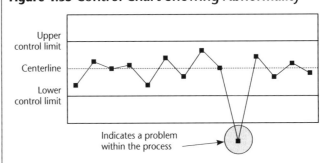

Control charts are closely related to histograms. Think of the histogram as a snapshot and the control chart as a movie. A control chart is a histogram plotted over time. (See figure 4.30.) It's a systematic way of continuously monitoring process and output quality by frequently plotting small samples over a period of time.

To better illustrate the connection between histograms and control charts, imagine that each point on this control chart is a bead that can slide along a horizontal wire, as demonstrated in figure 4.31.

Now, as shown by our happy-go-lucky gent in figure 4.32, as he rotates the control chart, the beads begin sliding down

When the beads have collapsed into a heap at the lower end as demonstrated in figure 4.33, it becomes clear that the control chart is a histogram plotted on a timeline. Therefore, a control chart can be likened to a stretched-out histogram.

In a normal frequency distribution, 99.73 percent of all points fall within ±3 sigma of the average. So it is with control charts, too. The upper and lower control limit lines are plotted 3 sigma on either side of the center line. Therefore, any plot points that fall outside these limit lines become a cause for investiga-

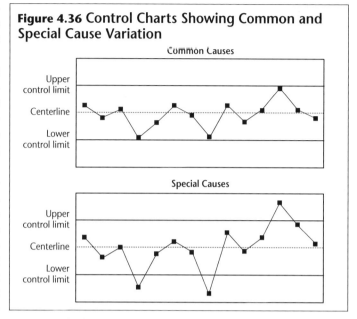

Figure 4.36 Control Charts Showing Common and Special Cause Variation

tion. For example, there are two plot points outside the control limits on the control chart shown in figure 4.34. Because 99.73 percent should be within the control limits, the points outside the control limits are a signal that the process is out of control.

Consider figure 4.35. Although only one point has gone outside the control limits, see how different it is from all the other plots? Clearly, something unusual has happened which needs investigation.

Control charts indicate whether a process is operating with common cause variations (also called chance causes)—which are normal and to be expected—or whether variations are due to special cause variations (also called assignable causes), which demand investigation and correction. In figure 4.36, the control chart on the top shows a process that has only common cause variations. The one on the bottom signifies that special causes are the problem.

Constructing an X̄-R chart

Let's look at the steps in constructing an X̄-R bar chart.

1. *Collect the data.* Figure 4.37 shows the form we will use to collect the data to make our control chart. For this and the following examples, we will use "Manufacturing Day" as the appropriate unit of time in which we collected the samples. For other processes it might be such units as hours or lot numbers.

2. *Compute the mean X̄ values.* In figure 4.38 we see how this is done for

Figure 4.37 Sample Data Sheet

Mfg. Day	Samples					Sum ΣX	Mean X̄	Range R
	X_1	X_2	X_3	X_4	X_5			
1	51	48	53	51	51			
2	53	47	48	50	52			
3	51	49	50	53	50			
4	40	52	50	48	45			
5	49	49	50	48	47			
17	52	52	51	51	51			
18	50	49	52	54	48			
19	46	51	48	49	48			
20	48	54	51	49	48			

Manufacturing Day No. 1. The total of the five units is 254. The total divided by five gives an average or X̄ value of 50.8.

3. *Compute the range (R) values.* The range is the variation between the largest and smallest of the samples for one set of Xs. Figure 4.39 uses the top row of our data sheet as an example. The difference between the largest number, 53, and the smallest number, 48, is five. This is the range.

4. *Plot the $\bar{X}$ and R data on graph paper.* The data are plotted with the X numbers directly over the R numbers. Figure 4.40 shows day six as an example.

5. *Compute the centerlines.* For an $\bar{X}$ line graph, we refer to the centerline as $\bar{\bar{X}}$. On the R line graph, it becomes $\bar{R}$, an average R. (See figure 4.41.)

6. *Determine the $\bar{X}$ control limits.* As was stated earlier, the control limits are set ±3 sigma distance from the center line. To simplify the means for determining 3 sigma, a table is used. A_2 provides the values for varying sample sizes. A_2 depends on the number of samples in each group. Figure 4.42 shows how the control limit lines were determined using the A_2 table.

7. *Determine the range control limits.* D_3 and D_4 are also tables to make it easier to calculate the 3 sigma limits for the range. In figure 4.43, we see

Figure 4.38 Computing the Mean Value

$\bar{X}$ and R Data Sheet

Mfg. Day	Samples					Sum ΣX	Mean $\bar{X}$	Range R
	X_1	X_2	X_3	X_4	X_5			
1	51	48	53	51	51			
2	53	47	48	50	52			
3	51	49	50	53	50			
4	40	52	50	48	45			
5	49	49	50	48	47			

1st day 51
48
53
51
+ 51
Sum = 254

$$\frac{\text{Sum } (\Sigma x)}{\text{Sample size (N)}} = \frac{254}{5} = 50.8$$

Figure 4.39 Computing the Range Values

$\bar{X}$ and R Data Sheet

Mfg. Day	Samples					Sum ΣX	Mean $\bar{X}$	Range R
	X_1	X_2	X_3	X_4	X_5			
1	51	48	53	51	51	254	50.8	5
2	53	47	48	50	52	250	50.0	6
3	51	49	50	53	50	253	50.6	4
4	40	52	50	48	45	245	49.0	7
5	49	49	50	48	47	243	48.6	3
17	52	52	51	51	51	257	51.4	1
18	50	49	52	54	48	253	50.6	6
19	46	51	48	49	48	242	48.4	5
20	48	54	51	49	48	250	50.0	6
Total							1,005.0	102
Average							50.25	5.10

Largest 53
Smallest -48

Difference 5
Or range (R)

Figure 4.40 Plotting Data Examples

$\bar{X}$ and R Data Sheet

Mfg. Day	Samples					Sum ΣX	Mean $\bar{X}$	Range R
	X_1	X_2	X_3	X_4	X_5			
1	51	48	53	51	51	254	50.8	5
2	53	47	48	50	52	250	50.0	6
3	51	49	50	53	50	253	50.6	4
4	40	52	50	48	45	245	49.0	7
5	49	49	50	48	47	243	48.6	3

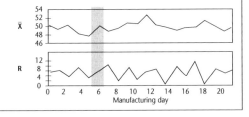

Figure 4.41 Calculating Averages

17	52	52	51	51	51	257	51.4	1
18	50	49	52	54	48	253	50.6	6
19	46	51	48	49	48	242	48.4	5
20	48	54	51	49	48	250	50.0	6
Total							1,005.0	102
Average							50.25	5.10

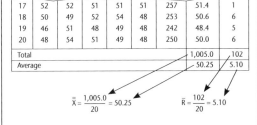

$$\bar{\bar{X}} = \frac{1,005.0}{20} = 50.25 \qquad \bar{R} = \frac{102}{20} = 5.10$$

the tables used to calculate the upper and lower range control limits of our example. Note the lower control limit will always be zero for sample sizes under seven.

8. *Indicate the size of samples.* Because the control limit lines are affected by the size of the samples (as noted in figure 4.44), always add the sample size notation to the chart.

Let's look at some examples of ways in which $\bar{X}$-R control charts signal there is a problem.

Interpretation methods

■ *Method one.* Because the control limit lines for a controlled process will encompass 99.73 percent of all plot points, even one plot point outside the limits is a signal. However, the example in figure 4.45 appears to be a unique event. Look for errors in measurement or some other one-time happening. The range example that's above the upper control limit illustrates the need to look at both $\bar{X}$ values and R values together. In this case, the $\bar{X}$ would not tell us there was a problem. The average is OK, but the R value varies too much not to examine it.

■ *Method two.* When at least seven connecting points are all on one side of the centerline, it's a signal that something unusual is happening. The laws of probability tell us that for a process to be under statistical control, the plot points should fall above and below the centerline in a somewhat regular pattern.

■ *Method three.* Figure 4.47 shows a process with four plot points beyond ±2 sigma from the centerline of the

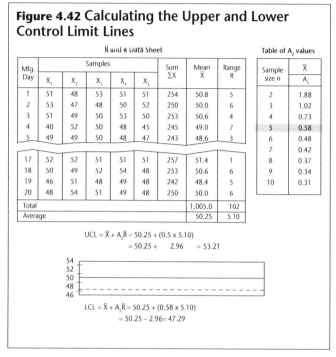

Figure 4.42 Calculating the Upper and Lower Control Limit Lines

$\bar{X}$ and R Data Sheet

Mfg. Day	Samples					Sum ΣX	Mean $\bar{X}$	Range R
	X_1	X_2	X_3	X_4	X_5			
1	51	48	53	51	51	254	50.8	5
2	53	47	48	50	52	250	50.0	6
3	51	49	50	53	50	253	50.6	4
4	40	52	50	48	45	245	49.0	7
5	49	49	50	48	47	243	48.6	3
17	52	52	51	51	51	257	51.4	1
18	50	49	52	54	48	253	50.6	6
19	46	51	48	49	48	242	48.4	5
20	48	54	51	49	48	250	50.0	6
Total							1,005.0	102
Average							50.25	5.10

Table of A_2 values

Sample size n	$\bar{X}$ A_2
2	1.88
3	1.02
4	0.73
5	0.58
6	0.48
7	0.42
8	0.37
9	0.34
10	0.31

$$UCL = \bar{X} + A_2\bar{R} = 50.25 + (0.5 \times 5.10)$$
$$= 50.25 + \quad 2.96 \quad = 53.21$$

54
52
50
48
46

$$LCL = \bar{X} + A_2\bar{R} = 50.25 + (0.58 \times 5.10)$$
$$= 50.25 - 2.96 = 47.29$$

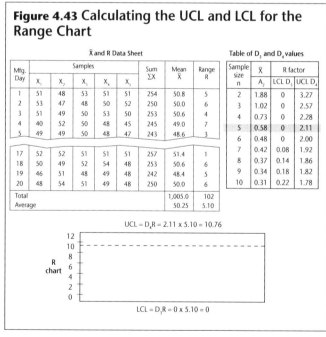

Figure 4.43 Calculating the UCL and LCL for the Range Chart

$\bar{X}$ and R Data Sheet

Mfg. Day	Samples					Sum ΣX	Mean $\bar{X}$	Range R
	X_1	X_2	X_3	X_4	X_5			
1	51	48	53	51	51	254	50.8	5
2	53	47	48	50	52	250	50.0	6
3	51	49	50	53	50	253	50.6	4
4	40	52	50	48	45	245	49.0	7
5	49	49	50	48	47	243	48.6	3
17	52	52	51	51	51	257	51.4	1
18	50	49	52	54	48	253	50.6	6
19	46	51	48	49	48	242	48.4	5
20	48	54	51	49	48	250	50.0	6
Total							1,005.0	102
Average							50.25	5.10

Table of D_3 and D_4 values

Sample size n	$\bar{X}$ A_2	R factor LCL D_3	R factor UCL D_4
2	1.88	0	3.27
3	1.02	0	2.57
4	0.73	0	2.28
5	0.58	0	2.11
6	0.48	0	2.00
7	0.42	0.08	1.92
8	0.37	0.14	1.86
9	0.34	0.18	1.82
10	0.31	0.22	1.78

$$UCL = D_4\bar{R} = 2.11 \times 5.10 = 10.76$$

R chart

12
10
8
6
4
2
0

$$LCL = D_3\bar{R} = 0 \times 5.10 = 0$$

control chart. Because we know that a statistically controlled process with ±2 sigma catches 95 percent of the plot points, only one plot point in twenty should land in the outer portions. Thus, this chart indicates a clear reason to investigate.

■ *Method four.* Trend lines also signal problems. The control chart in figure 4.48 suggests that someone was alarmed at the continuing upward trend, investigated the cause, and took successful corrective action as indicated by the line dropping back into a normal pattern.

■ *Method five.* The control chart in figure 4.49 indicates stable, well-controlled processes.

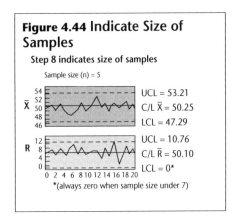

Figure 4.44 Indicate Size of Samples

Step 8 indicates size of samples

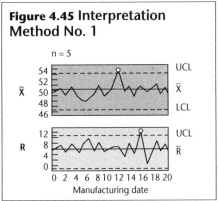

Figure 4.45 Interpretation Method No. 1

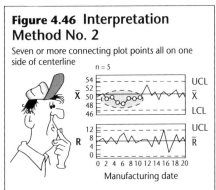

Figure 4.46 Interpretation Method No. 2

Seven or more connecting plot points all on one side of centerline

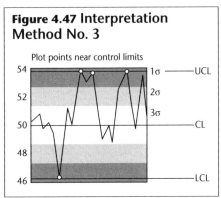

Figure 4.47 Interpretation Method No. 3

Plot points near control limits

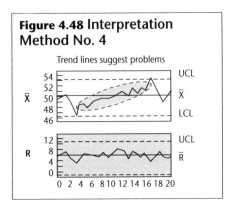

Figure 4.48 Interpretation Method No. 4

Trend lines suggest problems

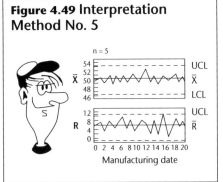

Figure 4.49 Interpretation Method No. 5

Summary of variables control charts

Control limits should not be confused with tolerances allowed on blueprints or specifications. Control limits are set by the natural variation of the process, whereas specifications are set by the product's use requirements. Control limits are derived from the average measurement of samples; specifications apply to unit measurements and are used for the product's acceptance or rejection.

An $\bar{X}$-R control chart is an important statistical tool that can be used to signal problems before large volumes of defective output have been produced. For an example of a completed variables control chart, see figure 4.50.

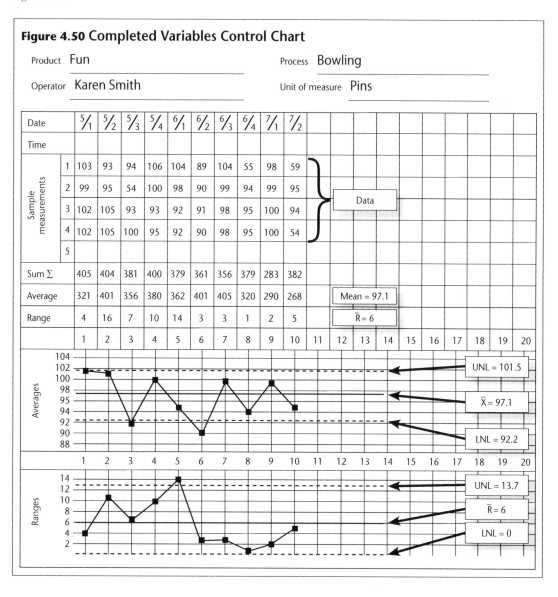

Figure 4.50 Completed Variables Control Chart

Product **Fun** Process **Bowling**

Operator **Karen Smith** Unit of measure **Pins**

Date		$^5/_1$	$^5/_2$	$^5/_3$	$^5/_4$	$^6/_1$	$^6/_2$	$^6/_3$	$^6/_4$	$^7/_1$	$^7/_2$										
Time																					
Sample measurements	1	103	93	94	106	104	89	104	55	98	59										
	2	99	95	54	100	98	90	99	94	99	95										
	3	102	105	93	93	92	91	98	95	100	94										
	4	102	105	100	95	92	90	98	95	100	54										
	5																				
Sum Σ		405	404	381	400	379	361	356	379	283	382										
Average		321	401	356	380	362	401	405	320	290	268										
Range		4	16	7	10	14	3	3	1	2	5										

Mean = 97.1
$\bar{R} = 6$

UNL = 101.5
$\bar{X} = 97.1$
LNL = 92.2

UNL = 13.7
$\bar{R} = 6$
LNL = 0

ATTRIBUTES CONTROL CHARTS

Attributes control charts plot attributes data of a process' performance. The parameter is usually determined by regular sampling of the product, service, or process as a function of time, unit number, or other chronological variables. This is a frequency distribution plotted continuously over time, which provides immediate feedback about the behavior of a process. A control chart will have the following elements:

■ Centerline (CL)
■ Upper control limit (UCL)
■ Lower control limit (LCL)

How to use attributes control charts

Control charts which record defective parts or units and control charts that record the number of defects are both attributes control charts. This is "counted" data. Control charts that record measurements are variables control charts. This is called "measured" data. (Variables control charts were presented in the previous section of this chapter.)

Attributes data are counted data that can be classified as yes/no, accept/reject, black/white, or go/no-go. These data are usually easy to collect because they only require counting. Attributes data don't measure the process, but they often require large samples.

Attributes data count defective units and are plotted on charts called p charts and pn charts. The difference between the two is that p charts are plotted in percentages of defective units and are used when the sample size varies. With a pn chart, the data are plotted in number of defective units. It's best used when the sample size is constant.

Attributes control charts count defects and are divided into two types: c charts and u charts. C charts plot the number of defects per sample with a constant sample size and u charts plot the number of defects per unit with a varying sample size. (See figure 4.51.)

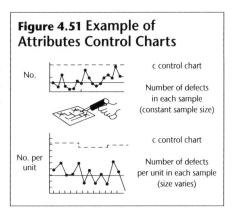

Figure 4.51 Example of Attributes Control Charts

No. — c control chart

Number of defects in each sample (constant sample size)

No. per unit — c control chart

Number of defects per unit in each sample (size varies)

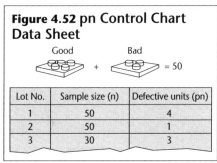

Figure 4.52 pn Control Chart Data Sheet

Good   Bad

+   = 50

Lot No.	Sample size (n)	Defective units (pn)
1	50	4
2	50	1
3	30	3

"Control without action is simply a hobby."
—Kaoru Ishikawa,
Introduction to Quality Control
(Quality Resources, 1993)

There is a difference between a defective unit and defects. A pn control chart addresses the number of defective units. Even if a unit contains 100 defects, it would still count only as one defective unit. Both c and u control charts deal in number of defects.

We will use pn control charts for our example. Constructing other attributes control charts differs only in the control limit formulas used. The steps to construct a pn control chart are:

1. *Collect the data.* Take a random sample of a set number of parts. (For a pn chart, the sample size is constant.) Measure the parts in the sample. Place the good ones in one container and the defective ones in another. Accurate measurement instruments, equipment, and techniques are a must if reliable data are to be obtained. Prepare a pn control chart data sheet. (See figure 4.52.) In pn control charts, the size of the sample from each lot must be the same. Enter the number of defects found in this sample and the other samples taken in this manner.

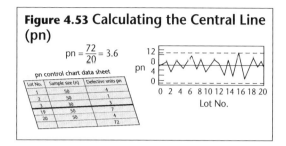

Figure 4.53 Calculating the Central Line (pn)

$$pn = \frac{72}{20} = 3.6$$

pn control chart data sheet

Lot No.	Sample size (n)	Defective units pn
1	50	4
2	50	1
3	30	3
19	50	7
20	50	4
		72

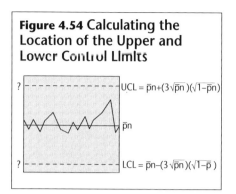

Figure 4.54 Calculating the Location of the Upper and Lower Control Limits

$$UCL = \overline{pn} + (3\sqrt{\overline{pn}})(\sqrt{1-\overline{pn}})$$

$$\overline{pn}$$

$$LCL = \overline{pn} - (3\sqrt{\overline{pn}})(\sqrt{1-\overline{p}})$$

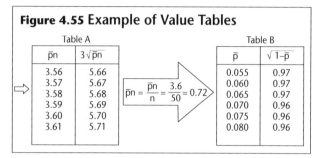

Figure 4.55 Example of Value Tables

Table A

$\overline{pn}$	$3\sqrt{\overline{pn}}$
3.56	5.66
3.57	5.67
3.58	5.68
3.59	5.69
3.60	5.70
3.61	5.71

$$\overline{pn} = \frac{\overline{pn}}{n} = \frac{3.6}{50} = 0.72$$

Table B

$\overline{p}$	$\sqrt{1-\overline{p}}$
0.055	0.97
0.060	0.97
0.065	0.97
0.070	0.96
0.075	0.96
0.080	0.96

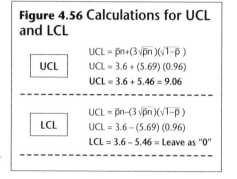

Figure 4.56 Calculations for UCL and LCL

UCL

$$UCL = \overline{pn} + (3\sqrt{\overline{pn}})(\sqrt{1-\overline{p}})$$
$$UCL = 3.6 + (5.69)(0.96)$$
$$\mathbf{UCL = 3.6 + 5.46 = 9.06}$$

LCL

$$UCL = \overline{pn} - (3\sqrt{\overline{pn}})(\sqrt{1-\overline{p}})$$
$$UCL = 3.6 - (5.69)(0.96)$$
$$\mathbf{LCL = 3.6 - 5.46 = \text{Leave as "0"}}$$

2. *Plot the pn control chart.* See figure 4.52.

3. *Calculate the central line (pn).* Find the mean of all defective units in all the lots. In the example shown in figure 4.53, the total number of defective units is seventy-two. Divide this by the number of lots (20) to determine the mean (3.6 defective units).

4. *Determine pn control limits.* Control limits are not imposed arbitrarily; they are the product of statistical formulas. The output of the process determines its control limits. The formulas for pn control limits are noted in figure 4.54. They may look complicated, but with tables or a simple calculator that can compute square roots, they are simple to use. Just as with variables control charts, the upper and lower control limit lines will be ±3 sigma from the central line. Note that pn = mean value; p = pn ÷ sample size.

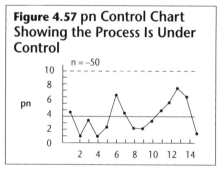

Figure 4.57 pn Control Chart Showing the Process Is Under Control

The following tables are excerpts from a more complete set of "value tables" that can be found in statistical manuals. (See figure 4.55.)

Using our $\overline{pn}$ value of 3.6, the value for $3\sqrt{\overline{pn}}$ can be determined by using table A in figure 4.55. The arrow shows that 5.69 is the figure needed.

To find the value for $\sqrt{1-\overline{p}}$ we first need to calculate $\overline{p}$, by dividing $\overline{pn}$ (3.6) by n (50). This gives us a $\overline{p}$ figure of .072.

Entering table B of figure 4.55 at the value closest to the $\overline{p}$ figure of 0.072, we find 0.96 as our value for $\sqrt{1-\overline{p}}$. Now we have all the information necessary to finish the calculations for both the UCL and LCL lines.

The formulas are repeated in figure 4.56 with the appropriate numbers inserted for each part of the formula. After a few calculations, we find that the upper control limit calculates to be 9.06 defective units and the lower control limit is -1.86. This is recorded as zero because, needless to say, you cannot have fewer than zero defects.

Figure 4.57 shows the completed pn chart. The sample size n = 50 has been added. Notice that all points are within the upper and lower limits and the process is under control.

Defining out-of-control points on pn control charts make use of the 7-7-1 rule. (See figure 4.58.)

Interpretation methods

In our example in figure 4.59, point one is out of control. Point two highlights seven connecting points on one side of the central line. Although all the points are within the control limit, it's statistically improbable that seven consecutive samples would all be on one side of the average line. An investigation is warranted.

A trend line such as the one depicted in figure 4.60 indicates a drift in the process. It will likely continue until it goes out of control. This is an alert that it's time to take action and investigate.

It's unusual for a pn control chart to have a positive value for a lower control limit. Given this condition, if a point penetrates the lower control limit, it's an indication of some special cause that you would like to duplicate because zero defects are what you are aiming for. (See figure 4.61.) Investigate this situation to determine how to repeat it.

With pn charts, it's important to realize that the goal of SPC is to have no defects. Although this process is under control, improvements to the system should always be sought.

Figure 4.58 The 7–7–1 Rule for Control Charts

Seven data points in a row steadily going up or down

Seven data points in a row on one side of the average

One data point that shows a large spike

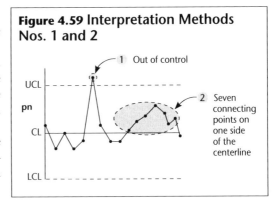

Figure 4.59 Interpretation Methods Nos. 1 and 2

1 Out of control

2 Seven connecting points on one side of the centerline

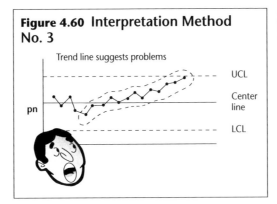

Figure 4.60 Interpretation Method No. 3

Trend line suggests problems

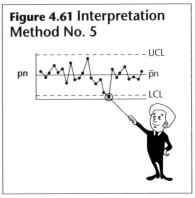

Figure 4.61 Interpretation Method No. 5

Application

Let's look at applying pn control charts. These control charts are used when the following conditions exist:

- There are no variables data or they are not readily available.
- There are many processes or products to monitor.
- Process output is in units.
- The production is consistently batched.
- More than one type of defect occurs.

When there are enough plot points to establish the limit lines, use them in monitoring future output. The purpose of control charts is to monitor; they don't solve problems. They only act as a signal. Standard problem-solving tools such as cause-and-effect diagrams will be needed to isolate problems.

After the cause or causes of a problem have been identified and corrected, compare the "after" condition with the "before" condition. The control limit lines on attributes control charts have no relationship to the specification limits because an attributes control chart by definition is not measuring a variable. However, the specifications do determine the go/no-go decision to count a unit as defective and these specifications may not always be correct.

Attributes control charts can be used in many circumstances. Wherever data can be counted, there is a potential for the application of an attributes control chart.

Examples

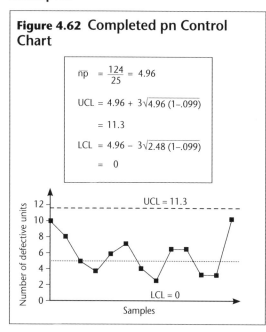

Figure 4.62 Completed pn Control Chart

$$\bar{np} = \frac{124}{25} = 4.96$$

$$UCL = 4.96 + 3\sqrt{4.96\,(1-.099)}$$

$$= 11.3$$

$$LCL = 4.96 - 3\sqrt{2.48\,(1-.099)}$$

$$= 0$$

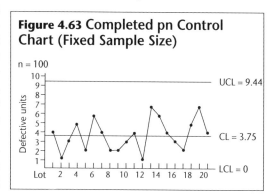

Figure 4.63 Completed pn Control Chart (Fixed Sample Size)

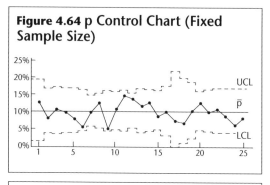

Figure 4.64 p Control Chart (Fixed Sample Size)

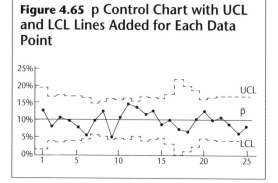

Figure 4.65 p Control Chart with UCL and LCL Lines Added for Each Data Point

SUMMARY

This chapter introduced your to basic statistical tools. There are a lot more statistical tools that your organization's Green Belts and Black Belts have been trained to use.

"Most bad decisions are made using statistically unsound data."

—HJH

CHAPTER 5

DMAIC OVERVIEW

"A problem can be a stumbling block or a stepping stone.
It is up to you what you make of it."

—HJH

The starting point for all improvement efforts is a problem that's experienced and/or recognized by at least one person. The desired result is to solve the problem by finding and eliminating its root cause. Only by doing so can you be sure that the problem is truly solved and that you won't be blindsided by it again. To get at the root of a problem efficiently and effectively—thereby improving a process—effective problem-solvers often use root cause analysis.

Root causes can be uncovered and analyzed using a variety of approaches, tools, and techniques that help the problem-solver get at the heart of the matter and find its root cause or causes. The process used in this book is based on the Six Sigma problem-solving approach known the world over as define-measure-analyze-improve-control (DMAIC). It's based on W. Edwards Deming's version of the Shewhart cycle, first introduced to the world in the 1940s and 1950s under the umbrella of the scientific methods of statistical process control (SPC) found in the plan-do-check-act (PDCA) cycle of continuous improvement. The methods were popularized and brought to the United States by the Union of Japanese Scientists and Engineers (JUSE) in the 1980s. It was popularized by Motorola and GE during the late 1980s and early 1990s.

Many of the problem-solving efforts performed by organizations have to be continually redone because they address symptoms, rather than causes. Knowing the difference between symptoms and causes is a matter of scale and insight. Root causes take time and detailed analysis to identify. This analysis ends when a cause large enough in scope to change the problem situation in a major way—and yet small enough in scope to be tackled by real-world teams—is found.

DEFINITION OF A PROBLEM

The common dictionary definition of "problem" is "a question proposed for solution; a state of difficulty that needs to be resolved." What these two definitions suggest are two characteristics that are important:

The DMAIC Process

Six Sigma's breakthrough strategy consists of a series of established steps that reveal how well products perform and how well services are delivered so that organizations improve their processes and maintain their gains.

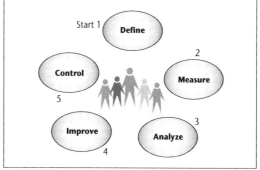

■ Having a problem causes difficulty or undesired conditions.

■ A problem that is resolved will establish more desirable conditions.

Beneath every problem lies a root cause or causes. To solve the problem we must first identify the cause(s) of the problem and then find ways to eliminate them from recurring. It's not easy to identify root causes, but without knowing them you will solve the problem only by luck or not at all. Once you've identified the true causes, eliminating them is a much easier task. Therefore, identifying a problem's cause is essential.

DIFFERENT LEVELS OF CAUSES

A problem is often the result of multiple causes at different levels. This means that some causes affect other causes that eventually create the eventual problem. Causes can be classified into four areas:

■ *Higher-level causes*, which are causes that lead to first-level causes

■ *First-level causes*, which are causes that lead directly to a problem

■ *Symptoms*, which are not regarded as actual causes, but rather as signs of existing problems

■ *Root causes*, which are the actual causes of the error

Although higher-level causes don't directly cause the problem, they form the links in the chain of cause and effect that ultimately create the problem. The highest-level cause of a problem is the root cause. If one attacks only the symptoms, the problem may only get worse while the problem remains and the symptom will no longer be easily recognized and monitored. On the other hand, eliminating first- or higher-level causes can temporarily alleviate the problem but the root cause will eventually find another way to manifest itself in the form of another problem. The solution is to systematically remove the root cause and monitor the symptoms to ensure that the problem will not recur.

CHARACTERISTICS OF EFFECTIVE PROBLEM SOLVING

There are seven characteristics of effective problem solving:

■ Problem solving requires patience and discipline.

■ Problem solving requires creativity.

■ Problem solving must embrace continuous improvement.

■ Problem solving requires repetition and honesty.

■ Problem solving requires facts.

■ Problem solving is all about cause-and-effect relationships.

■ Problem solving requires continuous learning to flourish.

At every step in the problem-solving process, the Six Sigma team (SST) will be challenged to do the following three critical activities: maximize creativity, apply scientific-thinking skills, and reach agreement on conclusions to be drawn from each step. During the problem-solving process, there are three key aids in the challenge to help understand the situation and perform problem analysis at its best:

■ The problem-solving process described in this application

■ The basic and the more advanced DMAIC problem-solving tools

■ An orientation to scientific thinking

APPLICATION OF SCIENTIFIC THINKING

In *Science for All Americans* (Oxford University Press, 1991), authors F. James Rutherford and Andrew Ahlgren note:

> "*Scientific habits of mind can help people in every walk of life to deal with problems that often involve evidence, quantitative considerations, logical arguments, and uncertainty . . . involving four key values: curiosity, openness to new ideas, skepticism, and critical thinking.*
>
> "*Curiosity means being filled with questions, seeking answers, and verifying how good the answers are. Openness means being discovery-oriented, even if the ideas are at odds to current beliefs. Skepticism means accepting new ideas only when they are borne out by the evidence and logically consistent. Critical thinking means not being swayed by weak arguments.*"

Some of the difficulties that arise in applying scientific-thinking principles are:

- Overcoming resistance to change
- Satisfying a diversity of viewpoints
- Thinking that any change using the DMAIC process would be an improvement in its own right
- Taking the time to meet the objectives of the problem-solving process once the change is agreed to
- Recognizing when a change is an improvement through proper testing and follow-through

These challenges can be overcome by using the DMAIC problem-solving process outlined in this application and by helping people overcome their mental roadblocks, which is the true focus of the art and science of this approach. Because all products, services, and outcomes result from complex interactions between people, equipment, and processes, it's crucial to understand the properties of such systems. Appreciation of the DMAIC problem-solving process helps us to understand the interdependencies and interrelationships among all of the components of a system and thereby increases the accuracy of prediction and the effect of recommended changes throughout the system. However, a person can use the methods described in this application without knowing the theory behind them just as a person can learn to drive a car without knowing how the engine operates. Deming once said that one doesn't have to be an eminent scientific thinker to apply scientific thinking.

PROBLEM SOLVING USING THE DMAIC PROCESS

Following the DMAIC methodology will help organizations achieve the stretch goal of Six Sigma, or 3.4 defects per million opportunities.

There are twelve tollgates and hundreds of elements involved in the five phases of the DMAIC process:

- *Define.* Select an appropriate project, organize the SST, define the problem (especially in terms of customer-critical demands), and develop a project plan to correct the problem.

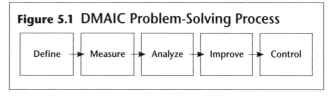

Figure 5.1 DMAIC Problem-Solving Process

Define → Measure → Analyze → Improve → Control

- *Measure.* Gain information about process performance and develop a problem statement.
- *Analyze.* Analyze the causes of the problem and verify suspected root cause(s).

■ *Improve.* Identify actions to reduce defects and variation caused by root cause(s) and pilot selected actions while evaluating the measurable improvement. If the improvement isn't apparent, return to phase one.

■ *Control.* Develop a control plan, implement the improvements, control the process to ensure continued improved performance, determine if improvements can be transferred elsewhere, and identify lessons learned and next steps.

Although figure 5.1 depicts the way the process is usually illustrated, figure 5.2 better represents how it actually works.

DMAIC is an iterative process of learning, understanding, and redefining. A measurement is taken and analyzed; if additional data are needed, we go back to the

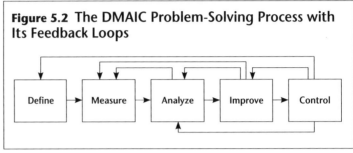

Figure 5.2 The DMAIC Problem-Solving Process with Its Feedback Loops

measure phase. In the improve phase, we might run a pilot project and find that it doesn't correct the problem, so we revert back to the analyze phase or measure phase to find the true root cause. This type of recycling occurs until the criteria defined in the team charter are met or the project is cancelled.

THE SIX SIGMA TOLLGATES

Each of the five DMAIC phases has blocks of work associated with them called tollgates. (See figure 5.3.) Each of these twelve tollgates indicates the specific work that the team must complete as it progresses through the DMAIC cycle. Think of the twelve tollgates as checkpoints or demarcations that you must pass on the "Quality Highway" to improved sigma performance.

1. Develop the team charter.
2. Develop high-level process maps and customer requirements.
3. Prepare the project plan.
4. Create the data-collection plan.
5. Implement the data-collection plan.
6. Analyze the data.
7. Analyze the process.
8. Analyze the root cause(s).
9. Generate solutions.
10. Select/test solutions.
11. Determine the method of control.
12. Implement the improvement plan.

At each tollgate the executive team or the project sponsor will review the status of the project to determine if:

■ The project should continue into the next phase.
■ The project should be dropped.
■ Parts or all of the current phase or past phases should be redone.
■ The effect of the project on other projects indicates that more information is needed.

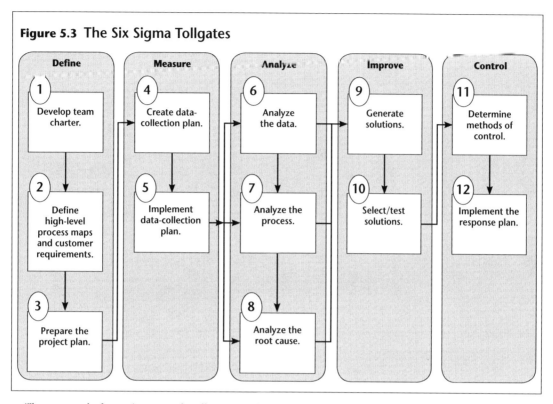

Figure 5.3 The Six Sigma Tollgates

The approval of a project at each tollgate signifies that the reviewers agree that:

■ Phase activities have been completed successfully.

■ The goals as defined in the charter can still be met.

■ The project is ready to progress to the next phase.

A lot of problem-solving work is completed before a problem is even assigned to a DMAIC SST. We will call this phase 0 because it takes place before the executive team approves the formation of a SST. The start of phase 0 is the identification of a potential problem or improvement opportunity. The potential problem/improvement opportunity is then evaluated to determine if it's a priority and if it meets the requirements to be assigned to an SST. To accomplish this, a preliminary charter and a cost-benefits estimate is prepared and presented to the executive committee. This business case should include ballpark estimates based on data; accuracies of ±30 percent are good enough at this point in the process. The business case should include:

■ A statement of the problem

■ A recommendation of the problem-solving approach that should be used:

   ☐ Lean Six Sigma

   ☐ DMAIC

   ☐ Define, measure, analyze, design, verify (DMADV)

■ Costs related to the present situation

■ The effect on external customers

■ The length of time needed to develop the future-state solution

Figure 5.4 DMAIC at a Glance

DMAIC Phase	Problem-Solving Equivalent	Purpose and Output	Tollgate
Phase I Define	Problem definition and understanding	For the assigned project, organize the SST, define the problem—especially in terms of customer-critical and mission-critical characteristics—and develop the project plan to correct it.	1. Develop the team charter with goals, project scope, and problem statement. 2. Identify stakeholders' critical-to-quality characteristics (CTQs) and define the current process using high-level process maps. 3. Prepare a project plan.
Phase II Measure	Problem cause generation, measurement, and data collection	Gain information about process performance, develop a measurement system, and collect data.	4. Create the data-collection plan. 5. Gather initial data, determine current performance, and develop project scorecard.
Phase III Analyze	Analyze data and identify root causes	Analyze the data and causes of the problem, and verify suspected root cause(s).	6. Analyze the data and report results. 7. Analyze the process. 8. Analyze the root cause(s) and develop cause-and-effect hypotheses.
Phase IV Improve	Improvement-oriented activities	Identify actions to reduce defects and variation caused by root cause(s), pilot selected solutions, and define the future-state solution. Develop an implementation plan.	9. Identify breakthroughs and generate solutions. 10. Test solutions, perform cost/benefit analysis, design future state, establish performance targets, gain approval to implement.
Phase V Control	Implementation and control-oriented activities	Implement the future state solution. Control the process to ensure continued improved performance and determine if improvements can be transferred elsewhere. Identify lessons learned and next steps.	11. Determine methods of control. 12. Implement the improvement plan. Measure the results. Project is closed out.

- Recommended improvement goals
- A qualitative estimate of the impact that meeting these goals would have on the organization
- An estimate of the resources required to develop the future-state solution
- A recommendation of who should lead the SST and the sponsor of the project

If the executive committee approves the project as a Six Sigma project, the outputs from phase 0 and the inputs to the phase I of the DMAIC cycle are:

- A project manager (Green Belt or Black Belt) is named and assigned.
- An executive sponsor is assigned.
- A budget is approved.
- A preliminary charter is approved.

DMAIC PHASE OBJECTIVES

Each of the five DMAIC phases has very specific objectives. As we defined earlier, there is a lot of interaction between the phases. The major objectives for each of the five phases are:

- Phase I (define) objectives:
  - ☐ Define the project problem.
  - ☐ Define the project approach.
  - ☐ Define the project outcome.
  - ☐ Define the project stakeholders.
  - ☐ Define customer requirements.
  - ☐ Define the SST members.
  - ☐ Train the SST.
  - ☐ Launch the project.
  - ☐ Define project risks.
  - ☐ Define project schedule.
  - ☐ Define project budget.
  - ☐ Prepare an approved team charter.
  - ☐ Prepare an project plan.
  - ☐ Develop high-level process maps.
  - ☐ Address "low-hanging fruit."
  - ☐ Define the cost and benefits.

- Phase II (measure) objectives:
  - ☐ Confirm key customer requirements.
  - ☐ Define required measurements.
  - ☐ Define measurement systems.
  - ☐ Evaluate the accuracy of the measurement systems.
  - ☐ Define sampling plans.
  - ☐ Define analysis methods.
  - ☐ Define data collection format and forms.
  - ☐ Develop a measurement plan.
  - ☐ Collect the required data.
  - ☐ Determine if the data are accurate.
  - ☐ Prepare a measurement report.
  - ☐ Validate the process flowchart and collect relevant process flow data.

- Phase III (analyze) objectives:
  - ☐ Analyze the measurement data.
  - ☐ Validate the process flowchart/maps.
  - ☐ Develop a cause-and-effect hypothesis.
  - ☐ Determine and validate root causes.

- Phase IV (improve) objectives:
  - ☐ Identify improvement solutions.

☐ Quantify improvement solutions.
☐ Select the best solution.
☐ Design the future-state solution.
☐ Perform a cost-benefit analysis.
☐ Plot the individual solutions.
☐ Develop a preliminary implementation plan.
☐ Gain approval to implement the future-state solution.

■ Phase V (control) objectives:
☐ Organize the implementation team.
☐ Prepare the control plan.
☐ Prepare the procedures.
☐ Train the employees.
☐ Implement the solution.
☐ Measure the results.
☐ Revise KPIs.
☐ Recognize the SST.
☐ Close the project.

TYPICAL SCHEDULE FOR A NINETY-DAY DMAIC PROJECT

The following is a typical schedule for a ninety-day DMAIC project; however, the length of these projects can differ dramatically. Some take as little as five days and others take more than six months. We recommend that you try to select projects that won't take longer than ninety days.

Typical DMAIC Schedule for a Ninety-Day Project

Phases		1	2	3	4	5	6	7	8	9	10	11	12	13
Phase I Define	Tollgate 1: Develop team charter.	▓												
	Tollgate 2: Define customer requirements and high-level process maps.	▓												
	Tollgate 3: Prepare project plan.		▓											
Phase II Measure	Tollgate 4: Create data-collection plan.			▓										
	Tollgate 5: Implement collection plan.			▓										
Phase III Analyze	Tollgate 6: Generate solutions.					▓								
	Tollgate 7: Analyze the process.						▓							
	Tollgate 8: Analyze the root cause.							▓						
Phase IV Improve	Tollgate 9: Generate solutions.								▓					
	Tollgate 10: Select/test solutions.									▓				
Phase V Control	Tollgate 11: Determine method of control.											▓		
	Tollgate 12: Implement the improvement plan.												▓	▓

SIX SIGMA TOOLS USED IN EACH DMAIC LEVEL

The following provides a quick look at the Six Sigma tools used in the DMAIC process. The Yellow Belt tools are marked with an asterisk.

DMAIC is the first approach used by Six Sigma practitioners and is the approach most used by Yellow Belts. There are two other major problem-solving approaches used in Six Sigma systems:

■ DMADV, which is part of design for Six Sigma
■ Lean Six Sigma

Yellow Belts can use these approaches with the assistance of a Black Belt or a Master Black Belt.

Tools of DMAIC

Tools	D	M	A	I	C
* Action plan W/S					
* Affinity diagram					
Benchmarking					
* Brainstorming					
CAP-Do					
* Cause-and-effect diagram					
Change management					
* Checksheet					
Contingency planning (PDPC)					
Contingency table analysis					
* Control charts					
Cost-benefit analysis					
Poor-quality cost analysis					
Countermeasures					
CTQ tree diagram					
Creativity methods/SCAMPER					
Critical pathway analysis					
Customer interview guide					
Customer prioritization table					
* Customer requirements table					
Cycle time analysis					
DMAIC storyboard					
Design of experiments					
* Failure mode and effects analysis					
Failure-to-follow analysis					
* Flowchart/process map/SIPOC					
* Force field analysis					
Gage R&R study					
GANTT chart					
* Histogram					
Implementation training matrix					

Tools	D	M	A	I	C
Interrelationship diagram					
Layout diagrams					
* Meeting agenda					
* Nominal group technique					
* Pareto charts					
Prioritization matrices					
Problem statement checklist					
Process book					
* Process capability analysis					
Process deficiency worksheet					
Process inventory					
Process management charts					
Process profile					
Process watch					
* Team charter worksheet					
Project launch checklist					
Project plan worksheet					
Project scorecard					
Quality function deployment					
Responsibility flowchart					
Responsibility matrix					
* Run chart					
* Scatter diagram					
Six Sigma operational definition					
* Sigma conversion table					
Taguchi methods					
* Team charter					
The 5 S's					
Tree diagrams					
Twenty questions					
* 5 Whys					

SUMMARY

People assigned to a DMAIC project or other Six Sigma activity must treat it as a part of their work assignment. They are being paid as much for each hour they work on the Six Sigma project as they get for doing other assignments, so it can't be treated as something they do when they have nothing else to do. They must make the time to meet these Six Sigma commitments, just as they would any other commitment. Management must remove other work assignments from the individual's normal activities to provide the time required to be an active participant on the project. Each member of an SST should have his or her performance measured and reported so that it will be reflected in his or her performance evaluation.

"DMAIC provides the roadmap to problem elimination."
—HJH

CHAPTER 6

THE SIX SIGMA DEFINE PHASE

"A problem well defined is half solved."
—HJH

The define phase of a define-measure-analyze-improve-control (DMAIC) project focuses on clearly specifying a problem or opportunity, the project's goals, and its scope. Identifying who the customers are and their requirements is also critical, given that the overarching goal for all Six Sigma projects is improving the organization's ability to meet the needs of its customers. The define phase has five major deliverables:

- Team readiness: A fully trained team is formed, supported, and committed to work on an improvement project with a fully developed charter.
- Critical-to-quality (CTQ) characteristics and customers are defined.
- High-level business process map
- Team charter
- Project plan

The first and one of the most important jobs the Six Sigma team (SST) leader has is to define the makeup of the SST. The type of skills that SST members need will vary based on the project. In most cases the people who make up the SST will be Yellow Belts, Green Belts, and/or Black Belts. Sometimes people who haven't been trained on Six Sigma tools will also become part of the SST if they have special skills.

An SST identifies a project based on business objectives as well as customer needs and feedback. The team identifies CTQs that the customer considers to have the most effect on quality. It also separates the "vital few" from the "trivial many" (the projects that will have the most impact vs. those that could stand improvement but are not critical). The define phase is vital to the overall success of any Six Sigma project. This is the phase where the current situation, the basic issue or problem, and desired outcome are assessed and documented.

Many organizations don't address the simultaneous, multimedia nature of data and records, and treat electronic documents, such as the Web, e-mail, and fax output from enterprise applications like enterprise resource planning and customer resource management separately from paper during the define phase. In other instances, organizations focus only on the paper document production process and ignore the need for electronic document integration.

An internal assessment should be completed to determine which kinds of data are being kept. The assessment should address and quantify several baseline data-gathering requirements, such as:

- Existing policies and procedures

- Records creation and recordkeeping
- Existing schedules and inventories, centralized controls or systems in use by specific departments, divisions, and subsidiaries
- If measurement systems do exist, include whether file plans, life-cycle controls, storage, and disposition management are in place.
- An inventory of measures and controls and a determination of the regulations that apply to records created and/or contained within them

The problem statement developed in the define phase will be refined as the project progresses and more information is collected in subsequent phases.

INTRODUCTION TO THE SIX SIGMA DEFINE PHASE

This chapter will provide the reader with an understanding of the activities that take place during the three tollgates that make up the DMAIC define phase:
1. Develop the SST charter.
2. Define high-level process maps and customer requirements.
3. Prepare the project plan.

The Yellow Belt tools most often used during the define phase are:
- Five whys (5Ws)
- Affinity diagrams
- Brainstorming
- Checksheets/checklists
- Gantt charts
- Nominal group technique
- Process mapping project planning matrix worksheets
- Project selection matrix
- Project stakeholder analysis worksheet
- Suppliers-input-process-output-customers (SIPOC) charts

THE PURPOSE OF THE SIX SIGMA DEFINE PHASE

The purpose of the define phase is to organize the SST, get a team charter approved, develop a high-level process map of the problem, and prepare an approved project plan. The charter is the collection of documents that provide definition, purpose, and motivation for the SST to do its work. The project definition is explicitly stated in the team charter, which also provides the project manager with the authority to apply organizational resources to project activities. The team charter typically includes:
- A description of the business need addressed by the project (i.e., the opportunity or threat presented to the organization that provided the stimulus to undertake the project)
- The product or outcome that will be produced by the project and the characteristics of the value (product or service) that the project will create
- The relationship between the business need and the product. The product/outcome should be described at a high level, but with sufficient detail to support subsequent project planning.

- The authorization to apply organizational resources to the project
- The problem statement to answer the question, "Why is it essential that this project be done now?" It should be specific enough to help the team identify the project's scope and major stakeholders.

Although the SST will develop a work breakdown structure (WBS) that will break large projects into smaller subprojects, problems of gargantuan proportions should be subdivided into smaller projects before they're assigned to SSTs. Senior leadership should put the problem statement in writing. The team charter should include a statement indicating the vision/mission of the SST and linking the project to the larger organization's strategic plan via the charter.

All Six Sigma projects must be managed efficiently and effectively. As a result, the Green Belt and/or Black Belt who is leading the SST serves as the project manager of the project. This requires that a project plan be prepared and followed. Often the project management plan that is prepared at this phase of the project is modified as more data are acquired, but it should never go beyond the boundaries defined in the team charter.

SELECTING THE SST

The executive committee (EC) will have defined the terms of reference, selected the team leader, and given some general direction about the composition of the SST. A team is more effective than an individual for problem solving because it can draw on a wider range of experience and skills. There are two types of skills required—technical and problem-solving skills. Team members must be chosen to ensure that someone on the team is knowledgeable in every aspect of the process being studied. Major stakeholders and customers should be represented. A low-level process team should have people from the working level because they have a better understanding of how a process actually works. Often the low-level SSTs are led by Green Belts and high-level process teams include managers to draw on their broader perspective. These SSTs are usually led by Black Belts and the team members are Green Belts and Yellow Belts.

All team members must be knowledgeable in team-building skills and understand the tools and strategies that can be used for problem solving. It's likely that time will have to be set aside at the first few meetings to provide training.

The SST should develop and agree to a set of operating rules. These rules will define how the SST will be run and what is expected of the SST members and the team leader.

Team readiness is evidenced by:

- A team sponsor, champion, or business leader is selected.
- Team members are trained on the basics of synergy, group dynamics, and Six Sigma basics.
- Team members fully participate in all team meetings.
- Project work is completed in a timely manner.
- Documentation is completed for each of the deliverables.
- Resources are provided on a regular basis.

BUILDING THE TEAM CHARTER (TOLLGATE NO. 1)

Next, the SST should review the scope of the charter and negotiate changes with the EC. The team should talk to the customer and end user to learn their problems and define their expectations. The scope of the project should include the statement of the problem, a definition of its boundaries, the improvement goals, a target date for completion, and the resources available.

The scope of the project may include a project timeline and project tasks and define the overall involvement of the organization in the project. If you make the project scope too narrow, you will have to create a series of smaller projects that will require more coordination and management problems. If you make the project too large, the project may never be completed because it will be too unwieldy.

Improvement comes from the application of knowledge—of medicine, engineering, teaching, driving a truck, serving a client, or merely the way that some activity is performed. Generally, the more complete the appropriate knowledge, the better the improvements will be when it's applied to making changes. Therefore, any approach to improvement must be based on building and applying knowledge.

This leads to a set of fundamental questions, the answers to which form the basis of improvement:
- What are we trying to accomplish?
- How will we know that a change is an improvement?
- What changes can we make that will result in improvement?

These questions form the basis of the DMAIC framework, which is modeled after a "trial and learning" approach. The term "trial" suggests that a change is going to be tested. The term "learning" implies that criteria have been identified that will be used to study and learn from the trial. Focusing on these three questions accelerates the building of knowledge by emphasizing a framework for learning, the use of data, and the design of effective trials and tests.

Project scope

The scope determines the success of the project: too narrow and the results will be lackluster; too broad and it never gets implemented. Here are some guidelines for defining the project scope:
- The project must have a direct effect on a key performance indicator (KPI) and have a champion.
- The project should tackle facility or divisional functional problems or opportunities.
- The project should be beyond the capability of the staff members to accomplish as part of their normal jobs.
- The project should have adequate historical data so that analysis can start immediately.
- External factors such as customers, technology, suppliers, regulations, politics, and other forces will often affect the project and its end product. These areas affect both the scope and the SST project objectives because the end product of the project needs to directly relate to the overall SST project purpose.
- The project should focus on current processes or systems instead of creating new ones.
- The project should save a minimum of $100,000 after the cost of the SST and implementation is subtracted.
- The project should have at least a six-to-one return on investment.

Tollgate No. 1 review

By reviewing the team charter, the EC will be able to determine how well the SST understands the project assignment it was given. The team charter is important, but the backup data the team used to prepare the charter and the caliber and makeup of the team are key indicators of the importance that is being placed on the project. The EC should check with each team member to be sure that his or her workload has been adjusted to allow full participation on the team. If the SST is not organized to successfully complete the project, the best time to stop the project is during this review. If the team charter is approved, the SST will start tollgate No. 2 activities.

Summary of tollgate No. 1

Tollgate No. 1 focuses on initiating improvement action and addressing an identified problem through a formal team charter and problem-solving process that addresses the project goal and scope. It also ensures that the right people are taking the most efficient and effective route to fixing the problem(s) being reviewed and that the project scope is well crafted and understood. Next, it addresses how the proper scope is defined.

The SST should develop a very narrow and broad view of the project as alternatives, then identify what has been deleted when moving from large to small. Deleted items could result in additional projects that could be addressed by other project teams after the initial project has been completed.

To determine if a work area falls under the project's scope, consider the following questions:
- How closely related is the work to the project?
- Would the same resources be used on the work and the project?
- If they are kept separate, what will be the advantages and disadvantages?

This tollgate requires an external effect analysis to evaluate that the problem is addressed and the process measurably improved. This analysis is often ignored or overlooked. Having defined the project goals, it's important to define the outcomes and boundaries of the project and to understand its environment. Why do this? Why not just start by defining more of the internal detailed characteristics of the project? The answer is because the project will be affected by external factors.

It's also important to validate the project objectives. Their achievement will result in some material change within and, perhaps, outside of the organization. Understanding the external environment helps to validate the objective.

TOLLGATE NO. 2 REQUIREMENTS

There are two parts to tollgate No. 2, and there is a lot of interaction between them:
- Tollgate No. 2, part 1: Define high-level process maps.
- Tollgate No. 2, part 2: Define customer requirements.

During this tollgate the SST will prepare high-level process maps related to the problem statement. These maps will be used to identify the customers of the outputs, the suppliers to the process, and as an overview of the process.

Purpose of tollgate No. 2, part 1
In this phase, you will produce SIPOC diagrams, level-one core process maps, and level-two support process maps. Organizations typically have between seven and ten core processes and ten to twenty support processes. They need to be mapped in enough detail to start the measurement and analysis processes.

Overview of tollgate No. 2, part 1
There are two approaches to understanding a process: descriptive and graphic. Describing processes is a good way of understanding them and it sometimes leads to the discovery of obvious problems and solutions that can be fixed quickly. A flowchart of the process is particularly helpful in obtaining an understanding of how the process works because it provides a visual picture. There are four types of flowcharts that are particularly useful:
- Top-down flowchart
- Deployment matrix flowchart
- Process map
- SIPOC diagram

Of the four types of flowcharts, the SIPOC diagramming method is the one that is most often used in the define phase. The SIPOC flowchart will assist with improvements and simplification by providing:

- A high-level description of the business process addressed by the project
- An accurate picture of how work is currently performed
- Knowledge that will allow the problem solvers to narrow the range of potential causes to be investigated in the measurement and analysis phases

Note: Creating SIPOC diagrams was discussed in chapter 3.

There are three reasons why a Six Sigma engagement frequently begins with building a SIPOC diagram:

- A SIPOC diagram quickly and easily captures the process' current state.
- The SIPOC exercise builds teamwork and momentum for the project.
- It allows the team to identify the most critical opportunities and the next steps.

Tollgate No. 2, part 2

The authors of software engineering literature and most Six Sigma management requirements often assume that users understand their requirements perfectly; they just can't articulate or document them. The SST needs only to clarify ambiguity to elicit the requirements. This prescription causes constant change, frustration, and failure to deliver solutions that address customer requirements. Project team members who are responsible for requirements development often start with four basic and usually erroneous assumptions:

- Customers can define their systems requirements.
- The software development organization is a customer—not the process owner.
- Requirements management starts after requirements have been defined.
- The customer owns the requirements.

The dichotomy between analysts who believe the customer is responsible for requirements definition and those who believe the customer isn't capable of providing this information—at least to the level of detail and precision that is required—leads to widely divergent courses of action. If you believe that customers are responsible for defining their requirements, you will primarily employ interviewing and other elicitation techniques to obtain requirements. However, customers often perceive these techniques as too intrusive. Also, these methods leave you at your customers' mercy—you know only what they tell you, and their stated requirements will almost certainly be incomplete. Even if customers appear unable to define their requirements, you may believe that the correct elicitation tools and techniques will achieve success. Too many organizations that produce and market requirements management tools self-servingly insist that requirements management begins after requirements have been identified. Requirements management begins at project inception, starting with problem identification and continuing through a request or feasibility process.

What problem(s) are you trying to solve? What business need(s) are you addressing? These questions determine your requirements. Problem definition must be managed. Requirements belong to the SST members. The team—not the customers—must develop solutions that meet those requirements. The customer must ultimately own the product but only if it meets his or her requirements.

Overview of tollgate No. 2, part 2

The measurement of key customer requirements tollgate is the collection of customer and stakeholder needs and wants that provide the basis for the CTQ requirements of the project. Every customer has needs from his or her supplier. The characteristics of the need determine whether the customer is happy with the service outcome.

Figure 6.1 CTQ Tree Diagram

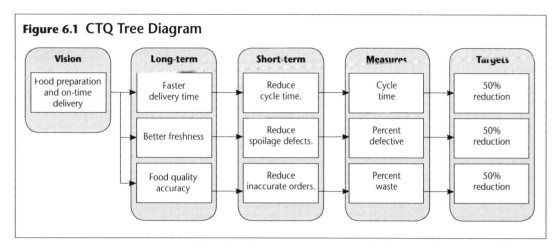

Discovering, understanding, and acting on customer requirements is vital to an effective Six Sigma initiative. However, capturing and analyzing the voice of customer (VOC) data is one of the hardest tasks for many SSTs. The SST leader may use a CTQ tree diagram to gather the VOC as it helps organizations to quickly and efficiently capture the data and identify the CTQ characteristics.

Also, Six Sigma teams often need the ability to create and deploy surveys, immediately analyze the results, and coordinate and drive responsive actions. Best-practice surveys ensure valid, reliable, and actionable customer insights.

Voice of the customer (VOC)

Every Six Sigma process-improvement project begins with the question, "What performance standards must be met to satisfy customers?" The VOC helps organizations listen to and understand their customers' needs. VOC is the customers' expression of their requirements in their own terms. It's a proactive, multidimensional approach that keeps organizations on top of customers' current and future needs, as well as their performance expectations in critical areas such as quality, delivery, responsiveness, and value. Gathering and understanding the VOC and accurately determining the CTQ requirements are vital to the business model and overall success of the company.

The method of determining CTQ requirements must be clearly defined prior to creating any further processes. It's well established that quantifying the VOC is necessary to understanding customers' CTQ requirements. To that end, the SST must establish continuous feedback and communication loops between the customer and the company. Having a customer-relationship management (CRM) system alone is not sufficient for a Six Sigma initiative unless the data and insight derived from CRM are combined with the insights gained from understanding the VOC.

Loyalty and satisfaction feedback processes are more consistent and accurate through regular deployment and analysis using customer satisfaction surveys. Surveys should also be fully customizable and scaleable regardless if there are thousands or millions of customers. Alerts can be sent to appropriate management to understand and identify problems—if necessary in real time—as respondents are completing the survey reducing response time.

Voice of the customer and voice of the business

It's important that the SST understands the VOC and the voice of the business (VOB), which describes the stated and unstated needs and requirements of the organization and its stakeholders. Call monitoring is one of many listening posts used to gather the VOC and VOB. Collecting the appropriate data will help identify strengths and opportunities for improvement. Having an effective quality monitoring process is equally as important. The information collected must be analyzed and reported to various levels of management. The appropriate scorecards and metrics must be in place to effectively drive actions and accountability throughout the organization. Below are examples of metrics used:

- Quality objectives
- Call quality (evaluation score)
- Errors and rework (data entry accuracy)
- Efficiency objectives
- Adherence to schedule
- Cost performance
- Cost per call
- Strategic impact
- Customer satisfaction scores
- Customer feedback
- Employee satisfaction
- Turnover
- Percent quality monitored
- Percent call back
- Percent sales conversion
- Average interviews per hire
- Percent first-call resolution

Once an organization has defined and collected the appropriate data, they can be used to identify process improvement projects that will ultimately be used to develop a project pipeline. These projects are prioritized and resources are allocated, but it's important to note that everyone in the company is responsible for quality, not just the quality department.

Tollgate No. 2 review

During review, the SST will present the high-level process maps of the process related to the EC. The focus is to define what the SST believes are the process' key inputs and outputs. The next part of the review will focus on how the SST determined the customer requirements and expectations.

TOLLGATE NO. 3: PREPARE A PROJECT PLAN

After the team charter and CTQs have been prepared, the following eight parts of the project management plan can be created:

- Create the project integration work plan.
- Develop the project scope management.
- Project time management
- Project cost control
- Project quality management
- Manage risk.
- Manage procurement.
- Implement organizational change management.

Overview of tollgate No. 3

Based on the project management body of knowledge (PMBOK), a project plan will contain the following documents and information:

- Team charter
- Project management approach
- Scope statement or statement of work
- Work breakdown structure (WBS)
- Cost estimates
- Scheduled start dates
- Targeted end dates
- Responsibility assignments
- Project organizational structure
- Schedule and cost performance measurement baselines
- Major milestones and target dates
- Key or required staff
- Key risks
- Open issues
- Subsidiary plans
- Tollgates

The charter serves as the foundation of the project plan. Because the SST's Green Belts and Black Belts have been trained in how to prepare it, Yellow Belts will just need to follow directions and input data to the project plan. The project plan should address the ten elements shown in figure 6.2 on page 147.

Project plan summary

The purpose of the project plan is to select a team that has the right people, power, performance parameters, and passion to create workable solutions. To launch the project, we also need to design and conduct an initial team strategy meeting that begins to build a solid infrastructure and a project plan. A good project plan should provide the basis for some of the following:

- Project organization
- Project manager selection
- Which organizations should be involved
- SST membership
- Project execution
- Tools to be used

One of the most frequently used outputs from this tollgate is a WBS, as shown in figure 6.3 (page 148). This document defines what will be done, when it will be done, and who will do it. It's prepared based on the team charter but in much more detail. Project plans prepared at this point in the DMAIC methodology are often updated as more data become available, but at no time should the project plan go beyond the limits set by the team charter. More projects fail due to poor project management than for any other single reason.

Tollgate No. 3 review

If tollgate No. 3's review is unsuccessful, funding for phases II, III, IV, and V won't be approved. During this review, the detailed project plan will be reviewed including the:

- WBS

- Budget
- Quality controls
- Risk analysis
- Scheduling
- Objectives and goals
- Scope
- Project controls

The project plan is the key document that defines what the SST will do and when it will be done. The approval of the project plan is a major commitment for the EC and the SST. When the project plan is approved by the EC, the budget for phase II is released and other resources are committed. The SST is then approved to start phase II.

Summary of tollgate No. 3

There is no right way to tackle a Six Sigma project. There are many ways and some will work better than others. The basic plan of action will be to identify root causes and develop solutions, then implement the changes and review the results. It would be difficult to create a single document that covers all aspects of both the processed and actual completion of your team's project, but this planning will reduce the risks of the project's failure.

SUMMARY OF THE SIX SIGMA DEFINE PHASE

There are five key elements in the define phase of the DMAIC process:
- Identify the process or product for improvement.
- Identify key customers and CTQ elements.
- Develop a team charter with problem/goal statement, project scope, business case, team roles, and milestones.
- Develop a high-level process map for the most significant four or five steps of the process.
- Develop the project plan using project management techniques.

Discuss the problem you examined. Explain how you identified your specific Six Sigma project. You might integrate visuals and data summaries with text using tools such as a Pareto chart or a summary report of current performance for a manufacturing or transactional process.

Some topics that should be included are:
- Discussion of the problem addressed in your project
- Discussion of the project scope
- Identification of key measures used to evaluate the success of your project (such as DPM, DPMO, process yield, error rates, processing or order-filling time, machine cycle time, number of complaints, etc.)
- Discussion of effect of your project on key business indicators

As an example, one of our client's team objectives was to increase the quality of patient care while reducing the average length of stay and costs for open-heart surgery. This had been the objective behind several initiatives in the past at this particular hospital, many of which—such as the implementation of critical pathways—had been successful. However, a comparison of the hospital's length-of-stay data to best-practice hospitals revealed an opportunity for further improvement.

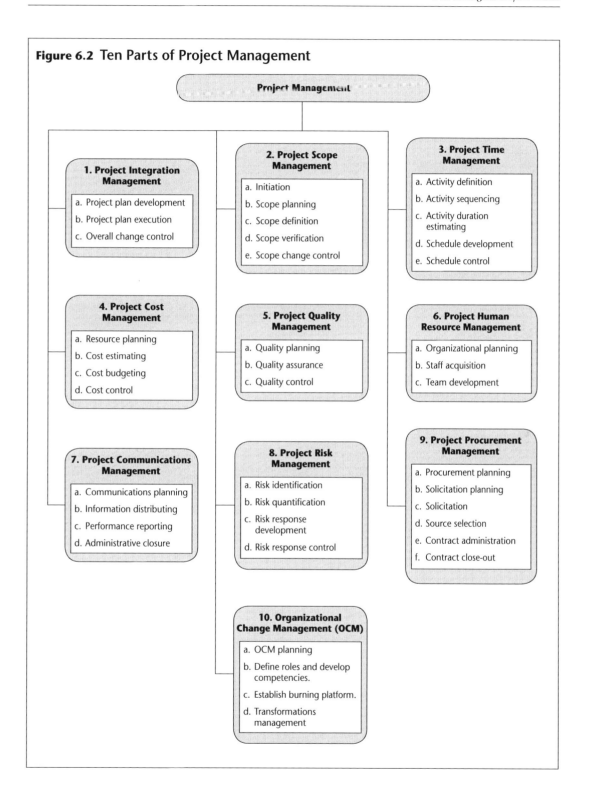

Figure 6.2 Ten Parts of Project Management

Figure 6.3 Typical Work Breakdown Structure (WBS)

ID	Task Name	Duration
1	Project start	37 days
2	Kick-off meeting with human resource executive.	1 day
3	The quality manager and management committee will select team members.	10 days
4	Review the project plan by human resources executive.	23 days
5	Phase I gap analysis	44 days
6	Collection	44 days
7	Gap analysis checklist	21 days
58	Distribute and provide a brief awareness session for human resources executive's gap analysis.	21 days
59	Human resources executive to interview each business unit individually.	3 days
60	Human resources executive to issue gap analysis report, present findings to EC.	1 day
61	Distribute human resources executive's change management assessment forms.	21 days
62	Analysis of the change management assessment forms.	10 days
63	Develop mitigation plan.	9 days
64	Issue the revised plan (subject to variation resulting from the gap analysis).	2 days
65	Phase I completed	0 days
66	Phase II training	329.05 days
250	Phase II completed	0 days
251	Phase III documentation	167 days
520	Phase III completed	0 days
521	Phase IV implementation	231.67 days
658	Phase IV completed	0 days
659	Phase V registration	37.33 days
669	Project completed	0 days

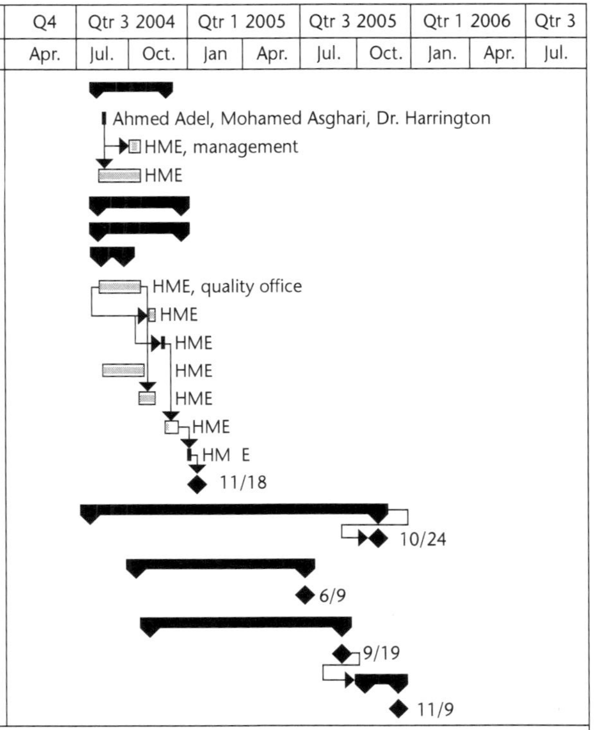

Project: ISO H
Date: Wed 9/13/06

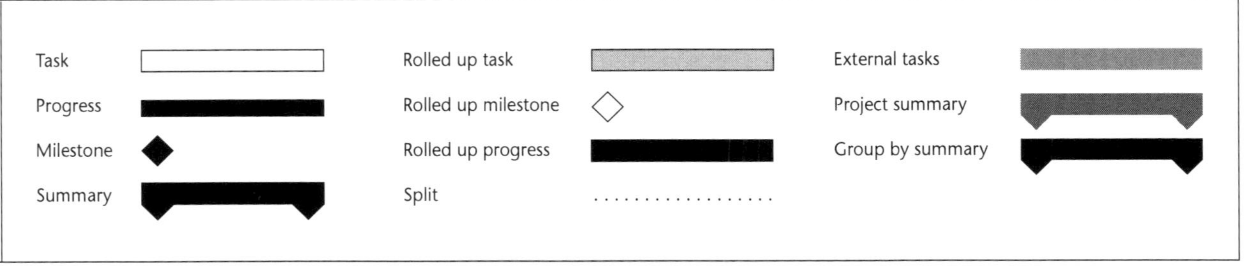

Task
Progress
Milestone
Summary

Rolled up task
Rolled up milestone
Rolled up progress
Split

External tasks
Project summary
Group by summary

The comparison indicated that 53 percent of the hospital's patients were discharged on or after the seventh post-op day compared to 18 percent for benchmark hospitals, as shown in figure 6.4. In addition to improving the quality of care, the potential economic opportunity to the hospital was estimated to be $400,000 annually. This financial value was calculated by multiplying the cost per day by the projected number of days to be saved through

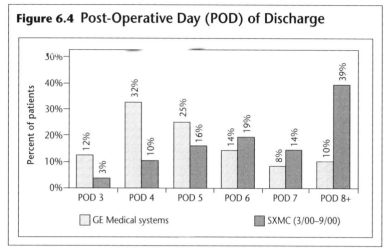

Figure 6.4 Post-Operative Day (POD) of Discharge

this performance improvement initiative. The economic effect to the hospital combined with increased competition from neighboring cardiovascular centers and declining program reimbursement convinced the hospital administration to charter a special project team to work on this initiative.

At the first team meeting, the project leader should review the charter with the team members to ensure clarity of purpose, goals, and the parameters or scope of work involved. A process flowchart should also be completed. The development of the process flowchart is always a valuable exercise, especially for team members who are getting their first view of the entire process and the role they play.

The define phase focuses on defining the as-is process. Processes are frequently understood by experienced personnel but are not documented. Simply gathering a group of key people in a room and asking them to define a process often improves it. Sometimes the improvements are significant, and the team decides that no further work is necessary.

The define phase shapes the SST. Be sure that there is a common understanding of the assignment and that you have developed a plan that will maximize the organization's improvement. Once this is accomplished, the SST is ready to start the measure phase.

- Phase I objectives:
  - ☐ Define the project problem.
  - ☐ Define the project approach.
  - ☐ Define the project outcome.
  - ☐ Define the project stakeholders.
  - ☐ Define customer requirements.
  - ☐ Define the SST members.
  - ☐ Train the SST.
  - ☐ Launch the project.
  - ☐ Define project risks.
  - ☐ Define project schedule.
  - ☐ Define project budget.
  - ☐ Prepare an approved team charter.
  - ☐ Prepare an approved project plan.
  - ☐ Develop high-level process maps.

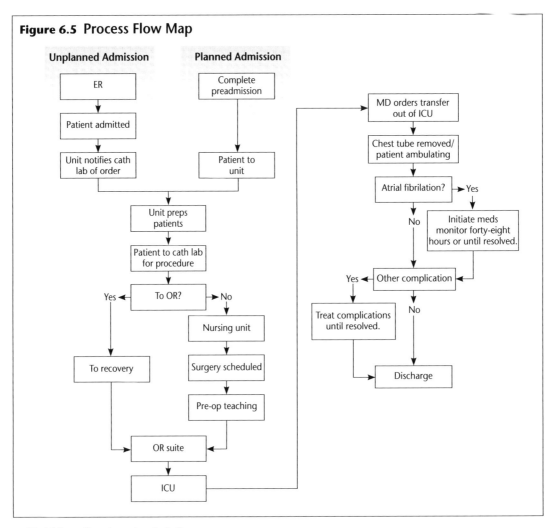

Figure 6.5 Process Flow Map

☐ Address "low-hanging fruit."
☐ Define the cost and benefits.

Figure 6.6 provides an overview of the highlights that occur during phase I.

"Proper planning prevents poor performance."
—HJH

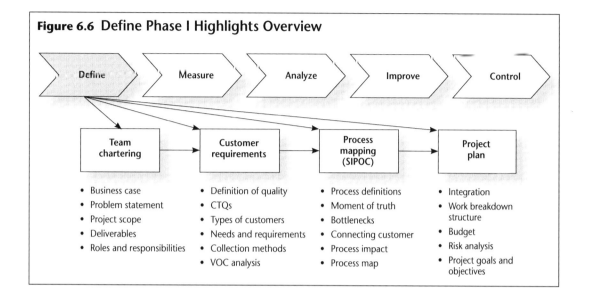

Figure 6.6 Define Phase I Highlights Overview

| Define | Measure | Analyze | Improve | Control |

| Team chartering | Customer requirements | Process mapping (SIPOC) | Project plan |

- Business case
- Problem statement
- Project scope
- Deliverables
- Roles and responsibilities

- Definition of quality
- CTQs
- Types of customers
- Needs and requirements
- Collection methods
- VOC analysis

- Process definitions
- Moment of truth
- Bottlenecks
- Connecting customer
- Process impact
- Process map

- Integration
- Work breakdown structure
- Budget
- Risk analysis
- Project goals and objectives

CHAPTER 7

THE SIX SIGMA MEASURE PHASE

"Don't collect data to prove your point, but to find the point."
—HJH

The second phase of the define-measure-analyze-improve-control (DMAIC) journey is to measure and gather information on the problem the Six Sigma team (SST) is studying. This involves identifying and prioritizing the metric using tollgate no. 4 and tollgate no. 5. First, establish a data-collection plan to determine what to measure, how to collect the data, how they will be measured, and how the data will be displayed. After validating the measurement systems, the next step is measuring the actual process to reach the final steps of identifying process capability and displaying the data.

The measure phase begins with the identification of the key process-performance metrics. Once the key process-performance metrics have been specified, related process and customer data are collected. The two commonly used process performance measures that are most often used are defects per million opportunities (DPMO) and process sigma.

The team identifies the key internal processes that influence critical-to-quality characteristics (CTQs) and measures the defects currently generated relative to those processes to determine the levels of variability. During the measure phase, quantitative and qualitative data are gathered to gain a clear view of the current situation. This serves as a baseline to evaluate potential solutions and typically involves interviews with process owners, mapping of key business processes, and gathering data relating to current performance (time, volume, frequency, effect, etc.).

If the organization has problems with its data and electronic records, this could be addressed using data flow diagramming, which is used to improve an understanding of process flow, address problems with cycle time, and reduce process costs. It involves either basic or detailed flow diagrams with value-adds and nonvalue-adds. Data "doors" in the diagram can help explain what creates variations in a process by using scatter plots or stratification. When you have variables data that can be divided into categories and analyzed, use stratification.

The next step is to find the reason for the variations. A scatter plot is a graph used to visualize the relationship between two variables. The dots on the scatter plot represent the data points and can either show a strong correlation between variables or no correlation at all. Scatter plots also show how one variable is affected by a change to another variable. Once the information is collected, the next step is to prepare the organization for change. To ensure success, it's important to require participation throughout the organizational hierarchy from administrative to senior executive levels. Activities at this point include determining and delegating individual responsibilities required by applicable requirements, providing detailed explanations of the project plan, and reviewing training requirements.

Measurement helps to define the improvement opportunities, and data stratification and prioritization are critical to project success. In many cases, the "low-hanging fruit" identified in this phase can help build the project team's credibility for months to come.

INTRODUCTION TO THE SIX SIGMA MEASURE PHASE

Stakeholder measurements summary

One of the major reasons improvement efforts fail is a lack of measurable results in all functions and areas of an organization. There's a real need to see the economic effect (e.g., the return on investment) for both the short term and the long term. The strategy, the objectives, and the associated measures are the keys to success. When all employees understand the relationship between their performance and the organization's success, they will strive to sustain their jobs and lifestyles.

The following shows how three types of organizations approach measurements:

- Attitude about measurement
  - ☐ *Losers:* It's not important.
  - ☐ *Survivors:* It's treated as an afterthought.
  - ☐ *Winners:* Sets up the measurement process at the beginning of the process so that a baseline is defined and progress can be measured.

- Targets
  - ☐ *Losers:* Management sets targets.
  - ☐ *Survivors:* Employees set targets for themselves.
  - ☐ *Winners:* Management sets business targets. The employees set more stringent challenge targets for themselves. The target is less important than the trend.

- Measurement communications
  - ☐ *Losers:* Data are collected so that management can keep things under control.
  - ☐ *Survivors:* Job-related measurements are shared with the employees.
  - ☐ *Winners:* All the improvement measurements are posted for everyone to see and reviewed with the employees as a team at least four times a year.

- Measurement use
  - ☐ *Losers:* To identify individuals who need to improve
  - ☐ *Survivors:* To define problems and measure progress
  - ☐ *Winners:* To help the individual understand his or her impact on the organization and align the individual goals to those of the organization

This chapter will provide the reader with an understanding of the activities that take place during the two tollgates that make up the DMAIC measure phase:

- Tollgate No. 4: Create a data-collection plan.
- Tollgate No. 5: Implement the data-collection plan.

The Yellow Belt tools most often used during the measure phase are:

- Brainstorming
- Checklists

- Control charts
- Cycle-time analysis
- Data-collection plan framework
- Data-flow diagrams
- Nominal group technique (NGT)
- Process capability analysis
- Run charts

THE PURPOSE OF THE SIX SIGMA MEASURE PHASE

The purpose of the measure phase is to collect data that will define the status of the situation that was assigned to the SST. This includes current-state measurements such as cycle time, processing time, error rates, costs, and customer satisfaction. Data needed to analyze the problem and define the root cause of the problem are also collected in the measure phase. While collecting this data the SST needs to understand the amount of error in the measuring equipment and the measurement system repeatability.

TOLLGATE NO. 4: CREATE DATA-COLLECTION PLAN

The data-collection plan helps the team improve the effectiveness and efficiency of the process it's working on. Effectiveness refers to the output measures that are important to the customers and the effectiveness of an organization's suppliers and sources. The efficiency measures refer to what occurs inside the process and the cycle time, cost, value, and labor occurring between the start and stop points in the process map.

During this phase, the SST will decide what data (balanced between input and output) to collect, determine the sample size, identify data sources, develop data-collection checksheets, and assign data-collection duties to team members. It will also develop operational definitions so that all team members apply the same definitions when gathering data.

Overview

The measure phase begins with an analysis of the output from phase I. Its major inputs are an approved team charter, a project plan, and a budget for phases II, III, IV, and V.

After these tasks are complete, the SST must develop a sound data-collection plan to gather data in the measure phase. There are several crucial steps that need to be addressed to ensure that this process and its related measurement systems are stable and reliable. Incorporating these steps into a data-collection plan will improve the likelihood that the data and measurements can be used to support the ensuing analysis.

Statistical data analysis is the process of analyzing objective data to determine performance of processes and to test hypotheses. Measurability is essential. To analyze data properly, it's essential to know what type of data you are collecting and analyzing.

The type of data analysis to perform is dependent on the type of data collected during the measure phase. There are two types of data that SSTs deal with: discrete data analysis and continuous data analysis. Discrete data are binary (e.g., off/on, good/bad, and male/female). Discrete data are also called "go/no-go data," and are collected using frequency distribution checksheets and analyzed with histograms. Statistical pictures of discrete data are created with Pareto diagrams.

Discrete data tell the team about the six major factors that affect the performance of the process or the data-collection system—the 5Ms and the 1P: machines, methods, measurement, materials, Mother Nature (the environment), and people.

Continuous data address relative characteristics such as height, weight, minutes, days, and length. They are also called "variables data." Continuous data are preferred over discrete data because they render more information about the process.

Three steps are involved in building a sound data-collection plan:

1. Clearly define the goals and objectives of the data-collection plan.
2. Agree on operational definitions and methodology.
3. Ensure data-collection (and measurement) repeatability, reproducibility, accuracy, and stability.

Step 1: Clearly defined goals

A good data-collection plan should include a brief description of the project, the specific data that are needed, the rationale for collecting the data, what insight the data might provide, and what will be done with the data once they have been collected. Being clear on these elements will facilitate the accurate and efficient collection of data.

Step 2: Operational definitions and methodology

The improvement team should clearly define what data are to be collected and how. It should dictate what's to be evaluated and determine how a numerical value will be assigned to facilitate measurement. The team should consider consulting with customers to see if they are already collecting the same (or similar) data. If so, comparisons can be made and best practices shared. The team should also formulate the scope of the data collection to determine:

- How many observations are needed
- What time interval the study should employ
- Whether past, present, and future data will be collected
- The methodologies that will be employed to record the data

The team should agree on the applicable definitions, procedures, and guidelines it will use to collect data. Serious problems can arise for the organization when business decisions are made based on potentially unreliable data.

If the team wishes to examine historical data to include as part of the study, it should pay careful attention to how reliable the data and its source have been. Suspect data should be discarded.

Step 3: Ensuring repeatability, reproducibility, accuracy, and stability

Data are repeatable if an operator can reach essentially the same outcome multiple times on one particular item with the same equipment. The data will be reproducible if all the operators who are measuring the same items with the same equipment reach essentially the same outcome. The degree to which a measurement system is accurate will generally be the difference between an observed average measurement and the associated known standard value. The degree to which a measurement system is stable is generally expressed by the variation resulting from an operator measuring the same item with the same equipment over an extended period.

Improvement teams should note all the factors that could potentially cause reductions in repeatability, reproducibility, accuracy, and stability that may produce unreliable data. It's a good practice to test—perhaps on a small scale—how the data collection and measurements will proceed. It should become apparent upon simulation of the potential factors that could be done to mitigate or eliminate them.

The fundamental question of data analysis is: "Is the variation (spread) of my measurement system too large to study the current level of process variation?" The vital follow-up question is: "Must I stop and correct my measurement system before proceeding on my project?"

Stratification and prioritization

Stratification is a technique used to divide data into homogeneous groups (strata) for analysis. Data collected from multiple sources often need to be treated separately. Stratifying data involves examining process data, splitting them into distinct layers, and analyzing them to identify a different process. For example, in an analysis of loans, you might begin by stratifying the data by loan size (e.g., less than $10 million and more than $10 million). If the central tendency metrics are different, it would indicate two entirely different processes or that one of the processes is broken.

Stratification is related to segmentation. A stratifying factor—also referred to as stratification or a stratifier —is one that can be used to separate data into subgroups. This is done to investigate whether that factor is a significant special-cause factor.

Testing the measurement plan

Once you've gathered feedback from colleagues, experts, and outsiders and implemented all their great advice, you should test the data-collection tool. This is the final step before you begin collecting data, and it's especially important if you haven't consulted your target population yet. If the data-collection tool is a survey, send it to four or five people in your target population and tell them to fill it out like they normally would and get back to you with any issues that came up. If you're doing an observational study, pick a few sample cases and try using your defined method to assess them. This testing process will help you adjust any final confusion or problem areas and adjust the language if necessary.

Testing is the only reliable way to evaluate the responsiveness and effectiveness of your data-collection plan and its associated elements. It identifies collection areas that need improvement or further evaluation, and it allows for dissemination of accurate information and development of meaningful sampling programs. It promotes decision making and resource allocation based on solid evidence rather than on isolated occurrences, assumption, emotion, or politics, so you can know what you don't know.

Tollgate No. 4 review

At the end of tollgate No. 4, the executive committee will conduct a review in which the SST will present its data-collection plan. The SST will explain why it's recording the data it chose and discuss the adequacy of its sampling plans. It will also explain how the data will be used and the cost of collecting them. At this review, the status of the project will be compared to the project plan. When the executive committee is satisfied that the data collection plan is adequate and cost effective, it will close out tollgate No. 4, allowing the SST to start tollgate No. 5.

This doesn't mean that the measurement plan won't be changed as a result of additional information collected during the remainder of the project. In fact, the measurement plan should always be updated whenever additional measurements are required.

TOLLGATE NO. 5: IMPLEMENT DATA-COLLECTION PLAN

The purpose of collecting data is to understand how the process works. Before the team can attempt to improve the process, it must understand how it currently works and what it's supposed to do. There are two approaches to understanding the present process. One is descriptive and the other is graphic. A good way to understand the process is to describe it. One benefit of describing the process is that it sometimes leads to the discovery of obvious problems and solutions that can be fixed quickly.

Overview

Once the data-collection process has been planned and defined, it's best to follow the process from start to finish to ensure that the plan is executed consistently and accurately. The SST members must be in close communication with all the data collectors and participants; often Yellow Belts will be part of the data-collection team. This could be followed up with some form of training or demonstration that will further enhance a common understanding of the data-collection process.

Someone from the SST should be present at the commencement of data collection to provide some oversight. This way the participants will know right away whether the plan is being followed properly. Once the data are available, the SST members should review the data to look for gross errors that can be immediately analyzed and corrected.

Failure to oversee the process at its beginning stages might mean that course correction will need to be made later in the project, which would waste a lot of the data-collection and/or measurement efforts. Depending on the length of time it takes to collect data—and whether the data collection is ongoing—periodic oversight will help to ensure that there are no shortcuts taken and that any new participants are properly oriented with the process to preserve consistency.

The project leader should check to see that the data and measurements are reasonable and that they meet the criteria to ensure that the measurement systems used are reproducible, repeatable, accurate, and stable. If the results don't meet the criteria, the project leader should determine where any breakdowns exist and what to do with any suspect data and/or measurements. Reviewing the operational definitions and methodology with the participants should help to clear up any misunderstandings or misinterpretations that may have caused the breakdowns.

As previously mentioned, the team needs to see how robustly the process performs according to the process variables that have the biggest affect on key customer requirements. Quality is judged based on the output of the process, and the quality of output is improved by analyzing inputs and process variables. This ensures that team members are all viewing the process in the same manner.

Summary of tollgate No. 5

This tollgate includes the implementation of the data-collection plan outlined in the previous tollgate. Based on a determination of sample size and identification of data sources, team members perform their data-collection duties. This is where operational definitions can be critical because the data often defy common wisdom, and people will challenge it if the data aren't well defined.

Agreeing on what to measure will play an important step in getting people to agree about the results. The ultimate goal of this tollgate is to calculate the baseline sigma of the process being improved, should sufficient data be available. In social services, the most common way to do this is to determine the process' fail points. The results of the data should be collected and formally documented in a report. This report should also include the data-collection method.

Based on the data, it may be necessary to update the team charter; it's usually appropriate to expand the project plan into greater detail for the analysis phase. Frequently, at this point the SST can identify simple, inexpensive solutions that can be implemented quickly.

SUMMARY OF THE SIX SIGMA MEASURE PHASE

During the measure phase, the SST collects data that define the current state of the assigned improvement opportunity. It also collects data needed to define the root causes during the analysis phase.

■ Phase II objectives:

☐ Confirm key customer requirements.

☐ Prepare a detailed process flowchart.

☐ Define required measurements.

☐ Define measurement systems.

☐ Evaluate accuracy of the measurement systems.

☐ Define sampling plans.

☐ Define analysis methods.

☐ Define data-collection format and forms.

☐ Develop a measurement plan.

☐ Collect the required data.

☐ Determine data accuracy.

☐ Prepare a measurement report.

☐ Validate the process flowchart and collect relevant process flow data.

"Good measurements are the foundation for all problem-solving activities."
—HJH

CHAPTER 8

THE SIX SIGMA ANALYZE PHASE

"Avoid analysis paralysis."
—HJH

The objective of the analyze phase is to use the data that were collected earlier in the process to discover the root causes of the gaps between the process' current performance and its desired performance. The team discovers why defects are generated by identifying the key variables that are most likely to create process variation. In the analyze phase, information gathered in the measure phase is studied to pinpoint bottlenecks and identify opportunities where nonvalue-added tasks can be removed. A business case is developed to determine if potential process improvements are cost-effective and worthwhile. The business case considers not only hard costs but also intangible benefits such as user productivity and satisfaction. At this point, providing resources for infrastructure, messaging, disaster recovery, business continuity, and data storage is sometimes required.

Through analysis, the team can determine the causes of the problem that need improvement and how to eliminate the gap between existing performance and the desired level of performance. This involves discovering why defects are generated by identifying the key variables that are most likely to create process variation. A common error that teams often make when they discuss Six Sigma is to assume that the define-measure-analyze-improve-control (DMAIC) process takes too long to accomplish improvements. However, "quick hits" are often established early in the project and frequently implemented by the time the team reaches the analyze phase. If the team has not already identified major improvements, the breakthrough often results from careful process analysis with data. Six Sigma analysis techniques are the proper tools to uncover the more complex and difficult solutions.

INTRODUCTION TO THE SIX SIGMA ANALYZE PHASE

This chapter will provide the reader with an understanding of the activities that take place during the three tollgates that make up the analyze phase:

- Tollgate No. 6: Analyze the data.
- Tollgate No. 7: Analyze the process.
- Tollgate No. 8: Analyze the root cause(s).

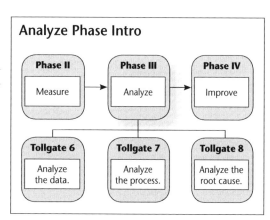

Analyze Phase Intro

The Yellow Belt tools that are most often used during the analyze phase are:
- 5 Whys (5Ws)
- Affinity diagrams
- Basic SPC
- Brainstorming
- Cause-and-effect diagrams
- Checksheets/checklists
- Control charts
- Customer requirements table
- Cycle-time analysis
- Flowcharts
- Histograms
- Nominal group technique
- Pareto charts
- Process capability analysis
- Run charts
- Sampling plans
- Scatter diagrams
- Sigma conversion tables

TOLLGATE NO. 6: ANALYZE THE DATA

Tollgate No. 6 activities are designed to organize data that will be used to define the current status of the problem. It's important to accurately define the current status so that improvement opportunities are well documented and the degree of improvement can be measured after the corrective action has been implemented. This analysis will later help isolate and validate the root cause(s).

The planning for data analysis took place in the measure phase. It's important to identify possible measurements needed to develop a solution for the problem. The Six Sigma team (SST) needs to know how to select the most important variables to measure, along with how to create a data-collection plan for each of the data types. These plans need to be designed so they meet the input requirements needed to analyze the data.

Overview
We analyze data to:
- Identify and verify root causes of problems.
- Identify and eliminate variation in processes.
- Become "defect detectives."
- Understand the current status of an activity or process.

Databases often become so large that they're difficult to handle. In these cases, data stratification can simplify analysis. Stratification involves breaking down the process data into smaller groups to find the most significant contributors to the performance gap, based on certain key characteristics. A key characteristic is an aspect of the data that might help explain when, where, who, and why a problem exists. This is needed to detect a pattern that localizes a problem or explains why the frequency of impact varies between times, conditions, locations, or other factors.

Data analysis challenges include:

- Moving too quickly from the measurement phase to the improve phase without considering all the relevant data
- Developing and confirming the best-case hypothesis
- Navigating through the iterative stages of exploring, hypothesis, and verifying causes smoothly and productively

Hypothesis testing refers to the process of using statistical analysis to determine if the observed differences between two or more samples are due to random chance (as stated in the null hypothesis) or to true differences in the samples (as stated in the alternate hypothesis).

Tollgate No. 6 review

The tollgate No. 6 review is the first time the executive committee is presented with organized information about how the process is performing. At long last, it has some business facts related to the problem/improvement opportunity that was assigned to the SST. Depending on the project, the type of information and the format that it is presented in will vary.

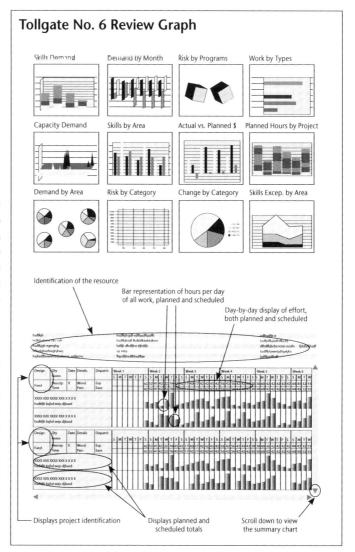

Tollgate No. 6 Review Graph

TOLLGATE NO. 7: ANALYZE THE PROCESS

The purpose of the analysis tollgate is to enable change efforts not only to begin, but also to persist. The activities that take place during this phase will sharpen the organization's ability to improve by focusing on the analysis of a particular process. This is done by increasing knowledge about the targeted process, in terms of both the expertise of specific individuals and the quantitative data on process performance. Only when this groundwork has been well defined can specific improvements be developed.

COMPONENTS OF SUCCESSFUL PROCESS ANALYSIS

Process analysis is always accomplished in conjunction with the two components to successful change: begin and persist. Given a powerful initial stimulus, it is relatively easy for an organization to begin change.

When a powerful constituency calls for change, organizations generally respond by launching a number of immediate initiatives. A list of ongoing initiatives can be used to demonstrate responsiveness and to promise quick results. However, most improvement initiatives that are undertaken without sufficient preparation either end inconclusively or quietly fail once the initial enthusiasm passes.

The analysis of processes is accomplished by applying the following steps:

1. Walk through the process.
2. Measure process performance.
3. Create data snapshots.
4. Envision process intersections.
5. Perform a poor-quality cost analysis.

This cycle is repeated continuously. Many organizations have demonstrated the benefits of using the DMAIC improvement methodology to help sustain change. Embedding an improvement method into an organization's culture turns the expectation and search for improvement into a standard operating procedure—the accustomed way of doing business.

Walk through the process

Process walkthroughs emphasizes the need to understand the needs of customers and the outputs of the particular logistics process under study. Detailed walkthroughs of the process by teams of technical experts are important for improving the organization's understanding of which procedures are currently followed and how they affect performance. Because many processes are complex, they need to be understood in great detail if the sources of performance problems are to be accurately identified and solutions correctly developed and implemented.

Figure 8.1 Typical Process Walkthrough Questions

- What inputs are required?
- How were you trained?
- What do you do?
- How do you know it is good?
- What feedback do you receive?
- Who are your customers?
- What keeps you from doing error-free work?

Group walkthroughs that draw membership from across organizational units also foster competitive improvement incentives while sharing expertise, experience, and insights. It can be eye-opening for the participants to discover that they all have different and limited views of the same process. Shared questions and suggestions lead to collective insights and develop a sense of common purpose. Even with the friendly competition, a broader organizational cohesion is developed that helps to break down organizational divisions or silos and disruptive process handoffs among units. As a result, improvement teams learn that previous improvement efforts focused on particular segments of the process may have been working at cross-purposes and minimizing their effectiveness and efficiency.

Many simple and easy-to-fix issues may be immediately exposed during walkthroughs, and this "low-hanging fruit" should, of course, be gathered. More important is the development of a group that collectively embodies a new level of expertise. The group's members should share an end-to-end understanding of the process, a common framework for assessing process performance that focuses on customer satisfaction, well-informed hypotheses about the sources of persistent performance deficits, and the collective authority to devise and recommend innovations to improve process performance. Such a cadre constitutes in and of itself an enhanced capability to change which the organization formerly lacked.

Walkthroughs need to be repeated periodically for several reasons. First, even seemingly simple changes to a process may change the flow of materials, information, and funds—sometimes in unexpected ways. As improvements are made, additional opportunities for improvement are exposed. Also, because Six Sigma projects take an average of ninety days to complete, there may be a need to train new and replacement members of the SST. Repeated walkthroughs provide training opportunities for new team members.

Figure 8.2 **Functional Flowchart of the Internal Job Search Process**

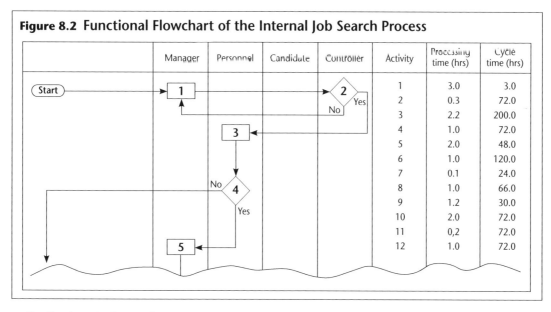

	Manager	Personnel	Candidate	Controller	Activity	Processing time (hrs)	Cycle time (hrs)
					1	3.0	3.0
					2	0.3	72.0
					3	2.2	200.0
					4	1.0	72.0
					5	2.0	48.0
					6	1.0	120.0
					7	0.1	24.0
					8	1.0	66.0
					9	1.2	30.0
					10	2.0	72.0
					11	0.2	72.0
					12	1.0	72.0

Finally, there is the need to re-emphasize that process analysis represents a continuous improvement effort and that as each local goal is achieved, it should be replaced by a new goal. Although the SST will only do one walkthrough during tollgate No. 7, periodic walkthroughs by the process owner after the Six Sigma project is completed provides visible evidence to the whole organization of this continuing commitment.

Figure 8.2 shows a typical analysis prepared after a walkthrough. Averages are often inadequate, and the SST will need to calculate the sigma values for the major activities.

Note: Process walkthroughs are sometimes part of the measure phase.

Measuring process perfomance

The most critical aspect of process analysis is the development and implementation of appropriate metrics that span the full process and reflect key customer values. These should have been developed during phase II. Metrics are the *lingua franca* by which all the stakeholders in a process communicate with one another about the goals and status of their improvement efforts. Six Sigma advocates the use of multiple metrics to guide improvement on all dimensions of process performance—time, quality, and cost. Because they aim to reduce the variability in process performance, metrics should measure median performance and variance, not just average performance.

The measure substep of the process analysis tollgate represents an investment an organization must make before a dramatically higher level of performance can be reasonably expected or achieved. The central activity to foster performance improvement is essential to driving and sustaining change. The choice of metrics is critical because what gets measured is what gets attention. But performance analysis must go beyond that; it must enable change agents to diagnose the drivers of weak performance. As changes are made, analysis must continue to determine which of the changes lead to improvement.

In addition, data sources to support the metrics must be identified and evaluated. Until this point, the Six Sigma implementation has been able to proceed using data that are available from standard information systems, though frequently these data have been combined and used in new ways. A beneficial byproduct of using data to support process improvement is that the quality of the data improves very quickly; those who are using the data often uncover previously unnoticed data quality problems, and those who are responsible for inputing and maintaining the data are alerted to the importance of its accuracy, completeness, and timeliness. These data improvements often benefit process performance by increasing the rate of successful transactions.

Create data snapshots

Because trends in performance are more interesting and useful than single snapshots, data must be archived and continually re-analyzed. Analysis is important not only for determining the sources of performance deficits, but also for monitoring and evaluating the effects of improvement efforts. Establishing baseline performance is essential for gauging improvement accurately. It's best to combine short feedback cycles with longer-term trend data to maximize the use of the data available. Prompt feedback permits a focus on controlling variability and implementing changes as intended, while the trend data help to identify opportunities for improvement and provide the historical perspective to track improvement.

Process analysis includes reporting, which is another activity critical to sustaining the continuous improvement aspects of Six Sigma. By displaying the value of an improvement initiative, measurement reporting helps to build support and maintain long-term momentum. Measurement offers maximum benefit when the results are widely shared among stakeholders in the process. Customers need to know the level of service they are getting from the different sources they use, and providers need to understand the processwide effects of their improvement efforts. Improvement is difficult to guide and sustain unless performance feedback is consistent and rapid. As reporting time lengthens, it becomes increasingly difficult to link a specific intervention to an outcome. In work settings where the activity to be improved occurs many times a day, daily feedback is most useful. For activities that are less frequent or more extended, weekly or even monthly feedback may be preferable. Feedback less frequent than monthly is often very difficult to use to evaluate specific improvement actions.

Figure 8.3 shows a process and its inputs (Ys) and outputs (Xs).

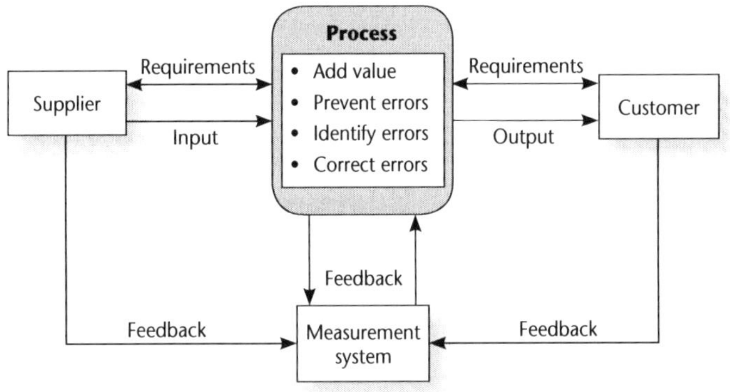

Note that the design of the process is based on agreed-to requirements between the process and its customer. It's a best practice if the requirements are documented. At the same time, the customer should agree to provide feedback to the process on the acceptability of the output. Once this is established, a value-added process can be designed that:

- Prevents errors
- Identifies errors
- Corrects errors
- Produces output to documented requirements

Figure 8.3 The Process Picture

The process inputs should be defined based on the process design. This allows the process owner to document the requirement for the inputs and find a supplier that will agree to meet its requirements. Too much of outsourcing is driven because the internal suppliers cannot meet the process input requirements. Part of the agreement with each supplier is the requirement for the ongoing feedback from the process on acceptability of the inputs from the supplier.

Envisioning the process intersections

Envisioning, the fourth step of the process analysis, capitalizes on the knowledge developed during the first three steps. By utilizing the DMAIC method, teams develop a much-improved understanding of the performance deficits in a process and where improvement efforts might most profitably begin. Through direct observation of the process as it's actually performed, the team acquires the detailed knowledge needed to develop innovative alternatives to current business methods and to identify sites where they can be implemented.

Through the use of mutually agreed-upon metrics, the team is able to envision and ultimately measure whether performance could improve after the implementation of process changes. Moreover, by comparing performance trends, it can create quasi-experimental demonstrations of the beneficial effects of a given intervention. When data are reported that show a clear potential performance advantage, a compelling motivation is created for other teams to join the process improvement initiative.

Tollgate No. 7 review

This review is conducted to prove to the EC that the SST performed a comprehensive analysis of the related process. It will want to see the detailed process flow diagrams and the data related to the key activities. It will also want to see a summary of the process walkthrough report.

TOLLGATE NO. 8: ANALYZE THE ROOT CAUSE(S)

Root cause analysis is often described as an essential step in the problem-definition process. Many organizations devote considerable resources to it. Root cause analysis aligns with W. Edwards Deming's dictum: "The most important numbers are unknown and unknowable, few appear to reap the due rewards of their efforts."

There are times when it's either not possible or not affordable to ascertain all the root causes underlying a problem. A simplified root cause analysis that requires less analysis time and effort should be used. It's usually capable of delivering powerful solutions.

Root cause analysis was addressed in detail in chapter 3.

Overview

The SST can now create a list of potential causes to determine what's causing the problem by focusing on the causal relationships between the factors that contribute to the variation in a process. The goal is to develop root cause theories so they can be confirmed with data. It's also necessary to identify all the potential causes and select the root cause(s) that the team will focus its improvement efforts on throughout the remainder of the project. It's important to consider how measurable each of these likely contributors is. In general, it pays to focus on the causes for which data can be gathered because knowing which potential causes can be changed will help to focus the analysis effort.

To different degrees, everyone in an organization solves problems and analyzes root causes, although many of us may prefer to think of our problem-solving process as something less fancy than "root cause analysis." Regardless of what we call this effort, we're all looking for the same things: root causes that eliminate and prevent problems. Whether our work is quality, engineering, safety, production, maintenance, or just about any other function in the organization, we should be comfortable with the concept of root cause analysis.

Let's clarify the term "prevention solutions." Fixing things, cleaning up, removing, reworking, redesigning, modifying, and fortifying are not prevention and control steps; they are correction steps. These actions may or may not be a result of prevention actions, but they in themselves are not prevention steps. Prevention has to do with why the design was inadequate, why the machine needs repair, and why cleanup is necessary. This is not to say that these responses are not important to the operation; certainly we want to discover immediately when things need early repair. Root cause analysis should uncover such opportunities to remedy, but the primary goal of the process should be to design the process to avoid the need for avoidable repair, rework, clean up, and expensive redesign.

Root cause coding worksheet

The root cause analysis system includes a coding system for the causes. Most lists contain general root causes, which don't provide the needed focus, as the problem buckets are too large and vague. For example, the general category of "people" can be listed in more detail as "supervision," which can be further classified into "definition" of work assignments. Your specific company list of assignable causes might be from 100 to 200 items in length. These are usually shown in subcategories under their more generic root causes and are useful in specifying causes and in the later determination of the nature of organizational problems.

The development of the proper understanding of the root cause(s) of the problem starts with a practical operational definition of quality that focuses on a set of measurable characteristics. This is sometimes called "measures of quality" or "quality characteristics." The following list identifies and defines a number of generic dimensions of quality that may assist in the determination of the root cause(s) of the problem at hand (developed by A.V. Feigenbaum and David Garvin):

- *Performance:* Primary operating characteristics
- *Features:* Secondary operating characteristics
- *Time:* Cycle time, time spent waiting, time to complete a task, service, or product
- *Reliability:* The degree of failure-free operations over a certain time period
- *Uniformity:* The state of low variation among system components or repeated outcomes of a certain process
- *Flexibility:* The ability to adapt, customize, or accommodate changes
- *Durability:* The amount of repeated use before a replacement is preferred to a repair
- *Serviceability:* The degree of resolution of problems and complaints
- *Usability:* The ergonomic relationship to the logical and natural use of a product or service
- *Aesthetics:* Relating to the senses, such as color, taste, fragrance, fit, or finish
- *Personal interface:* Such as punctuality, professionalism, courtesy
- *Consistency:* The degree of fit with standards, documentation
- *Perceived quality:* The inferences about reputation and other dimensions
- *Harmlessness:* The relationship to safety, health, or the environment

The suggested use of the above dimensions of quality is to develop scenarios around input from customers and then compare these measures against the list, using the fourteen dimensions as categories for investigating the possible root causes of the problem in terms of customer needs and wants. Root cause codes can then be developed for a small number of the items on the list. Although all or many of the dimensions may seem to apply, the problem solvers must focus on a small number of critical items to arrive at a proper understanding of the possible root causes.

Table of typical root cause codes

- Training
- Qualifications
- Work practices
- Organization
- Planning

- Communications
- Supervision
- Management methods
- Resource allocation
- Change management
- Physical conditions
- Ergonomics/machine-person interface
- Design
- Purchased product
- Manufacturing
- Installation
- Operation
- Maintenance
- Testing
- Documentation
- External
- Other

Develop opportunity/problem statement and project

Use brainstorming, cause-and-effect diagrams, or the structure tree to develop a list of possible causes. Begin by defining the problem and then generate ideas as to the cause. To begin building the project scorecard and get at the root cause, you need to ask the question, "What is the cause of the cause?" For instance, if some manufactured parts are defective, find out why—maybe it's because of a supplier problem. Keep asking "Why?" until the team can't think of another question to ask.

When the team has determined what it thinks the root causes are, it should verify the conclusions with data. The team should think about why it's collecting data and what data it needs to verify the conclusions. It's easy to draw the wrong conclusions from erroneous data. Use charts and graphs to analyze the data and have the conclusions checked by others who are knowledgeable in the process. If there are obvious root causes that can be fixed easily, then fix them immediately.

Clearly state the 5Ws and 2Hs of the opportunity/problem—what, why, where, who, when, how, and how much—of a proposed improvement project. The goal is to ensure that all data collectors look at the problem in the same way by removing ambiguity and reducing variation in the scorecard measurements. The more specific the definition is, the better the definition. Plan on refining the problem statement after you try it out.

The SST should verify that the defined root causes are the true root causes. This is best done by controlling the insertion of the root cause into the process and verifying that it causes the problem to occur. This is usually done by running a controlled experiment where items are processed together with and without the suspected root cause inserted.

Tollgate No. 8 review

At tollgate No. 8, the SST will present its root cause report along with an explanation of how it reached its conclusions. If the EC is satisfied that the list identifies the major root cause(s), it will approve the SST to start phase IV.

SUMMARY

During the analyze phase, the SST works with the data collected during the measure phase and condenses them into meaningful charts, graphs, and reports so that the root causes of the problems and improvement opportunities are identified.

■ Phase III objectives:

☐ Analyze the measurement data.

☐ Validate the process flowchart/maps.

☐ Develop cause-and-effect hypotheses.

☐ Determine and validate root causes.

Figure 8.4 provides an overview of the highlights that occur during the analyze phase.

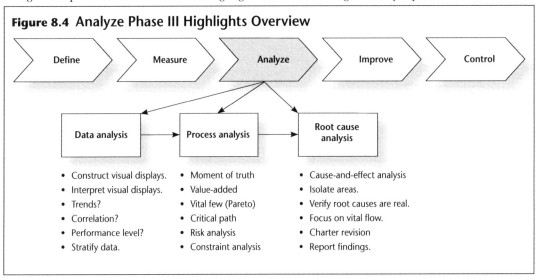

Figure 8.4 Analyze Phase III Highlights Overview

"Treat the symptom and the problem will be put to bed only to wake up later.
Treat the root cause and the problem will be buried, never to come back."

—HJH

CHAPTER 9

THE SIX SIGMA IMPROVE PHASE

"A good solution poorly implemented can be
worse than no solution at all."

—HJH

The primary purpose of the Six Sigma define-measure-analyze-improve-control (DMAIC) improve phase is to develop, pilot test, and evaluate the solutions developed from the data during analyze phase. Using tollgate No. 9 (generate solutions) and tollgate No. 10 (select/test solutions), the team prioritizes and generates solutions and performs a cost-benefit analysis of proposed solutions. Next, it selects the solution, assesses the related risks, and operates a pilot program to ensure that the chosen solution works. Implementation can be run in three phases: original test, pilot, and full-scale. The final step is deploying the implementation; planning the tasks and subtasks; planning when, where, and who is involved; and identifying the resources needed. These steps are part of the control phase.

It's during the control phase that the recommended solutions are installed. During the improve phase, a pilot implementation plan is developed and implemented, beginning with a pilot program and culminating in full-scale, organizationwide deployment during the next phase. Where appropriate, new technology is implemented, workflows are streamlined, paper-based processes are eliminated, and consulting services are initiated. Key factors of success during the last two phases often include involvement of the information technology (IT) organization, acceptance by end users, and organizationwide change without any degradation of current productivity levels.

This phase is often the most fun; it can also be the most demanding and difficult. After root causes are determined in the analyze phase, the Six Sigma team (SST) finds new improvement solutions. More often than not, simple process experimentation and simulation bring the SST big gains in this step.

After requirements, awareness, and sponsorship are secured, implementation can begin. As the majority of implementation content is in both physical and electronic formats, the team may need to recommend the purchase of new software and hardware. In these cases, the selection of a single-vendor, integrated solution is highly recommended, though specialized "point" solutions may be required to address specific requirements not offered by the integrated solution. Involvement of the IT organization (i.e., those involved with server, network, storage, security, and e-mail infrastructure components) is a requirement at this stage if new software is required. An initial pilot implementation—based on work done in previous phases—should focus on business areas that are most exposed, subject to immediate compliance mandates, or seeking to minimize risks associated with current organizational practices.

Overlaps and territorial lines of business interest will arise at this step, because corporate involvement is highlighted across many parts of the organization. The SST should expect to spend time working with end users on system ergonomics (e.g., interfaces and procedures) and the creation of indices and taxonomies established for organizationwide use. Audits should be performed against key groups participating in the project, and evaluations should address redundancies, inefficiencies, and complementary technologies. The team should identify the maximum acceptable ranges of the key variables and validate a system for measuring deviations of the variables, then modify the process to stay within the acceptable range.

INTRODUCTION TO THE SIX SIGMA IMPROVE PHASE

This chapter will provide the reader with an understanding of the activities that take place during the two tollgates that make up the DMAIC improve phase:
■ Tollgate No. 9: Generate the solutions.
■ Tollgate No. 10: Select/test the solutions.

The Yellow Belt tools that are most often used during the improve phase are:
■ Brainstorming
■ Cause-and-effect diagrams
■ Cost-benefit analysis
■ Flowcharting
■ Force-field analysis
■ Gantt charts
■ Nominal group technique
■ PERT charts
■ Planning tools brainstorming

THE PURPOSE OF THE SIX SIGMA IMPROVE PHASE

The purpose of the improve phase is to define what action should be taken to bring about the changes required to meet the targeted improvements defined in the team charter. Once the proposed changes are defined, they will be tested in a pilot application to verify that the estimated improvements produce the desired results. The SST will also prepare a cost-benefit analysis and an implementation plan. The solutions will be implemented during the control phase.

TOLLGATE NO. 9: GENERATE SOLUTIONS

The purpose of this tollgate's activities is to develop and evaluate creative solutions that will significantly (not incrementally) reduce or eliminate the problem. It also identifies the approaches that will most significantly reduce or eliminate the root cause(s). It's also to express the financial effect of a selected improvement approach that addresses the root cause and the implications of the solution.

Overview

Thanks to the analyze phase in the DMAIC cycle, the root causes of failure have been uncovered and analyzed. In the improve phase, the SST gleans the important bits of data and begin to develop ingenious solutions. One by one, the improve phase addresses the root causes for failure, brainstorms solutions, and implements new processes for improving product design and manufacturing.

In the improve phase, the SST feverishly seeks out the possibilities, looking for the budding solutions hidden in every problem. This phase is broken down into five steps:

1. Use the data from the analyze phase to brainstorm innovative solutions.
2. Explore the effect these solutions potentially have, including value and cost benefit, process benefit, and customer satisfaction.
3. Use the solution design matrix to pinpoint the solution that will have the greatest effect. (This is a tool that the Black Belt will show the SST how to use.)
4. Ensure that the chosen solution is mistake proof.
5. Develop a corrective final solution that is pilot tested to ensure effectiveness.

When people are faced with problems, they often grasp at the first reasonable solution that presents itself. However, the first idea may not be the best, and it might not work out at all. The key is to generate as many alternatives as you can; go beyond the obvious solutions and come up with many ideas. A quick way to gather many alternative solutions is to conduct a brainstorming session with your management team. With more people involved, it's more likely that the best solution will emerge. Because different people have different perspectives, they may come up with alternatives that would never have entered your mind. You can also encourage your group to build on each other's suggestions and work together to come up with creative solutions to the problem. Brainstorming creative solutions to the causes of failure can sometimes twist and turn into a convoluted exercise.

Remember that you reserve the right to make the final decision. The solution design matrix will ensure that innovation stays in motion, on track, and pumped with creative juices.

Using the root cause to correct the problems

Defining the root cause(s) of the problem(s) is required to permanently correct them. The SST will prioritize the list of root causes based on each estimated effect upon the problems or improvement opportunity being addressed. This prioritization is often just major classifications, such as high, medium, or low because at this point in the process, it's just the SST's best estimate of what the individual root cause's effect will have on the improvements. Brainstorm and record a list of potential improvement opportunities for each root cause. Using the list of improvement opportunities, reduce the list for each root cause to a few creative improvement solutions.

The SST should then analyze options to select the best ones using narrowing/screening techniques. One improvement opportunity can correct a number of root causes. Keep this interaction in mind as you note down the improvement opportunities for each root cause. Often a matrix of root causes vs. improvement opportunities is an effective way of visualizing these interactions. (See figure 9.1.)

Select the group of improvement opportunities that the SST estimates will produce the required transformation to meet the project objectives. The SST will then evaluate the effect and cost of implementing each improvement opportunity. Next, the SST will estimate the effect each improvement opportunity will have on the project's goals. It will also estimate the cost and cycle time related to implementing each of the improvement opportunities.

Figure 9.1 Root Cause/Improvement Opportunity Matrix

Improvement Opportunities	Root Causes								
	1								
1.	X								
2.									
3.	X								
4.									
5.									

Mistake proofing

Wouldn't it be ideal if mistakes were impossible, particularly when you consider that 20 percent of the failures in a product or process are responsible for 80 percent of poor performance? Mistake proofing is a process used to ensure that mistakes don't happen again. Detection and prevention are used in the improve phase to remove all potential for human error. Examples of brilliant mistake-proofing ideas include bar codes, spell check, color codes, electric door locks, and optical readers. A technique called negative analysis can be used to help identify mistake-proofing ideas.

Now that the analyze phase has exposed all the causes for failure, it's up to the improve phase to make "lemonade out of lemons." The improve phase seeks out and identifies ingenious opportunities in every troublesome nook and cranny. Creative solutions abound, implementation is mistake-proofed, and Six Sigma moves design and manufacturing closer perfection.

Common Mistakes to Avoid During Idea Generation

Mistake	Suggested approach
Too few alternative solutions are generated.	• Keep brainstorming until people have genuinely run out of ideas. • Be a positive force, with comments like, "Great stuff," "Let's keep going," and "This is a big help." • Make sure every idea, no matter how far-fetched, is listened to and written down.
Ideas are evaluated as they are generated; this may lead to good ideas being rejected too quickly.	• At the start, tell the group that you're looking for every possible idea, no matter how silly or unlikely it may seem at first. • Ask the group to hold off on commenting, either negatively or positively, until lots of ideas have been generated.
A dominant person takes over and inhibits other people from suggesting alternatives.	• Don't criticize a dominant person, as that will discourage other quieter people from speaking up. • Call on a quiet person by name, asking for his or her ideas. • Have each person speak in turn.

After generating ideas, the SST should compare the estimated improvements to the goals set in the team charter if the selected improvement opportunities will meet the goals.

The SST will then create an improvement proposal. This proposal will define the improvement and action that the SST suggests should be taken to meet the project goals. It will also include a rough estimate of the cost and cycle time required to make the transformation. This estimate should be in error by no more than 20 percent.

Tollgate No. 9 review

By the time the SST reaches this activity in the improve phase, it has generated a list of potential improvements based on the root causes that were developed during the analyze phase. The executive committee will want to discuss the effect each of these improvements will have on the assigned problem or improvement opportunity. It will also want to know how difficult it will be to install each change and what effect it will have on the morale of the employees. When the executive committee is satisfied with the proposed preliminary solutions, it will close out tollgate No. 9.

TOLLGATE NO. 10: SELECT/TEST SOLUTIONS

The purpose of the select/test solutions tollgate activities is to design the most efficient and effective work process that improves the value of the products and services, and includes the identified corrective action to the causes of the problem. In other words, to make changes in the process that result in improvement from the viewpoints of the stakeholders and meet the goals defined in the team charter.

Overview

Once tollgate No. 10 is reached, the hardest part of the project is finished. The team has identified the problem, determined its root cause, and generated numerous alternative solutions with the help of the Six Sigma advisor and others. Now it will select the best alternative. To do this, the SST will select the improvement opportunities that have the highest probability of making the needed improvements. It's important to note that improvement opportunities may overlap, and as a result, they are not always additive. For example, if improvement opportunity A (IOA) renders a 10-percent improvement and improvement opportunity B (IOB) renders a 15-percent improvement for the same measurement, implementing both IOA and IOB will produce an approximate 15-percent improvement, not necessarily a 25-percent improvement (IOA 10% + IOB 15%). It's during this step that the SST will combine the selected improvement opportunities together to estimate the impact on the goals that were set forth during the preparation of the charter.

Estimating improvement can be a tricky business. There are many factors that need to be considered. Financial estimates should be validated by the financial department, and work-effort reduction estimates should be validated by the affected manager before they are presented to the executive committee. If the SST is estimating that the solution will reduce workload in a department by thirty hours per week, that's the equivalent to the elimination of one employee's job. In this case, the affected manager should have his or her department reduced by one employee and the department budget adjusted accordingly. If this doesn't occur, there are no savings.

The SST will then test its solutions to be sure that the estimated improvements are correct. This will require the solutions to be systematically piloted usually using a control sample to validate the findings. The SST will need to develop a plan to pilot the solution to be sure that the proposed solution results in the required improvement. It's often best to evaluate one improvement opportunity at a time so its effect on the total process can be measured. Sometimes, one improvement opportunity has a negative effect on other measurements, and if all the improvement opportunities are evaluated together, this negative effect may not be recognized. (See figure 9.2.)

In figure 9.2 improvement opportunities one, two, four, and five have positive effects on cycle time, but improvement opportunity three had a negative effect. If all five improvement opportunities were evaluated at the same time, improvement opportunity three's negative effect wouldn't have been identified.

If the solution is complicated or requires a lot of work to implement the pilot, the team might want to prepare an action plan outlining the necessary steps

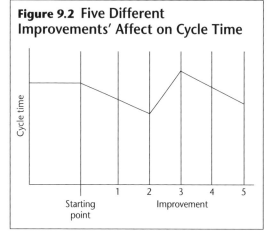

Figure 9.2 Five Different Improvements' Affect on Cycle Time

to be taken. This plan should indicate who is responsible for each action and the target date for completing it. You might want to include the resources the person responsible will have and any other information that will be helpful when implementing your solution.

One final point: Be sure that the team revisits the action plan to ensure that the people responsible are performing their duties as planned.

Analyzing the pilot data

Pilot Steps

	What action?	By whom?	By when?	What resources?
1.				
2.				
3.				

As you implement the pilot project, be sure to run the control sample along with the improved process approach. Special evaluations almost always cause employees to work more diligently, which can skew the SST's perception of the processes. We have seen situations in which the control sample outperformed the improvement sample, completely eliminating the improvement approach. Here again, the data must be professionally collected to ensure that they are accurate and can be effectively analyzed. As much care should be taken during this step as was taken during the measurement phase. You must have good data to base your recommendation for change to the executive committee.

Once the data are collected, the control sample and the improved sample should be compared. The individual improvement opportunities should be evaluated separately. This allows the effect of each improvement opportunity to be defined, along with the total effect of the combination of all the changes.

Adjust the results to consider the long-term drift. It's important to note that the pilot is a one-time slot database and doesn't reflect the drift over time. Often, the measurements made during the measurement phase reflect long-term drift. The normal reporting system used by management to measure performance reflects long-term drift. As a result, the SST needs to downgrade the results of the pilot by at least ±1.5 sigma to account for the long-term drift. The result of this analysis will be a set of improvement opportunities that effectively match together to provide a change in the key measurements that would meet the goals set forth in the charter.

Perform a cost-benefit analysis

After the SST has made a preliminary selection of the changes it wants to make, it will perform a final cost-benefit analysis of each solution and the combined solutions. This will include its best estimate of the cost to implement the solution, the resources required, and the benefits that will result from implementing the solutions.

Implementation plan

The SST will also prepare a preliminary implementation plan. The plan will be part of an update to the project plan. It will include a definition of the proposed solutions, the cost-benefit analysis, the cycle time required, and any risk related to the implementation. It will also include recommendations about any changes the SST feels are needed to implement the solutions and a budget for the control phase.

The implementation plan and the updated project plan will be submitted to the executive committee for its approval. When it's approved, the project will move into the control phase.

Tollgate No. 10 review

During this critical review, the SST will present to the executive committee the following:
- A review of the approach it used to select the recommended changes
- The estimated effect each change will have on key measurements
- The result of the pilot activities
- The implementation plan

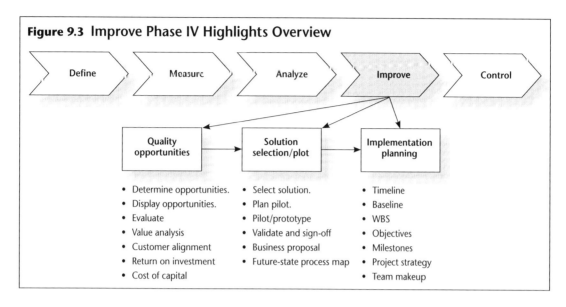

Figure 9.3 Improve Phase IV Highlights Overview

- An updated project plan
- An estimate of the cost and time to complete the implementation of the changes
- An estimated ROI

When the executive committee approves the improvement plan and the implementation plan, tollgate No. 10 is complete, and the SST will start on the control phase.

SUMMARY

During the improve phase, the SST analyzed the root causes and defined actions that could be implemented to offset the defined root causes. The SST then analyzed these proposed actions to define which had the best chance of correcting the assigned problem(s). The proposed solutions were then piloted to measure their effect on the problem(s). Based on the pilot, a cost-benefit analysis was conducted to define a final list of recommended solutions. The project plan was updated to include an implementation plan. The major output from the improve phase is the updated project plan, the implementation plan, and an approved budget to complete the project.

- Phase IV objectives:
  - ☐ Identify improvement solutions.
  - ☐ Quantify improvement solutions.
  - ☐ Select the best solution.
  - ☐ Design the future-state solution.
  - ☐ Perform a cost-benefit analysis.
  - ☐ Pilot the individual solutions.
  - ☐ Gain approval to implement the future-state solution.
  - ☐ Update project plan.

Figure 9.3 provides an overview of the highlights of the improve phase.

"There is nothing quite as rewarding as solving a difficult problem."
—HJH

CHAPTER 10

THE SIX SIGMA CONTROL PHASE

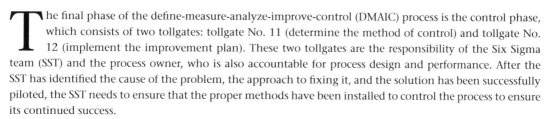

"If you don't 'control the fix,' you will be solving the same
problem over and over and over and over again."

—HJH

The final phase of the define-measure-analyze-improve-control (DMAIC) process is the control phase, which consists of two tollgates: tollgate No. 11 (determine the method of control) and tollgate No. 12 (implement the improvement plan). These two tollgates are the responsibility of the Six Sigma team (SST) and the process owner, who is also accountable for process design and performance. After the SST has identified the cause of the problem, the approach to fixing it, and the solution has been successfully piloted, the SST needs to ensure that the proper methods have been installed to control the process to ensure its continued success.

The solution also needs to be documented and standardized in training manuals and training curriculum; the operating procedures need to be prepared. An improvement plan process chart is used to document how standards are maintained. The chart has the product or program name, process name and code, date of issue, the issuer, who gave approval, revision date, reason for revision, and a signature. The improvement plan should also include a flowchart that shows the plan and what needs to be done. Each step will have its own work instructions, control and check points, and output requirements.

The SST needs to define the upper and lower control limits, process change management, and the evaluation of project results. In the control phase, tools are put in place to ensure that the key variables remain within the maximum acceptable ranges over time. At the point of enterprisewide implementation, the SST must collaborate with the organization's multiple lines of business and affected subsidiaries; this collaboration should address various enterprise-content applications, including data imaging, document management, and enterprise resource planning (ERP), etc. Further, any new content-related initiatives must include input from enterprise records management. After enterprise processes are developed and implemented, their refinement, enhancement, expansion, and auditing should be initiated. This includes quantifying value in the form of reduced risks, increased discovery and production, and avoidance of fines and penalties.

Success in this phase depends upon how well the team did in the previous four phases. If it used proper change management methods—starting with identifying key stakeholders—it should be on its way to success. In the control phase, tools are put in place to ensure that the key variables remain within the acceptable ranges over time so that process improvement gains are maintained. The team develops a project hand off process, reaction plans, and training materials to guarantee performance and long-term project savings. Finally, the team identifies what the next steps are for future Six Sigma process improvement opportunities.

Audits should be performed against all groups involved in and affected by the Six Sigma project; evaluations should address redundancies, inefficiencies, and complementary technologies. The next step is to place the necessary controls to ensure that improvements are maintained for the long term. This involves monitoring and publicizing key process metrics to promote continuous improvement and to guard against regression. In many cases, it's wise to revisit the implementation after three to six months to review key metrics and evaluate if the initial progress has been sustained.

A common practice is to put key metrics into service-level agreements. These are kept in full view to provide continuous feedback to the organization and enable decision makers to assess the level of success as the project moves forward. Managing implementation and control should, at this point, be an enterprisewide endeavor with diverse teams formed to work on structures and solutions. These team members, from backgrounds as varied as quality assurance or control, legal, finance, human resources, information technology, engineering, production, auditing, and records management, need a standard approach or model that can be understood and applied in a systematic way. After the project is closed, a lessons-learned document is prepared covering the results, what was learned, and recommendations for future actions.

INTRODUCTION TO THE SIX SIGMA CONTROL PHASE

This chapter will provide the reader with an understanding of the activities that take place during the two tollgates that make up the DMAIC control phase:
■ Tollgate No. 11—Determine the methods of control
■ Tollgate No. 12—Implement the response plan

The tools that are most often used during the control phase are:
■ Brainstorming
■ Checklists
■ Control charts
■ Flowcharts
■ Histograms
■ Implementation checklists
■ Implementation training matrices
■ Nominal group technique
■ Operational definitions
■ Pareto charts
■ Process capability analysis
■ Project planning worksheets
■ Project scorecards
■ Run charts
■ Sampling plans

The purpose of the Six Sigma control phase

The purpose of the control phase is to make improvements in the process and install the required controls that will maintain the improvements, while providing ongoing feedback about how the process is performing. This control system will also be used to measure the degree of improvement that resulted from the changes. The control system will also prepare the process to begin a continuous improvement phase conducted by the people that work within the process.

TOLLGATE NO. 11: DETERMINE METHODS OF CONTROL

To ensure that the team's improvements stick, process control plans are developed according to the amount of throughput that goes through the new process, along with how much standardization the new process has. The intent of a process control plan is to control the product characteristics and the associated process variables to ensure process capability and the stability of its output over time. The process' failure mode and effects analysis (FMEA) identifies the risks associated with something potentially going wrong in the production of the product that creates a defect. The FMEA identifies what controls are placed in the production process to catch any defects at various stages on the processing. Every completed Six Sigma project should have not only a control chart (if applicable), but a process control plan. This ensures that the process doesn't revert to the way it previously operated.

Overview

Inputs from the improve phase, including the improvement plan and budget, trigger the beginning of the control phase. The control phase is where the "rubber meets the road." It measures the SST's effectiveness at developing improvement solutions that are capable of bringing about the changes defined in the team charter. The SST starts phase V by completing an approved implementation plan and budget. Often, the makeup of the SST has changed at this point to include individuals that will be making the required changes to the process.

Most modern quality practitioners understand that quality cannot be inspected into products; quality must be designed into the products and services and built into processes. Once this is done, process control can be used to ensure that products meet or exceed customers' expectations. The process control plan documents a company's strategy for a specific product or service, or both. This plan systematically describes the process flow, operating procedures, control points, product or process specifications, test methods, and contingency plans. It can be developed with the following steps:

1. Management commits.
2. Personnel are instructed in statistical process control (SPC) and continuous improvement.
3. The team commits to following the Six Sigma 6-Principle method:
   - Define the product and output objectives for the product.
   - Describe the process.
   - Develop a control strategy.
   - Determine if the process variation is predictable and if the process is capable of meeting all standards and specifications.
   - Implement the control plan.
   - Maintain the quality control plan and continuously improve the system.

Only by developing and implementing a comprehensive plan can management be assured that processes will meet performance requirements which result in producing products and delivering services with the quality levels customers expect, as defined by the critical-to-quality (CTQ) characteristics.

How control plans work

Process control plans describe the actions required at each step in the process to ensure that all process outputs will remain controlled. During regular production runs, process control plans provide the process monitoring and control methods used to control part or product characteristics. During product development, the plan is used to document and communicate the initial plan for process control. During production, it guides manufacturing in how to control the process and ensure product quality. The process control plan is updated as the design changes, the process changes, and as control methodologies are improved. Process control plans are conceptually similar to the fourth phase of quality function deployment (QFD).

Technically speaking, the process control plan sets requirements that ensure the organization delivers products and services as promised. Specific quality control procedures are included and the plan is reviewed annually, updated and expanded as necessary, and refined. The plan should be developed in conformance to American National Standards Institute (ANSI) requirements and in accordance with ISO 9001, if possible. This will ensure consistency and effectiveness of the quality assurance operations. Thus, the process control plan documents the controls implemented on a particular process to ensure the resulting product meets or exceeds expected quality measures. It improves overall quality and productivity by reducing process variation. Ideally, it will also show the correlation between the process controls and improved overall quality and productivity through reduced process variation and increased customer satisfaction.

Formulate and issue new policies resulting from solution implementation

The change should now be documented in the related paperwork (e.g., operating procedures, set-up instructions, training requirements, and specifications). The measurement and reporting systems must be designed so that appropriate people are informed through the use of appropriate dashboards and exception reports. The improvement plan should be scheduled so that solutions are grouped so that the effect of each solution can be evaluated. Sometimes the pilot program does not totally reflect the performance of a normal operating unit. As a result, the pilot results should be validated during the control phase.

It's usually necessary to include a two-level measurement system. Level one is very comprehensive, as it's used to measure the effectiveness of the improvement program. It includes many secondary effects measurements that are important during start up, training, and implementation. This measurement system is used until the process has stabilized and historical data are available related to variation. Once this is accomplished, a more relaxed system can be used to maintain the process performance. This more-relaxed system typically will rely on control charts to adjust the process before it goes out of control, with exception reporting used to indicate positive and negative trends.

The process control plan and implementation plan are reviewed with the executive committee (EC) to obtain its concurrence related to how they are integrated to provide the organization with a high degree of confidence that the data that are collected will be adequate to validate the success or failure of the project. The EC will also wave assurance that adequate controls are in place that will contain any gains that are made.

With the control phase in full swing, an organization can permanently eliminate the roadblocks that have previously made improvement difficult. Monitoring plans, standardized processes, documented procedures, and response plans are all implemented to keep problems in their rightful places. This is important to note because the control phase is vulnerable to process slippage. As a result, impeccably designed control systems are crucial and the effectiveness of these systems must be continually challenged.

The key deliverables in the control phase are:
- Updated processes, standards, and procedures
- Training as needed
- Process control plan
- Control metrics
- Communication of success stories
- Team evaluation

Executing change requires that the new discipline for the work process can be established and maintained. Developing this discipline and transitioning the new process into routine operation are the objectives of the DMAIC control process. Two aspects of control that must be addressed are business and process control.

Business control vs. process control

A system for management of daily activities that integrates business controls with process controls needs to be developed that delivers the desired outcomes in a consistent, predictable manner. These controls ensure constancy of purpose in an organization's direction and consistency of critical work activities. The business controls and process controls must be complementary to establishing a practical and efficient daily management system. Business controls define an organization's shared system of management. They describe the rights and authorities for taking action in an organization and define its system of governance. Effective business control requires organizations to:

- Set the direction and strategy for the organization.
- Define responsibilities for oversight of the organization.
- Allocate decision rights and spending authority.
- Manage work processes to accomplish the sub-tasks that deliver the strategy.
- Review results and act to correct the organization so it stays focused on its goals.
- Adapt dynamically to changing circumstances.
- Evaluate performance and hold people accountable for delegated responsibilities.

Process controls are applied to manage the routine work of an organization; they define how work is done and the set of tasks and activities that collectively deliver performance results.

The fundamental skills of process management include:

- Make process steps visible and specify what is required to deliver process results.
- Measure process performance at each step that influences performance.
- Optimize flow and production by eliminating bottlenecks, decreasing set-up and waiting times, and assuring repeatable quality.
- Evaluate progress to ensure achievement of common direction and shared goals.

Measurement is critical to process control, as it indicates potential defects in the system, identifies places where the process is inefficient (too much time or resource consumed), and focuses people on improving areas where significant opportunities exist for performance improvement (defect, cost, or cycle time reduction). Process measures provide early warning of potential customer problems and contribute to process controls that ensure reliability in the routine activities of a business. By discovering the sources of process variation and determining how to control them, an organization uses its business and process control systems to drive performance gains. Sustained success occurs when root causes of problems are eliminated from work and statistical controls are integrated into the management system. Sustained success requires sound management of daily work processes.

Report scorecard data and create a process control plan

Teams sometimes use scorecard data to visually demonstrate the effect of a project's countermeasures and to create or revise the process control plan. The plan helps to deploy Six Sigma across large work forces and to coach groups through the major quality control processes. In ordinary systems, the data are dead until someone interprets them. In Six Sigma deployment, data are alive and direct the use of the process control plan.

Establishing control

The control process begins with the improvement factors identified in the improve phase and converts these improvements into an action plan for control that is measured, monitored, and managed by the organization. The following activities transition the improvement recommendations into reality:

- Develop a long-term measurement system that is effective for controlling processes, assuring business control, and delivering performance results.
- Define standard work and operating procedures that evaluate progress and maintain the work system in the most efficient and effective manner.
- Mistake proof and safeguard the work process to ensure that opportunities to make errors are eliminated or mitigated by preventing these problems from escaping the process activities and affecting customers.
- Document and train workers in the new process to assure that everyone understands it and has the skills necessary to perform it.

The key for creating a manufacturing control system is a process control plan that describes what must be controlled to maintain quality, what measures indicate that the process is maintained under control, the sample size that must be taken to determine that control is being effectively maintained, the decision rules for evaluating these samples, and the countermeasures to be employed whenever a sample indicates that an out-of-control condition exists.

The process control plan is based on the original failure study of the process and the findings of the improve process that dictate the mechanism for work process control. The plan is the key document that links the process control mechanisms to the business control and accountability system of management reviews.

Tollgate No. 11 review

The EC will conduct the tollgate No. 11 review, and the SST will present the control plan and an updated implementation plan. It will also present the updated project plan for tollgate No. 12. A detailed review of the implementation cost, cycle time, resources, and improvement projection will be made. This is the last change that the EC will have to kill the project, so it should be very thorough in its review. It is a good practice to have members of the SST sit down with key individuals on the EC to answer any questions they may have ahead of time.

This review provides the EC with an understanding of how the new process will be controlled to minimize out-of-control conditions and to maintain process improvements. Based upon the results of this review, the final decision will be made to implement the changes. When this review is completed successfully, the SST will start tollgate No. 12.

TOLLGATE NO. 12: IMPLEMENT THE IMPROVEMENT PLAN

Installing the improvement plan and implementing controls are the most complex parts of the DMAIC cycle. People need to be prepared to accept new ways of operating; they will need to be trained and they will need to understand how they fit into the new process. If productivity is improved, the organization needs a plan on how to handle surplus employees. As improvements are implemented, they need to be evaluated to ensure that they have no negative effects. In addition, records of the cost of installation and improvement savings need to be collected so that a true cost/benefits analysis can be conducted.

Overview

As the SST prepares to start to implement the improved process, the first critical step is to train the affected employees related to their new responsibilities and activities. This can be difficult; employees who are faced with a situation where they have to change behavior patterns will generally resist. The SST needs to work closely with the affected individuals to help them understand why it is important for them to embrace the proposed solutions.

Care must be taken to continuously monitor the key measurements as the solution is being implemented. Be sure that the data are being collected correctly and analyzed regularly. Carefully monitor control charts because long-term drift needs to be considered in drawing final conclusions. Remember that when a complex solution is implemented, there maybe a short-term negative effect while individuals are progressing through the learning curve.

The SST should develop a list of opportunities that the team could not address. Often a number of excellent improvement opportunities are identified directly or indirectly related to the project, but were outside the scope of the project. At this point the SST should document the list of all the opportunities that should be considered for future projects or future corrective actions. The list should be presented to the EC during the tollgate No. 12 review.

Tollgate No. 12 review

If the activities before tollgate No. 12 activities were conducted correctly, this review should be a celebration. During this review, the following items will be discussed:

- Performance of the new process
- Cost of the implementation
- The new process' effect on the customer
- Review of the effect on all the related key performance indicators (KPIs)
- Further opportunities
- Problems that were encountered during the project and how they were handled
- Return on investment

PROJECT CLOSURE

The EC and the champion of the project should at this point reward the SST members for their efforts. The SST should conduct a post mortem reviewing the entire DMAIC process to identify negative and positive aspects of the way the project was conducted. A report of these finding should be prepared and shared with the rest of the organization to help future projects take advantage of the positive activities and avoid the negative activities.

An official final report should be prepared to close out the project and document its results. The organization's Six Sigma champion should collect these final reports and summarize them on a continuous basis to track and report the success of the Six Sigma program to the executive team and the board of directors.

SUMMARY

- The SST has installed the new process and it meets all the project goals. The EC has rewarded the SST for its outstanding effort. As a Yellow Belt, we hope you learned some new ways to tackle the problems you face every day. Don't stop using them just because you are not working on a Six Sigma project. Use the tools that you have learned in your every day work to solve the problems you face. It can give you a head start over the other people you work with. But even better, share what you have learned with the people you work with to help them get better. It will return back to you tenfold.

■ Phase V objectives:

☐ Organize the implementation team.

☐ Prepare the control plan.

☐ Prepare the procedures.

☐ Train the employees.

☐ Implement the solution.

☐ Measure results.

☐ Revise KPIs.

☐ Recognize the SST.

☐ Close out the project.

Figure 10.1 provides an overview of the highlights that occur during the control phase.

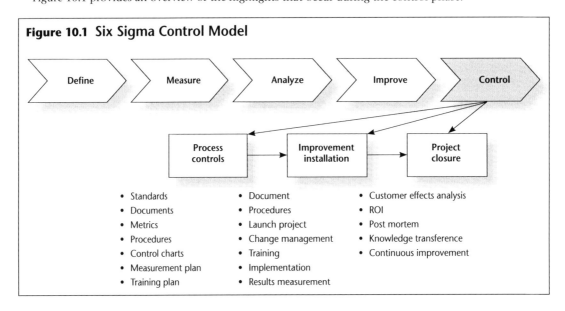

Figure 10.1 Six Sigma Control Model

SUMMARY OF DMAIC

DMAIC is an approach that was first used with Six Sigma systems, and it's an approach that Yellow Belts should master. There are two other approaches that are used in the Six Sigma system:

- Define, measure, analyze, design, verify (DMADV), which is part of design for Six Sigma
- Lean Six Sigma

Yellow Belts may become involved in either or both of these approaches as part of a SST led by a Master Black Belt or a Black Belt, in which cases the team leader will provide you with the required training.

DMAIC is a powerful approach to solve Six Sigma problems, but don't limit your use of it to Six Sigma projects. It works well in solving many of your day-to-day problems.

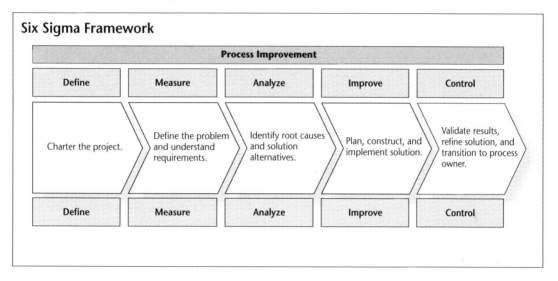

"A job well done is its own reward, but a little money helps."
—HJH

APPENDIX A

GLOSSARY

5W's and 2H's: A structured approach that probes into and defines a problem by asking a specific set of questions related to a previously defined opportunity or problem statement. The 5W's and 2H's stands for:
- What?
- Why?
- Where?
- Who?
- When?
- How did it happen?
- How much did it cost?

Acceptable quality level (AQL): The percentage or proportion of defects or defectives that is considered satisfactory quality performance for a process or product.

Acceptance decisions: The process of making the choice to accept or reject an output based on the risk related to accepting it and/or your evaluation of the output that is provided. Acceptance decision is the highest number of nonconforming units or defects found in a sample that permits the acceptance of the lot.

Accumulative distribution function: The area beneath the probability density function to the left of X.

Activity-based costing (ABC): A technique for accumulating product cost by determining all costs associated with the activities required to produce the output.

Activity plan: A simple chart that shows a list of implementation activities listed in sequence. It identifies the individual responsible for a particular activity and the projected timing of that activity.

Adaptability: The flexibility of a process to handle future changing customer expectations and special customer requirements.

Advantage/disadvantage technique: Lists of advantages and disadvantages of each proposed solution are made and the solution with the most favorable ratio of advantages to disadvantages is assumed to be the best solution.

Advocate: An individual/group that wants to achieve change but does not have sufficient sponsorship.

Affinity diagrams: A technique for organizing a variety of subjective data (such as options) into categories based on the intuitive relationships among individual pieces of information. It is often used to find commonalties among concerns and ideas.

Appraisal costs: The costs that result from evaluating already-completed output and auditing the process to measure compliance to established criteria and procedures.

Area activity analysis (AAA): A proven approach used by natural work teams (areas) to establish efficiency and effectiveness measurement systems, performance standards, improvement goals, and feedback systems that are aligned with the organization's objectives and understood by the employees involved.

Area graphs: Convenient methods of showing how 100 percent of something is apportioned. The most commonly used area graph is the pie chart.

Arrow diagrams: A way to define the most effective sequence of events and control the activity in order to meet a specific objective in a minimum amount of time. It is an adaptation of the program evaluation and review technique (PERT) or the critical path method (CPM).

Assumption evaluation: Provides a way of redefining problem statements, analyzing solutions, and generating new ideas.

Attributes control chart: A plot of attributes data of some parameter of a process' performance, usually determined by regular sampling of the product, service, or process as a function (usually) of time or unit numbers or other chronological variables. This is a frequency distribution plotted continuously over time and gives immediate feedback about the behavior of a process. A control chart will have the following elements: center line, upper control limit, and lower control limit.

Attributes data: This is counted data that can be classified as either yes/no, accept/reject, black/white, or go/no-go. This data is usually easy to collect because it requires only counting instead of measuring the process, but it often requires large samples.

Automation: The use of robots, machinery, or software to eliminate repetitive and boring jobs previously done by people.

Average incoming quality (AIQ): The average quality level going into an inspection point.

Average outgoing quality (AOQ): The average quality level leaving an inspection point when the rejected parts have been removed.

Axiomatic design: This approach provides a framework of principles that guide the design engineers of products, services, or processes. It reduces the complexity of the design process. Its purpose is to make designers more creative by reducing the random search process, thereby minimizing the trial and errors that are made during the design process.

Bar graphs: Graphs in which horizontal bars or vertical columns, by their height or length, show variations in the magnitude of measurements.

Bathtub curve: A picture of an item's failure vs. rate time.

Bell-shaped curve: The shape of a normal distribution curve.

Benchmark: A reference point for which other items can be compared.

Best practice: A process or method that is superior to all other known methods.

Best value future-state solution: A solution that results in the most beneficial new item as viewed by the item's stakeholders. It represents the best combination of implementation cost, implementation cycle time, risk, and performance results.

Bivariate distribution: A three-dimensional plot where the X and Y axes represent the independent variables, and the Z axis represents the frequency for discrete data or the probability of continuous data.

Black Belts: Highly trained team leaders responsible for implementing process improvement projects within an organization. They have a deep understanding of statistical methods and have a detailed understanding of how to use DMAIC and DMADV. Black Belts coach Green Belts and receive coaching support from Master Black Belts.

Block diagrams: A pictorial method of showing activity flow through a process, using rectangles connected by a line with an arrow at the end of the line indicating direction of flow, and a short phrase describing the activity is recorded in each rectangle.

Brainstorming: A technique used by a group to quickly generate large lists of ideas, problems, or issues with emphasis on quantity of ideas, not quality.

Budget: Provides the resources required to implement the tactics.

Bureaucracy elimination method: An approach to identify and eliminate checks and balances activities that are not cost justified.

Business case development: An evaluation of the potential effect a problem has on the organization to determine if it is worthwhile to invest resources to correct the problem or take advantage of the opportunity.

Business objective: Defines what the organization wishes to accomplish over the next five to ten years.

Business plan: A communication, planning, and business system that reaches and involves every employee in support of common goals and objectives.

Business process improvement (BPI): A breakthrough methodology that includes process redesign, process reengineering, process benchmarking, and fast-action solution teams.

Cp: See *process capability index.*

Cpk: See *time-related process capability index.*

Calibration: Comparing an instrument or measurement equipment performance to a standard of known accuracy that is usually based on National Institute of Standards and Technology standards.

Cause-and-effect matrix: A tool used to evaluate the net impact of potential Xs vs. various Ys or goals to make a first pass at setting aside potential Xs that are not likely to impact the Ys, thereby eliminating elements that do not have to be statistically evaluated.

Cause-and-effect diagram: A visual presentation of possible causes of a specific problem or condition. The effect is listed on the right side and the causes take the shape of fishbones. It is sometimes called a "fishbone diagram" or an "Ishikawa diagram."

C-charts: Plot the number of defects per sample, with a constant sample size.

Central composite design: Contains an embedded factorial or fractional factorial matrix with a center point augmented with a group of star points that allows the curvature to be estimated. This design contains twice as many star points as there are factors in the design, representing the extreme high and low of each design factor.

Central tendency: A measure of the center of the distribution.

Certification: Applies to a single operation or piece of equipment that's producing products to specification standards. Typically, a Cpk of 1.4 is required to be certified.

Change agent: Individual/group that is responsible for implementing the change.

Changee: Individual/group that must change. A changee is also called a change target.

Checksheet: A simple form on which data is recorded in a uniform manner. The forms are used to minimize the risk of errors and to facilitate the organized collection and analysis of data.

Collecting data: A systematic way of acquiring information about a specific point of interest.

Common cause: A source of errors that is always present because it is part of the random variation in the process.

Communication techniques: The many processes available to deliver and send messages through an organization by various channels, such as e-mail, meetings, gossip, newsletters, etc.

Comparative analysis: A systematic way of comparing an item to another item to identify improvement opportunities and/or gaps.

Competitive benchmarking: A form of external benchmarking that requires investigating a competitor's products, services, and processes and analyzing them to identify competitive advantages.

Confidence limits: A calculated measure of the accuracy of results obtained from pulling a sample of a complete population.

Conflict resolution: An approach to find a win-win solution when two or more parties are in disagreement with each other. It often ends with both parties making compromises.

Consensus: An interactive process involving all group members, where ideas are openly exchanged and discussed until all group members accept and support a decision.

Constants: Independent variables that are deliberately held constant during an experiment.

Continuous flow manufacturing (CFM): A manufacturing system that is set up so there is no buffer between individual activities. The product is continuously moving without going into a storage area.

Control chart: A graphic representation that monitors changes that occur within a process by detecting variation that is inherent in the process and separating it from variation that is changing the process (special causes).

Controllable poor-quality costs: The costs that management has direct control over to ensure that only acceptable products and services are delivered to the customer. It is divided into two subcategories: prevention costs and nonvalue-added costs.

Corrective action: Action that is taken to prevent reoccurrence of a problem.

Correlation coefficient (r): Used to quantify the degree of linear association between two variables. Its value can range from a negative one to a positive one.

Cost driver: Any factor which causes a change in cost of an activity.

Cost of quality: Developed by Val Feigenbaum when he was quality director at a General Electric division in the 1950s and put all the quality-related activities into a single cost base that could be added together. It is made up of four parts: prevention costs, internal defect costs, external defect costs, and appraisal costs.

Cost, quality, features, and availability (CQFA): Customers evaluate and select suppliers based upon the four factors of cost, quality, features, and availability. An organization must excel in one of these to stay on the market. The more of these four factors that an organization excels in, the greater value it provides.

Creative thinking: A methodology designed to stimulate and encourage creativity and innovation within an organization and by individuals.

Critical path methodology: Normally used with a project work breakdown structure where there is one path through the complex process that determines when the process is completed. By identifying this path the project manager can focus on ensuring that cycle time and cost are optimized, thereby minimizing the risk of not completing the budget on schedule.

Critical-to-quality (CTQ): Key measurable characteristics of a product or process that are set to ensure customer satisfaction. They help ensure that improvement activities are in line with internal or external customer requirements.

Cultural roadblocks: Unacceptable behavioral patterns that will have a negative effect upon a project.

Current-state maps: Flow diagrams of the present process as it operats prior to implementing a change.

Customer requirements: Stated or implied terms that the customer requires to be provided in order for him or her to be satisfied.

Customer surveys: Customers' opinions related to the service or products supplied by phone calls, written surveys, focus groups, one-on-one meetings, etc.

Customer-dissatisfaction poor quality costs: Customers buy competitive products because they perceive that the competitor's product is better quality or because the customer has had or knows someone that has had an unsatisfactory experience with the organization.

Customer-incurred poor quality costs: The costs that the customer incurs when a product or service fails to perform to the customer's expectations.

CuSum control charts (cumulative sum): This type of control chart is an alternative to the Shewhart concept of control charts. To create a CuSum chart to collect m sample groups, each the size of an m and compute the X Bar sub i of each sample. Determine Ssubm or S prime subm using the appropriate formulas. CuSum control charts are very effective at discerning shifts in the process mean that are less than 2 sigma.

Cycle time: The time from the point when all of the input has been received by the task until an output has been delivered to the next task.

Cycle time analysis: An approach to reduce the time it takes to move an item through a process.

DMADV: Define-measure-analyze-design-verify is Six Sigma's approach to using data for designing products and processes that are capable of performing at the Six Sigma level.

DMAIC: Define-measure-analyze-improve-control is Six Sigma's version of Shewhart's plan-do-check-act problem analysis technique.

DMEDI: Define-measure-explore-develop-implement is equivalent to the design for Six Sigma approach under a different set of titles.

Decision-making matrix: The team defines the desired results, then makes a list of the criteria that are "givens" (must have) and "wants" (would like to have). The alternative solutions are compared to the "givens" and "wants" list, and a risk analysis is made.

Defects per million opportunities (DPMO): The average number of errors that occur in a million opportunities for error.

Delphi narrowing technique: Team members' priorities are used as guidelines to reduce the list of alternatives to a select few of the most important alternatives.

Dependent variable: A variable that is measured as a result of changes in the independent variables.

Design for maintainability and availability: A methodology and tool set that is directed at analyzing the maintenance of a product to minimize the time to repair it and to maximize its total reliability with the object being to minimize downtime. It involves modular replacement rather than individual component replacement.

Design for manufacturing and assembly (DFMA): A methodology that is used to determine how to design a product for ease of manufacturing. It's usually done by performing concurrent engineering, where manufacturing engineering develops the manufacturing process along with the design.

Design for Six Sigma (DFSS): See DMADV.

Design for X (DFX): An approach in which the design team develops a product or service with as many desirable characteristics as possible, when viewed from the consumers' standpoint. It includes characteristics such as: safety, friendliness, serviceability, reliability, quality, maintainability, cost, and features; and including factors like: safety, quality, reliability, testability, manufacturability, design for assembly, environmental, serviceability, maintainability, repair ability, user-friendliness, ergonomic appearance, packaging, features, and time-to-market.

Design of experiments (DOE): A method that determines the relationship between factors affecting a process and the output of that process. It's a structured evaluation designed to yield the maximum amount of information at a defined confidence level with the least expense.

Direct poor-quality costs: Costs that can be identified in the organization's ledger.

Discrete data: Data that is based on count, and can't be broken down into subdivisions, such as the number of customer complaints that are received per week. It's also referred to as qualitative data.

Effectiveness: The extent to which the output of a process or subprocess meets the needs and expectations of its customers. Effectiveness, or quality, is having the right output at the right place at the right time at the right price.

Efficiency: The extent to which resources are minimized and waste is eliminated in the pursuit of effectiveness.

Equipment certification: An evaluation of each piece of equipment to define its accuracy, repeatability, drift, and capabilities so that it can be matched to product specifications.

Equipment poor-quality costs: The cost invested in equipment used to measure, accept, or control the products or services, the cost of the space the equipment occupies, and its maintenance costs. It also includes any costs related to preparing software to control and operate the equipment.

Error proofing: Designing processes and products so that it is difficult for errors to occur during creation and delivery to customers.

Establish the burning platform: Define why the as-is-process needs to be changed, and prepare a vision that defines how the as-is pain will be lessened by the future-state solution.

Executive error rate reduction (E2R2): A way to establish acceptable executive behavior standards and measure compliance to them.

Experiment: A sequence of trials that consist of independent variables set at pre-designed levels, which lead to measurements and observations of the dependent variables.

Experimental design: The building blocks of process definition, development, and optimization.

Exponential distribution: A process used to model items that consist of failure rates, usually electronic items. It is usually used to model the mean time between occurrences, and measures probability of occurrence per time interval.

External and internal customers: The person who receives the input is the internal customer. External customers are individuals or organizations that are not part of the organization that is producing the product. They typically buy the product for themselves or for distribution.

F test: An evaluation of two samples taken from different populations to determine if they have the same standard deviation at a specific confidence level.

Failure mode and effects analysis: Identifies potential failures or causes of failures that may occur because of process design weaknesses.

Fast action solution technique (FAST): A breakthrough approach that focuses a group's attention on a single process for a one- or two-day meeting to define how the group can improve the process over the next ninety days. Before the end of the meeting, management approves or rejects the proposed improvements.

First-time yield (FTY): The number of good parts that go into an operation divided by the number of acceptable parts going out of the operation without any rework. First-time yield for a total process is calculated by multiplying the first-time yield at each activity by the first-time yield at each activity in the process. It is also called roll-through yield (RTY).

Five Ss (5Ss) or five pillars: A system designed to bring organization to the workplace. It originated in Japan and includes five requirements:
- *Seiri*—Organization
- *Seiton*—Orderliness
- *Seiso*—Cleanliness
- *Seiketsu*—Standardized cleanup
- *Shitsuke*—Discipline

In English, the 5Ss are sort, set in order, shine, standardize, and sustain.

Five whys (5Ws): A technique to get to the root cause of a problem. It requires asking at least five times why the failure has occurred. Each time an answer is given, you ask why that particular condition occurred.

Flowchart: A method of graphically describing an existing process or a proposed new process by using simple symbols, lines, and words to pictorially display the sequence of activities in the process.

FOCUS: An acronym for:
- Find a process to improve.
- Organize an effort to work on improvement.
- Clarify current knowledge of the process.
- Understand process variation and capabilities.
- Select a strategy for continuous improvement.

This process was based on Shewhart's plan-do-check-act approach and was developed by W. Edwards Deming.

Focus groups: A group of people who have a common experience or interest brought together to discuss items being analyzed to define the group's opinion/suggestions related to the item being discussed.

Force-field analysis: A visual aid for pinpointing and analyzing elements which resist change (restraining forces) or push for change (driving forces).

Fractional factorial: An experiment where selected combinations of factors and levels are analyzed. It is useful when a number of potential factors are involved in causing an error to occur because it reduces the total number of runs required to define potential root causes.

Full factorial: An experiment that measures the response of every possible combination of factors and levels and provides information about every main effect and each interacting effect. This is not recommended for five or more factors.

Full factorial design: A design in which every setting of every factor appears with every setting of every other factor. This is not recommended for five or more factors.

Function diagrams: A systematic way of graphically displaying detailed tasks related to broader objectives or detailed issues.

Future-state mapping: Future-state maps are generally produced by flow diagrams or simulation models in which a proposed change is displayed graphically. A resulting simulation model can help predict how effectively the future state will operate.

Gantt chart: A bar chart on its side, typically used for conveying a project schedule.

Gap analysis: A gap analysis is used to compare a present item to a proposed item. It compares efficiency and effectiveness measurements of one product to a competitor's product or one process to another process.

Graeco-Latin design: This design is often useful in eliminating more than two sources of variability in an experiment. This is an extension of the Latin square design with one additional blocking value resulting in a total of three blocking variables.

Graphs: Visual displays of quantitative data that summarize a set of numbers or statistics.

Green Belt: Someone who has been trained in Six Sigma process improvement methodologies and can lead or participate on a process improvement team. Green Belts maintain their full-time positions and perform their Green Belt duties as-needed. They work under the guidance of Black Belts.

Hard consensus: When all members of the team absolutely agree with the outcome or solution.

High-impact team (HIT): A methodology that designs and implements a drastic process change in twelve days.

Histograms: Visual representations of spread or distribution where the values are represented by a series of rectangles or bars of equal class sizes or width. The height of the bars indicates the relative number of data points in each class.

Hoshin kanri: A planning process that is used to annually develop the *hoshin* plan or policy development. It is used to set the direction of the improvement activities within the organization. *Hoshin* is made up of two Chinese words: *ho*, which means "method" or "form," and *shin*, which means "shiny needle" or "compass." *Kanri* means "control" or "management."

House of quality: A matrix format used to organize various data elements, so named for its house-like shape. It is the principle tool of quality function deployment (QFD).

Hypothesis testing: The process of using statistical analysis to determine if the observations that differ between two or more samples are caused by random chance or by true differences in the sample. A null hypothesis (Ho) is a stated assumption that there is no difference in the parameters of two or more populations. The alternate hypothesis (Ha) is a statement that the observed differences or relationships between the populations are real and are not the results of chance or an error in the sampling approach.

Independent variable: An input or process variable that can be set directly to achieve a desired result during an experiment.

Indirect cost: The support costs imposed on outputs that aren't directly related to the cost of the incoming materials or the activities that transform it into an output, such as the cost of accounting, personnel, or ground maintenance.

Indirect poor-quality costs: Costs that are incurred by the customer or that result from the negative effect poor quality has on future business.

Inherent process capability: The range of variation that will occur from the predictable pattern of a stable process.

Initiating sponsor: The individual or group with the power to initiate and legitimize change.

Innovation: The conversion of ideas into tangible products, services, or processes.

Intangible benefits: Gains attributed to an improvement project that are not documented in the formal accounting process. Sometimes called "soft benefits," they are frequently savings that result from preventive action.

Internal error costs: The cost of errors detected before the organization's customer accepts the output.

Interrelationship diagrams: A way to graphically map the cause-and-effect links between related items.

Interviewing: A structured discussion with two or more people to collect information related to a specific subject or person.

ISO 9000 series: A group of standards released by the International Organization for Standardization that define the fundamental building blocks for a quality management system and its associated accreditation and registration.

Information technology (IT) applications: The tools used for performance improvement. They are usually used to eliminate tedious but required jobs and to reduce the potential for errors.

Just-in-time: A strategy that allows an organization to produce only what is needed, when it's needed to satisfy immediate customer requirements. Implemented effectively, the just-in-time concept will almost eliminate in-process stock.

Kanban: A printed card that contains specific information related to parts, such as the part name, number, quantity needed, etc. It is the primary communication used in just-in-time manufacturing and maintains an effective flow of materials through a manufacturing system while minimizing inventory and work in process.

Kaikaku: A revolutionary activity that's similar to process reengineering or redesign.

Kaizen: A Japanese term that means "continuous improvement." *Kai* means "change" and *zen* means "good" or "for the better."

***Kaizen* blitz:** A sudden effort to take a process, system, product, or service apart and put it back together so it's more efficient.

Kano model: A model that was created by Noriaki Kano that classifies customer preferences into five categories: attractive, one-dimensional, must-be, indifferent, and reverse. This model classifies product attributes based on how they are perceived by the customer.

Key performance indicators (KPI): The key performance parameters related to a process, organization, or output. They are the ways by which that item is measured and are usually used to set performance standards and continuous improvement objectives.

Knowledge management: A system for capturing the knowledge of an organization. It groups knowledge into two categories: The first is tacit, or soft knowledge, which is made up of undocumented, intangible factors embodied in an individual's experience. The second is explicit, or hard knowledge, which is documented and quantified.

Kruskal-Wallis one-way analysis: A method of examining differences among a population's medians that offers nonparametric alternatives to the one-way analysis of variance.

Latin square designs: Fractional factorial experiments that require less experimentation to determine the main impacting areas. They are used to allow for two sources of nonhomogeneity in the conditions affecting the test. This approach is limited by two conditions: There should be no interactions between rows and column factors because these can't be measured; and the number of rows, columns, and treatments must be the same.

Lean manufacturing: A focus on eliminating all waste in a manufacturing process. Lean principles include zero inventory, batch to flow, cutting batch size, line balancing, zero wait time, pull instead of push production control systems, and cutting actual process time.

Level (of a variable): The point at which an independent variable is set during a trial.

Line graph: Line graphs display the relationship of one measurement to another over a period of time

Loss function: The mean-square deviation of the object's characteristics from their targeted values. It is used to determine the financial loss that will occur when the quality characteristic deviates from the target value.

Lost-opportunity poor quality costs: Lost profits caused by poor internal performance.

Mean time between failures (MTBF): The average time between mechanical breakdowns.

Machine capability index (Cmk): A short-term index derived from observations from uninterrupted production runs. The preferred Cmk value is greater than 1.67. The long-term index should be greater than 1.33.

Mann-Whitney U test: A hypothesis test used as a nonparametric alternative to the two-sample t-test. It tests the equality of two population medians and calculates the corresponding point estimates and confidence intervals.

Master Black Belt: A Six Sigma expert responsible for the strategic implementation of Six Sigma throughout the organization, training and mentoring Black Belts and Green Belts; conducting complex Six Sigma improvement projects; developing, maintaining, and revising Six Sigma materials; and applying statistical controls to difficult problems.

Matrix diagrams: A way to display data to make it easy to visualize and compare.

Mean: The average data point value within a data set. It's calculated by adding all of the individual data points together, then dividing that figure by the total number of data points.

Measure of dispersion: Dispersion within data is calculated by subtracting the high value from the low value (range).

Measurement error: The error that is inherent in every measurement. Measurement error can be caused by many factors, including human error, equipment precision, and equipment calibration.

Measurement systems analysis: An evaluation of the accuracy of a measurement. There are four characteristics that need to be examined. They are:

- Sensitivity—this should be no greater than one tenth of the total tolerance in the specification being measured
- Reproducibility—the ability of the measurement to repeatedly get the same answer
- Accuracy—how near the true value (the international standard value)
- Precision—the ability to get the same value using the same operator and the same set up

Measurement tools: Any object that is used to compare another object to a set of defined standards. It can be a ruler, a gauge, an oscilloscope, a scale, etc.

Median control charts: Median charts are used when an odd number of readings are made. This makes their median value more obvious. Another version records the data and plots the median value and range on two separate graphs.

Method of least squares: A statistical procedure to define the best fit's straight line for a series of points plotted on a graph.

Mid range: The mid point between the highest and lowest value of a set of data. It is calculated by adding the highest value and the lowest value together and dividing by two.

Milestone graph: Shows the goals or target to be achieved by depicting the projected schedule of the process. A primary purpose is to help organize projects and to coordinate activities.

Mind maps: Unstructured cause-and-effect diagrams. Also called mind-flows or brain webs.

Mixture design: In this type of experiment the measured responses are assumed to depend upon the relative proportions of the ingredients or components in the mixture and not upon the amount of the mixture.

There are a number of different mixture design methodologies. The most frequently used one is the simplex-lattice design.

Mood's median test: This tests the equality of medians from two or more populations. It is sometimes called the "median test."

Multiple linear regressions: An extension of the linear regression approach where only one independent variable is used. By increasing the number of independent variables, a higher proportion of the variation can be analyzed.

Multivariance analysis: Often variation within the output is different from piece to piece and time-to-time variation. Variation analysis uses a chart to investigate the stability or consistency of a process. The chart contains a series of vertical lines or other schematics, along a y time scale. The length of each line represents the range of values detected in each of the samples.

M$\bar{X}$ and MR charts (moving range charts): Used in place of an $\bar{X}$-R chart when the data is not readily available. These are two separate but related charts, one that plots averages and one that plots range. Typically the last three parts are added together and averaged to plot the most recent plot.

Negative analysis: A method used to define potential problems before they occur and develop countermeasures.

Nominal group technique (NGT): A special purpose technique that's useful for situations where individual judgments must be tapped and combined to arrive at decisions.

Nonvalue-added costs: The cost of activities that the customer would not want to pay for because they add no direct value to him or her. They can be further divided into business-value-added, nonvalue-added, bureaucracy costs, and appraisal costs.

Normal distribution: Occurs when frequency distribution is symmetrical about its mean or average.

Normal probability plots: Used to check whether observations follow a normal distribution of $P > 0.05$.

One-piece flow: Describes the practice of moving work-in-progress between work stations.

On-off technique: A method of directing attention to information on a screen or to the presenter during a presentation.

Operational process capability: Determined by the manner in which the process is operated in respect to how this predictable pattern meets specification requirements.

Opportunities for error: The way Six Sigma error rates are measured.

Opportunity cycle: A problem-solving cycle developed in support of total quality management (TQM) that consists of five phases: protection, analysis, correction measurement, and prevention.

Organizational change management: A methodology designed to lessen the stress and resistance of employees and management to critical changes.

Organizational cultural diagnostics (cultural landscape): An organizational change-management survey tool used to define strengths and weakness related to the organization's culture.

Organizational excellence: Also called the "five pillars," which must be managed simultaneously to continuously excel. The five pillars are: process management, project management, change management, knowledge management, and resource management

Origin: The point where the two axes on an X-Y graph meet.

Parts per million (PPM): In Six Sigma applications, this is used to identify defects per million opportunities. It is also referred to as defects per million opportunities (DPMO).

Pareto diagram: A type of chart in which the bars are arranged in descending order from the left to right. It is a way to highlight the vital few in contrast to the trivial many.

Pattern and trend analysis: Charts are typically used to analyze positive and negative changes in processes and outputs. Data is usually presented in either summary (static) or time sequence. Analyzing these graphs and/or charts helps to detect upward trends.

Policy deployment: An approach to planning in which organizationwide long-range objectives are set, taking into account the organization's vision, its long-term plan, the needs of customers, the competitive and economic situation, and previous results.

Poor-quality cost (PQC): An improvement on the quality cost system that expanded the concept from direct quality cost only to direct and indirect quality costs.

Lost-opportunity cost: A methodology that defines and collects direct and indirect costs related to resources that are wasted as a result of the organization's inability to do everything correct every time.

Portfolio project management: A technique used to simultaneously manage several projects within a specific area.

Positive correlation: This occurs when both variables increase or decrease together. When one variable increases while the other one decreases it is called negative correlation.

Prevention costs: The cost of preventing errors and helping employees do the job right every time.

Preventive action: Action taken to eliminate the possibility of errors occurring rather than reacting to them. A long-term, risk-weighted approach that prevents problems from occurring based on a detailed understanding of the output and/or the processes that are used to create it.

Primary functions: Those for which the process was designed.

Probability density function: A part of a histogram used to calculate the probability that a single sample drawn randomly from the population will be more or less than a specific value.

Probability plots: Plots in which the value of the item being measured is divided into small segments across the horizontal axis and the number of occurrences within that measurement segment is plotted on the vertical axis (e.g., histogram).

Problem tracking log: A systematic way to categorize, monitor, and measure a corrective action process.

Process benchmarking: A method of identifying superior processes to reduce cost, decrease cycle time, minimize inventory, and improve satisfaction for internal and external customers.

Process capability index (Cp): A measure of the ability of a process to produce consistent results. It represents the ratio between the allowable process spread (the width of the specified limits) and the actual process spread at the ±3 sigma level.

Process capability study: A statistical comparison of a measurement pattern or distribution to determine if a process can consistently deliver products within certain specification limits.

Process control: Refers to monitoring a process to maximize its cost effectiveness.

Process decision program chart (PDPC): A method that maps events and contingencies that may result from proposed solutions to problems. It uses a tree diagram to identify risks and counter measures.

Process elements: The various tasks that make up a process.

Process flow animation: A process model that shows the movement of transactions within a process and illustrates how outside functions affect its performance.

Process maturity grid: A six-level grid that sets standards for a process as it matures in its overall performance. The six levels are:

- Level 6—Unknown
- Level 5—Understood
- Level 4—Effective
- Level 3—Efficient
- Level 2—Error-free
- Level 1—World-class

Process owner: The individual responsible for a process' design and performance.

Process performance analysis: The collection of performance data at the activities or task level of a flowchart that is used to calculate the performance of the total process.

Process performance matrix: The efficiency, effectiveness, and adaptability measurements related to the process.

Process qualification: A systematic approach to evaluating a process to determine if it's ready to ship its output to an internal or external customer.

Process redesign: A methodology used to streamline a current process with the objective of reducing cost and cycle-time by 30 to 60 percent while improving output quality from 20 to 200 percent.

Process reengineering: A methodology that challenges all of an organization's process paradigms, typically takes six to nine months to complete, and is used when cost and cycle time need to be reduced by more than 60 percent.

Process simplification: A methodology that takes complex tasks, activities, and processes and bisects them to define less-complex ways of accomplishing the defined results.

Process simulation: A technique that pictorially processes resources, products, and services in a dynamic computer model.

Project champion: The individual who ensures that a project has the resources and cross-functional support it needs to be successful. He or she is also the most accountable to the executive team for the overall results of the project.

Project communications management: A subset of project management that includes the processes required to ensure timely and appropriate generation, collection, dissemination, storage, and ultimate disposition of project information.

Project cost management: A subset of project management that includes the processes required to ensure that the project is completed within the approved budget.

Project decision analysis: An approach used in deciding whether to start or continue a project. It includes a cost-benefit analysis, an impact analysis about the organization and its support of the strategic plan, an evaluation of the risks associated with the project, and its effect on the customer.

Project financial benefit analysis: Used at least at each checkpoint in the improvement process, it evaluates the potential savings compared to the cost of making the proposed change.

Project human resource management: A subset of project management that includes the processes required to make the most effective use of the people involved with the project.

Project integration management: A subset of project management that includes the processes required to ensure that the various elements of the project are properly coordinated.

Project quality management: An analysis of whether a project will satisfy the needs for which it was undertaken.

Project risk management: A subset of project management that includes the processes concerned with identifying, analyzing, and responding to project risk.

Project scope: The boundaries within which the project will work.

Project scope management: A subset of project management that includes the processes required to ensure that the project includes all the work required—and only the work required—to successfully complete a project.

Project selection matrix: A graphical analysis of the various improvement opportunities to define the factors that should be approved or continued. Typical factors are:

- Customer satisfaction
- Existing strategic objectives
- Potential financial returns
- Competitive advantage

Project time management: A subset of project management that includes the processes required to ensure timely completion of the project.

Pugh concept selection/Pugh matrix: A scoring matrix used to prioritize the selection of improvement opportunities and to select options in the design phase.

Pugh technique: A method of comparing alternatives to a process.

Pull system: A production control system that replaces parts and components only when the previous part or component has been consumed.

Plan understand-streamline-improve-continuous improvement (PUSIC): The basic ingredient of business process improvement used with reengineering, redesign, benchmarking, and fast-action solution teams.

Qualification: Formal notice that a process produces acceptable performance or meets certain specifications.

Qualitative data: Data related to the number of items.

Quality function deployment: A structured process for taking the voice of the customer, translating it into measurable requirements and counterpart characteristics, and deploying those requirements into each level of the process design and all customer service processes.

Quality plan: A document that includes the specific quality practices, resources, and sequence of activities relevant to a particular product, project, or contract.

R chart: A simple range chart plotted to control variability of a variable.

R control chart: An important statistical tool that can be used to signal problems very early and thus enable action to be taken before large volumes of defective output have been produced.

Randomized block plans: An analysis approach used when there are a large number of factors that need to be evaluated and it is desirable to keep all other conditions constant during each individual factor evaluation. The factors are grouped into categories where only one condition is varied and the other is held constant.

Regression analysis: A statistical analysis of the association between two variables.

Reliability analysis: A technique used to estimate the probability that an item will perform its intended purpose for a specific period of time under specific operating conditions.

Reliability management system: A system with a high probability of producing items that function correctly under stated conditions for a specific period of time.

Resultant poor-quality costs: The costs that result from internal and external errors.

Reverse engineering: The process of purchasing, testing, and disassembling competitors' products to understand their design and manufacturing approach and using this data to improve.

Risk analysis: An evaluation of the possibility of harm or loss, or a measure of uncertainty.

Risk assessment: A quantitative analysis of risks and conditions to prioritize their effects on the project objectives or the organization's performance.

Robust process: A robust process operates at the Six Sigma level, producing very few defects even when the inputs to the process vary. It has a very high, short-term Z value and a small Z shift value. The critical element in a robust process is the u element.

Robustness: The characteristics of a process output and process design that make it insensitive to the variation in inputs.

Roll-through yield (RTY): See first-time yield.

Root cause analysis: The process of identifying the various causes that effect a particular problem, process, or issue and determining the underlying reasons that caused the condition.

Run chart: A graphical display of data used to assess the stability of a process over time or a sequence of events, such as the number of batches produced.

Suppliers-inputs-processes-output-customers (SIPOC): Used to help ensure that a person remembers all the factors when mapping a process.

Single minute exchange of die (SMED): A lean tool that is a key part of just-in-time programs. It helps minimize the amount of time it takes to change a process to produce another output.

Substitute-combine-adapt/adopt-modidy/magnify-put to other uses-eliminate (SCAMPER): A checklist technique developed by Michael Michalko used to generate ideas.

Scatter diagram: A graphic tool used to study the relationship between two variables and to test for possible cause-and-effect relationships.

Secondary functions: Results of primary functions.

Seven basic tools:
- Cause-and-effect diagrams
- Checksheets
- Control charts
- Histograms
- Pareto charts
- Scatter diagrams
- Stratification

Shewhart cycle: Another term for the plan-do-check-act (PDCA) cycle.

Short-run chart: A type of chart used when it's difficult, if not impossible, to obtain a large enough sample size for a standard control chart.

Sigma: A Greek letter statisticians use to refer to the standard deviation of a population. "Sigma" and "standard deviation" are used interchangeably as a scaling factor to convert upper and lower specified limits to Z.

Sigma conversion tables: A set of tables used to convert sigma value into percent of product that should meet requirements under normal conditions.

Signal-to-noise ratio (S/N ratio): A calculation to quantify the effects of variation in controllable factors resulting from variation in output.

Simple language: Indicates the grade level that a person who is reading the document should have reached in order to understand the document. It produces documents that can be read at two grade levels lower than the lowest educational level of the person who will be reading them.

Simple linear regression: A method that allows the determination of the relationship between a continuous process output (Y) and one factor (X). Its mathematical equation is $Y = b + mX$.

Simplification approaches: A series of techniques that focus on simplifying processes. They include combining similar activities, reducing handling, eliminating unused data, clarifying forms, using simple wording, eliminating nonvalue-added activities, and evaluating information technology activities to determine if they are necessary.

Simulation modeling: The use of computer programs to mimic the activity, process, or system under study to predict or control how it will perform.

Six Sigma matrix: A four-part matrix that includes measuring customer opinion, determining customer critical-to-quality factors, measuring product outcomes, and correlating product outcomes to critical-to-quality factors.

Six-step error-prevention cycle: A process to prevent problems from occurring rather than fix them afterwards.

Six-step problem-solving cycle: A basic procedure for understanding and correcting a problem and analyzing the results.

Six-step solution-identification cycle: A procedure for defining how to solve a problem or take advantage of an opportunity.

Soft consensus: The status of a team when some of its members would prefer a different solution but are willing to support the majority's decision.

Soft savings: The benefits of a change not directly reflected in the accounting system. This includes components such as reduced cycle time, cost avoidance, improved employee morale, lost-profit avoidance, and improved customer satisfaction.

Solution analysis diagram: A diagram that assists in the analysis of all the possible effects of a proposed solution or cause.

Spearman rank correlation coefficient: A nonparametric measure of correlation that's often denoted by the Greek letter ρ (rho).

Spider diagram/radar chart: Used to show or compare one or more sets of data. Often used to compare the current state to the future state.

Stakeholder analysis plan: Identifies key stakeholders or individuals that have a stake in the overall success or failure of a process.

Standard deviation: An estimate of the spread of the total population based on a population sample. Sigma (σ) is the Greek letter used to designate the estimated standard deviation.

Statistical process control (SPC): A mathematical approach to understanding and managing activities that make their outputs more predictable. This includes design of experiments, control charts, and characterization.

Statistics: The collection, analysis, interpretation, and presentation of numerical data.

Storyboard: A series of pictures and accompanying narrative used to show how something is done or describe a related problem or situation.

Strategy: The approach employed to meet performance goals.

Stratification: A technique used to analyze data where the universal population is divided into homogeneous subgroups that are analyzed independently.

Structural roadblocks: Obstacles that must be overcome for a process or an organization to transform from one state to another.

Student's t-distribution: A combination of standard normal random variables and the chi-square random variables analysis. It's calculated by dividing the standard, normal-random variable by the square root of chi-squared random variable by the related degrees of freedom.

Supplier controls: Preventive measures that minimize the possibility of suppliers providing unacceptable product.

Supply chain management: The flow of items from raw materials to accepted products at the customer location. Effective supply chain management reduces cost, lead times, and inventory while increasing customer satisfaction.

Survey: A systematic way to collect information about a specific subject by interviewing people.

Strengths-weaknesses-opportunities-threat (SWOT) analysis: Analysis used to help match an organization's resources and capabilities to the competitive environment in its market segment.

Systematic design: A structured, four-phase design approach.

t test: The t test employs the statistic (t) with n-1 degrees of freedom to test a given statistical hypothesis about a population parameter. It is used when the population standard deviation is unknown and is effective in small sample sizes (less than 30 items).

Taguchi methods: Design of experiment approaches in which the output depends on many factors without having to collect data using all possible combinations of values for these variables. This provides a systematic way of selecting variable combinations so that their individual effects can be evaluated.

Takt time: The rate at which a completed item leaves the last step in the production process. It drives the pull system in a lean operation and should be equivalent to the rate at which customers, internal or external, require the output.

Team charter: The team's project objectives, project process boundaries, limitations, key deliverables, outside resources, and indicators/targets.

Theory of constraints (TOC): A method of identifying and eliminating bottlenecks within a process. It consists of a number of tools, including: transition tree, prerequisite tree, current reality tree, conflict resolution diagram, and future reality tree.

Three-factor or three-level experiments: This provides a three-dimensional look at a process or problem and is useful after screening a large number of variables. These experiments may be full or fractional factorials.

Throughput yield (TPY): The yield at the end of a process after any errors have been scrapped or reworked. Effective rework procedures can often increase first-time yield from 10 percent to a throughput yield of 100 percent.

Time-related process capability index (Cpk): An index that accounts for the drift that a product will have over time caused by common variation. A Cpk of at least 1.33 is standard unless the product is screened.

Tollgate: The process checkpoints at which deliverables are reviewed and measured, and readiness to move forward is addressed.

Total cost management: A comprehensive management philosophy for proactively managing an organization's total resources (material, capital, and human resources) and the activities that consume them.

Total productive maintenance (TPM): A methodology used to keep equipment at peak operating efficiency, thereby eliminating equipment downtime.

Total productivity management: A methodology designed to direct the organization's efforts at improving productivity without decreasing quality.

Total quality management (TQM): A methodology designed to focus an organization's efforts on improving quality of internal and external products and services.

Tree diagram: An illustration of each phase of a problem-solving process.

Trial: An observation made with all of the variables set at predesigned levels and held constant during the duration of the observation.

Tribal knowledge: Unwritten information not commonly known by others in the organization. Unlike other forms of intellectual assets, tribal knowledge cannot be converted into company property unless it's transformed into a hard knowledge base.

Theory of innovative problem solving (TRIZ): An approach that is effective at identifying low-cost improvement solutions during the define or identify phases.

Types of data: There are two major groupings of data: attributes data, which is counted, not measured; and variables data, which quantifies measurement data and therefore provides a more accurate measurement.

u-chart: A plot of the number of defects per unit with a varying sample size.

Value stream: All of the steps/activities (both value-added, business value-added, and nonvalue-added) in a process that the customer is willing to pay for.

Value-added analysis (VA): A procedure for analyzing every activity within a process, classifying its cost as value-added, business value-added, and nonvalue-added, and then eliminating the nonvalue-added costs and minimizing the business value-added.

Value-stream mapping: A tool used to help understand the flow of materials and information as an item makes its way through the value stream.

Variable control chart: A plot of variables data of a process' performance, usually determined by regular sampling of the product, service, or process as a function (usually) of time or unit numbers or other chronological variable.

Variables data: Data that are always measured in units, such as inches, feet, volts, amps, ohms, centimeters, etc.

Variation: A measure of the changes in the output from the process over a period of time.

Vision: A description of the desired future state of an organization, process, team, or activity.

Vision statement: A brief formal statement of an organization's desired future business environment.

Visual factory/visual office: A system of signs, information displays, layouts, material storage, and equipment storage that uses color-coding and error-proofing devices to visually organize a working environment.

Vital few: The 20 percent of the independent variables that contribute to 80 percent of the total variation.

Voice of the business (VOB): The stated and unstated needs and requirements of the organization and its stakeholders.

Voice of the customer (VOC): The customer's expression of his or her requirements.

Voice of the employee (VOE): The stated and unstated needs and requirements of the employees within an organization.

Voice of the process (VOP): Describes what the process is telling you about what it is capable of achieving

Weibull distribution: A continuous probability distribution with the probability density function frequently used in analyzing field-life data rate due to its flexibility.

Work breakdown structure (WBS): A Gantt chart used in project management to monitor and plan project activities and to define their interrelationships and present status.

Work-flow monitoring: A computer program used to track individual transactions as they move through the process to minimize process variation.

Work standards: Include documentation methods and engineering standards for performance expectations and measurement matrices.

World-class operations benchmarking: A form of external benchmarking that extends the benchmarking approach outside the organization's direct competition to involve dissimilar industries.

X value: The inputs required to produce the output Y. It includes the materials, procedures, process, and suppliers.

$\bar{X}$: The mean of a population.

$\bar{X}$-S chart ($\bar{X}$ sigma charts): Control charts used for increased sensitivity to variation.

X-MR chart: A chart that includes individual readings; a moving range may be used for short runs and in the case of destructive testing.

X-Y axes graph: A pictorial presentation of data on sets of horizontal and vertical lines called a grid. The data are plotted on the horizontal and vertical lines, which are assigned specific numerical values corresponding to the data.

Y value: Process outputs

Z value: Data points positioned between the mean and another location as measured in standard deviations. Z is a measure of process capability and corresponds to the process sigma value.

Zero defects: A system directed at eliminating all defects from a product.

Z_{min}: The distance between the process mean and the nearest specification limit (upper or lower) measured in standard deviation (sigma) units.

APPENDIX B

THE SIX SIGMA BODY OF KNOWLEDGE

The following is a list of the Six Sigma body of knowledge. Under the columns marked Green, Black, or Master, the following symbols are used:

- "A" means they are *almost always used*. At least 90 percent of the projects will use these tools. (The related belt must be trained on how to use these tools or already have been trained in the use of these tools.)
- "O" means *often used*. It is used in more than 50 percent of the projects. (The related belt should be trained on how to use these tools or already have been trained on these tools.)
- "S" means *sometimes used*. It is used in 25 percent to 49 percent of the projects. (The related belt should know what they are used for and know where to go to get more information on how to use them.)
- "I" means *infrequently used or never used*. It is used in less than 24 percent of the projects. (These tools are nice to know but not required and not part of the belt's training or certification test.)

Body of knowledge		SIX SIGMA BELTS			
		Yellow	Green	Black	Master
5Ss		I	O	O	O
Acceptance decisions		I	I	S	S
Activity network diagrams		I	S	S	S
Affinity diagrams		O	O	O	O
Area activity analysis (AAA)		I	S	I	I
Automation		I	I	S	S
Axiomatic design		I	I	S	S
Bar charts/graphs		A	A	A	A
Benchmarking		S	S	O	O
Bessel function		I	I	S	O
Binomial distribution		S	O	O	O
Bivariate distribution		I	I	S	O
Box plots		I	S	O	O
Brainstorming		A	A	A	A
Bureaucracy elimination		S	S	O	O
Business case development		O	A	O	O
Business process improvement		O	O	O	O
Calibration		S	O	O	O
Cause-and-effect (fishbone) diagrams		O	O	O	O

Body of knowledge		SIX SIGMA BELTS			
		Yellow	Green	Black	Master
Cause-and-effect matrix		O	O	O	O
Central limit theorem		O	O	O	O
Chi-square distribution		S	O	O	O
Coefficient of contingency		I	I	S	S
Collecting data		A	A	A	A
Communication techniques		O	O	O	A
Confidence interval for the mean/ proportion/variance		O	O	O	O
Conflict resolution		O	O	O	O
Continuous flow manufacturing (CFM)		S	S	O	O
Control charts					
	X̄-R charts	S	O	O	O
	Run charts	S	O	O	O
	MX̄-MR charts	I	S	O	O
	X-MR charts	I	S	O	O
	X̄-S charts	I	S	O	O
	Median charts	I	I	S	O
	Short run charts	I	S	S	O
	p charts	S	O	O	O
	np charts	S	O	O	O
	r charts	I	S	O	O
	u charts	I	S	O	O
	Cusum control charts	I	I	S	S
Correlation coefficient		S	O	O	O
Cp		O	O	O	O
Cpk		O	O	O	O
CQFA (cost, quality, features, and availability)		I	S	S	O
Critical-to-quality (CTQ)		A	A	A	A
Critical path method		S	O	O	O
Culture roadblocks		I	I	O	O
Cumulative distribution function		I	S	O	O
Current state mapping		O	O	O	O
Customer requirements		O	A	A	A
Customer surveys		S	S	O	O
Cycle-time analysis		S	O	O	Master
Design for maintainability and availability		I	I	S	S
Design for Six Sigma (DFSS)		I	I	S	O
Design for X (DFX)		I	I	S	O
Design of experiments					
	Three-factor, three-level experiment	I	I	O	O
	Randomized block plans	I	I	S	O
	Latin square designs	I	I	O	O

Body of knowledge		Yellow	Green	Black	Master
		SIX SIGMA BELTS			
	Graeco-Latin designs	I	I	S	O
	Full factorial designs	I	I	O	O
	Plackett-Burman designs	I	I	S	O
	Taguchi designs	I	I	O	O
	Taguchi's robust concepts	I	I	S	O
	Mixture designs	I	I	S	O
	Central composite designs	I	I	S	S
	EVOP evolutionary operations	I	I	I	S
DMADV (define, measure, analyze, design, verify)		S	S	O	O
DMAIC (define, measure, analyze, improve, control)		O	O	O	O
Effort/impact analysis		I	I	O	O
Equipment certification		I	S	S	S
Error proofing		S	O	O	O
Exponential distribution		I	I	O	O
External and internal customers		O	O	O	O
F distribution		I	I	S	S
Facilitation of teams		I	O	O	
Factorial experiments		I	I	S	O
Failure mode and effects analysis		O	O	O	O
Fast action solution team (FAST)		S	O	O	S
First-time yield (FTY) or rolled-through yield (RTY)		O	O	O	O
Five whys (5Ws)		O	O	O	O
Flowcharts		O	O	O	O
Focus groups		S	S	O	O
Force-field analysis		O	O	O	O
Frequency distribution		O	O	O	O
Future-state mapping		S	O	O	O
Gantt charts		O	O	O	O
Gaussian curves		I	I	S	S
General surveys		O	O	O	O
Histograms		O	O	O	O
History of quality		I	S	S	S
Hypergeometric distribution		I	I	S	O
Hypothesis testing					
	Fundamental concepts	I	S	O	O
	Point and interval estimation	I	I	S	O
	Tests for means, variances, and proportions	I	I	O	O
	Paired comparison tests	I	I	O	O
	Analysis of variance	S	O	O	O
	Contingency tables	I	S	O	O

Body of knowledge		SIX SIGMA BELTS			
		Yellow	Green	Black	Master
	Nonparametric tests		S	O	O
Interrelationship diagraphs (ID)		I	S	O	O
Interviewing techniques		I	O	O	O
IT applications		O	S	O	O
Just-in-time		S	S	S	S
Kaizen blitz		I	I	I	I
Kanban		S	S	S	S
Kano model		I	S	O	O
Kendall coefficient of concordance		I	I	I	S
Knowledge management		I	I	S	O
KPIs		O	O	O	O
Kruskal-Wallis one-way analysis		I	I	S	S
Lean thinking		I	S	O	O
Levene test		I	I	S	S
Lognormal distribution		I	I	S	S
Loss function		I	S	O	O
Management theory history		I	I	S	O
Mann-Whitney U test		I	I	S	S
Market segmentation		I	S	S	O
Matrix diagrams		S	O	O	O
Measure of dispersion		S	O	O	O
Measurement error		S	O	O	O
Measurement systems analysis (MSA)		S	S	O	O
Measurement tools		O	O	O	O
Method of least squares		S	O	O	O
Mood's median test		I	I	S	S
Motivating the work force		S	S	O	O
Multi-vari analysis		I	S	O	O
Multiple linear regression		I	S	O	O
Negotiation techniques		S	O	O	O
Nominal group technique		O	O	O	O
Normal distribution		O	O	O	O
Normal probability plots		S	S	O	O
Null hypothesis		I	S	O	O
Opportunity cycle (protection, analysis, correction, measurement, prevent)		S	S	S	S
Project management		I	A	A	A
Organizational change management		O	O	O	O
Organizational culture diagnosis		I	S	O	O
Pareto diagrams		A	A	A	A
Pattern and trend analysis		I	I	S	S
Plan-do-check-act (PDCA)		S	S	S	S
Plan-understand-streamline-implement continuous improvement (PUSIC)		I	S	O	O

Body of knowledge	SIX SIGMA BELTS			
	Yellow	Green	Black	Master
Poisson distribution	I	S	O	O
Poka-yoke	I	S	S	S
Poor-quality cost	I	S	S	O
Portfolio project management	I	I	S	O
Prioritization matrices	S	O	O	O
Probability concepts	O	O	O	O
Probability density function	I	I	S	O
Probability plots	S	O	O	O
Process capability studies	O	O	O	O
Process decision program charts (PDPC)	S	S	O	O
Process elements	O	O	O	O
Process failpoints matrix	S	S	S	S
Process mapping	O	O	O	O
Process performance matrix	S	S	O	O
Process redesign	S	S	O	O
Program evaluation and review technique (PERT)	I	I	S	S
Poisson series	I	I	S	O
Project decision analysis	I	I	S	O
Project financial benefits analysis	A	A	A	A
Project selection matrix	I	I	S	A
Pugh concept selection	I	I	I	I
Quality function deployment (QFD)	I	S	O	O
Qualitative factor	S	O	O	O
Quantitative factor	S	O	O	O
Reengineering	I	I	S	O
Regression analysis	S	S	O	O
Reliability analysis	I	I	S	O
Response surface methodology (RSM)	I	I	S	S
Rewards and recognition	I	S	O	O
Risk analysis	O	A	A	A
Risk assessment	O	A	A	A
Robust design approach	I	S	O	O
Root cause analysis	A	A	A	A
Rotation patterns	I	I	S	M
Run charts	O	O	O	O
Sampling	O	O	O	O
SCAMPER	S	S	S	S
Scatter diagrams	O	O	O	O
Seven basic tools	O	O	O	O
Sigma	O	O	O	O
Sigma conversion table	O	O	O	O
Signal-to-noise ratio	I	I	S	O

Body of knowledge		SIX SIGMA BELTS			
		Yellow	Green	Black	Master
Simple language		S	S	O	O
Simple linear regression		I	S	O	O
Simplification approaches		O	O	O	O
Simulation modeling		I	I	S	O
Single minute exchange of die (SMED)		I	I	S	O
Six Sigma metrics		I	I	S	O
Spearman rank correlation coefficient		I	I	S	O
Stakeholders		O	O	O	O
Statistical process control		O	O	O	O
Statistical tolerance		S	S	S	O
Stem and leaf plots		I	I	S	O
Strengths, weaknesses, opportunities, and threats analysis (SWOT)		S	S	O	O
Structural roadblocks		S	S	O	O
Student's T distribution		I	I	S	O
Supplier controls		S	S	O	O
Supplier, inputs, process, outputs, customers (SIPOC) diagrams		O	O	O	O
Systematic design		I	S	S	O
Takt time		S	S	S	O
Team building		O	O	O	O
Team charter		O	A	A	A
Team management		I	A	A	A
Theory of constraints		S	S	S	O
Throughput yield (TPY)		S	S	S	S
Tollgates		O	0	A	A
Total productive maintenance (TPM)		I	S	S	O
Tree diagrams		O	O	O	O
TRIZ		I	I	I	I
Types of data		O	O	O	O
Types of teams		I	I	S	O
Value/nonvalue-added activities		S	S	O	O
Value stream analysis		S	S	O	O
Variance (o^2, s^2)		I	I	O	O
Variation analysis					
	Rational subgroups	S	S	O	O
	Sources of variability	S	S	O	O
	Randomness testing	S	S	O	O
	Pre-control techniques	I	I	S	O
	Exponentially weighted moving average (EWMA)	I	I	S	S
	Moving average	S	S	O	O
Visual factory/visual office		S	S	O	O
Voice of the customer (VOC)		O	A	A	A

Body of knowledge			SIX SIGMA BELTS			
			Yellow	Green	Black	Master
Voice of the supplier (VOS)			O	O	O	O
Weibull distribution			I	I	O	O
Wilcoxon-Mann-Whitney rank sum test			I	I	S	S
Work breakdown structure			S	O	O	O
Work standard			I	I	S	O
Z value			I	I	S	O

INDEX